I dedicate this book to all the Muslims in Iran who have accepted Jesus Christ as their Lord and Savior, to those who have endured hardship for the cause of their faith in Christ, and to all the martyrs of the church of Jesus Christ in Iran. Their seed of faith and their love for their Lord have paved the way for a bold and uncompromised declaration of the truth.

THE COMING FALL OF ISLAM IN IRAN

REZA SAFA

A STRANG COMPANY

Most STRANG COMMUNICATIONS/CHARISMA HOUSE/SILOAM/FRONTLINE/
REALMS products are available at special quantity discounts for bulk purchase for
sales promotions, premiums, fund-raising, and educational needs. For details,
write Strang Communications/Charisma House/Siloam/FrontLine/Realms, 600
Rinehart Road, Lake Mary, Florida 32746, or telephone (407) 333-0600.

THE COMING FALL OF ISLAM IN IRAN by Reza Safa
Published by FrontLine
A Strang Company
600 Rinehart Road
Lake Mary, Florida 32746
www.frontlineissues.com

Unless otherwise noted, all Scripture quotations are from the New King James
Version of the Bible. Copyright © 1979, 1980, 1982 by Thomas Nelson, Inc.,
publishers. Used by permission.

Scripture quotations marked KJV are from the King James Version of the Bible.

Unless otherwise noted, quotations from the Quran are from *The Qur'an Translation,* 7th edition, by Abdullah Yusuf Ali (Elmhurst, NY: Tahrike Tarsile Qur'an,
Inc., 2001).

Library of Congress Cataloging-in-Publication Data

Safa, Reza F.
  The coming fall of Islam in Iran / Reza Safa.
      p. cm.
  ISBN 1-59185-988-3 (trade paper)
  1. Missions to Muslims--Iran. 2. Islam--Controversial literature. 3. Iran--Reli-
gion. I. Title.
  BV2625.S235 2006
  261.2'7--dc22
                                    2006015866

First Edition

06 07 08 09 10 — 9 8 7 6 5 4 3 2 1
Printed in the United States of America

Acknowledgments

First of all, I would like to thank my Lord Jesus Christ, without whom I could do nothing. Lord, You are so good, and I love You so much. I also want to thank the Holy Spirit of God for inspiring me and giving me knowledge and understanding beyond my natural ability. I love You so much, Spirit of truth. Then I would like to thank the God and Father of my Lord Jesus Christ, my heavenly Father. His love has changed me. I love and trust Him so very much. And I give Him all the glory.

On the human side, I would like to especially thank three people who have worked hard alongside me in making this book a reality. First of all, many thanks go to Barbara Dycus, my editor. Barbara, I appreciate your hard work; you studied almost as hard as I did on this project, plus some. Thank you so very much. May the Lord greatly bless you and your labor of love for Him.

Then I would like to thank my beloved wife, Marilyn. If it wasn't for you, I wonder if I could speak any language properly. Thank you for your hard work of correcting me and inspiring me.

And I want to thank Amy, my secretary, for being patient and working very hard on typing, reading, and correcting this manuscript.

I also want to thank my beautiful children who had to put up with Daddy many nights, staying calm and quiet so Daddy could write. I love you two so much.

Then last but not least, I would like to thank all of our supporters who have made Nejat TV and our ministry among the unreached people a reality. I know on the day of the Lord, you will be standing next to me welcoming possibly millions of souls to God's kingdom. Your reward is preserved by the King. Thank you for standing with me throughout the years. You are precious, and I am so proud of your love for the Lord. May the Lord richly bless you all.

Contents

❧

Introduction

An era of warfare with the radical Islam, or the true Islam, has begun. In 1995, the Lord told me that the radical Islam was going to come against America and that the people in this great land were not prepared to deal with its force. That became the focus of my book *Inside Islam*, first published in 1996. Only three thousand copies sold in the first few months after its release. I wondered if I had missed God or perhaps it wasn't God who spoke to me. However, after September 11, 2001, some thirty thousand copies were sold in a matter of weeks. This massive influx of responses tells me, first, that indeed we were not prepared for the events of 9/11, and, second, we do not know how to deal with Islam—just as the Lord had spoken to me.

On the matter of preparedness, I believe that President George W. Bush and his cabinet have done a fantastic work in securing the land from further attacks by the radical Muslims. From the events of September 11, 2001, until now, he has never backed down in his resolve to do whatever it takes to secure America from attack. In a speech on the war on terrorism at the National Endowment for Democracy in Washington DC on Thursday, October 6, 2005, he reiterated his resolve of just days after the 9/11 attack: "Against such an enemy, there's only one effective response: We never back down, never give in, and never accept anything less than complete victory."[1]

However, on the issue of *how to deal with Islam*, we have a long road ahead of us. This is mainly due to our lack of understanding of the Islamic ideology and the Islamic mind-set, which resides in the hearts of millions of Muslims worldwide. I believe that not even our president understands clearly how to deal with the issues of radical Islam. In the same speech he gave above, he likened the ideology of Islamic militants to Communism, saying that they were attempting to "...overthrow all moderate governments in the region and establish a radical Islamic empire that spans from Spain to Indonesia."[2] Yet, for the past few years, President Bush has made it his custom to break

I

Iftar (breaking of the Muslim fast) with the Muslim leaders at the White House. This past October 17, 2005, after breaking the Islamic fast with a large group of Muslim leaders in the White House, our president in his speech to the most welcomed Muslim leaders said:

> And I want to thank the Muslim—American Muslim leaders who are with us today. Thanks for taking time out to celebrate this important dinner.
>
> Ramadan is the holiest time of the Muslim year. According to Islamic teaching, this month commemorates the *revelation of God's word to the Prophet Muhammad in the form of the Koran*. For more than a billion Muslims, Ramadan is a time of heartfelt prayer and togetherness. It is a time of fasting and personal sacrifice. It is a time to give thanks for God's blessings through works of charity.
>
> One Muslim leader said: "It's a national and Islamic obligation to assist one's neighbors when they are in need." The American people saw that spirit as we recovered from Hurricanes Katrina and Rita. The world sees that spirit, that compassion of Islam, through the countless acts of kindness following the recent earthquake in southeast—in South Asia.
>
> *America is fortunate to count such good-hearted men and women among our fellow citizens.* We have great respect for the commitment that all Muslims make to faith, family, and education. And Americans of many backgrounds seek to learn more about the rich tradition of Islam. To promote greater understanding between our cultures, *I have encouraged American families to travel abroad, to visit with Muslim families. And I have encouraged American families to host exchange students from the Muslim world. I have asked young Americans to study the language and customs of the broader Middle East. And for the first time in our nation's history, we have added a Koran to the White House Library* (emphasis added).[3]

I will give him the benefit of the doubt that, as a president, Mr. Bush must be in right relationship with *all* the citizens of the land. And, facing the formidable enemy of the radical Islam, our president is pursuing hope and peace with the leaders of this religion. This is admirable. But is what is admirable also wise?

The intention is right, but it lacks wisdom because his action makes the radical Muslims even more furious. They consider his action an example of his pandering to Islam and a mockery of the Islamic faith. It reminds me of the many publicity stunts that the shah of Iran used to arrange. He would invite many nominal Imams (mullahs) to his palace and celebrate Friday prayer while the TV cameras broadcast it across Iran. This made us radical Muslims more furious at the infidelity of the shah toward the Islamic faith. To the radical Muslims, it was mocking the religion of Islam.

And the mixed message from the White House has also raised the skepticism of many Americans as well—including Arab Americans who do not practice the teachings of Islam. In a *World Net Daily* report submitted October 31, 2003, nationally syndicated columnist Joseph Farah admitted to being "increasingly Islamo-skeptical." He continued by saying: "As a descendant of refugees from that world, let me tell you the Islamic world does not respect nor honor such tributes. They see them only as a sign of weakness. . . . So why do we pussyfoot around with Islam?"[4]

Please know that I am not criticizing our beloved president. I greatly appreciate and admire him. He is the only president that I believed enough to vote for. I love America, and I am proud to be an American citizen. I believe that I carry more patriotic blood than many who claim to be American but lack the understanding of the value system that has made America great. My reason for writing this book, *The Coming Fall of Islam in Iran*, is to bring more awareness and more knowledge about our enemy, the Islamic faith, and its adherents, the radical Muslims. I have always believed that knowledge is the key to strength. Napoleon Bonaparte, the great conqueror of long ago, has been credited with instructing his armies, "Know your enemy!" The more we know, the stronger we are.

In the midst of a severe battle, waving a flag and charging to the enemy's front with shouts of glory will not bring us victory; it will bring us death. Emotion is good *after* the battle is won. Wisdom and knowledge are the keys we need to use to win this violent conflict that has begun with radical Islam.

A few years ago, I was invited to speak at a conference in Florida to a group of Charismatic leaders about Islam. After my lecture on Islamic radicalism and an evaluation of the war in Iraq and its outcome, I faced staunch opposition from several of the attendees. They felt that their *patriotic senses* had a better likelihood of success than my knowledge of Islam and the Muslim people. Last year the leader of that group sent me a letter and acknowledged the accuracy of my lectures. The point is this: we must have knowledge and not only emotional goose bumps.

Iran, the Next Axis of Evil!

At the time of this writing our emotions about Iran are becoming as heightened as they were about Iraq prior to the start of the U.S./Iraq war. Iran will soon become a dangerous nation with nuclear power capability. Labeled as the "axis of evil" and positioned with the stance that its president, Mahmoud Ahmadinejad, has toward Israel, Iran is on the threshold of an assault either by United States or Israeli forces.

Many fear the consequences if Iran is not stopped before it passes the point of no return in acquiring a nuclear weapon. In my opinion Iran has already passed the point of no return—with or without nuclear ability.

If the United States decides to bomb Iran's nuclear power plants, Iran will become stronger in its resolution against America. It will also gather momentum and raise greater support from radical groups in Iraq and other Muslim nations. Until now, Iran has been isolated from the Arab nations due to its Shi'ite belief, which is followed by only a small minority of the overall Islamic world. Our military aggression against Iran will most possibly raise stronger sympathy and support from the majority of the Muslim people. Our action will take us out of a pit and put us in a deep well of hatred by the Muslim communities.

I believe that we have already set something in motion by threatening the Iranian government. In early January 2006 Iran pulled all its assets out of the banks in Europe, an action confirmed by Iran's Central Bank governor Ebrahim Sheibani on January 21, 2006.[5] Late in January, Iranian President Mahmoud Ahmadinejad met with the leaders of the Palestinian groups Hamas and Islamic Jihad in Syria, and the two governments expressed support for Iran's right to the peaceful exploitation of nuclear power, criticizing what they called "the selective and double-standard policy practiced by some international powers in this regard."[6] What would a cooperation between Iran, Libya, Syria, Hamas, Muslim Brotherhood in Egypt, Hezbollah in Lebanon, and other renegades do to the spread of radical Islamic terrorism?

I believe that the U.S. government's war on terrorism in recent years has empowered radical Islam to respond with increasing animosity and violence. You must understand the spirit and the mind-set of the Islamic faith. The harder you hit them, the stronger they will become. As a young boy growing up in a radical Muslim family in Iran, I used to get into a lot of fistfights. All my fights were with young boys from families I knew. I never fought someone whose family I didn't know. There was a saying back in Iran that said: "Do not slap a man who has more than four brothers!" If you slap one, you must be ready to slap them all. Are we ready to wage a war against 1.3 billion Muslims?

The more we overpower the radicals, the greater they will become. Muhammad, the prophet of Islam, couldn't get a following of more than three hundred adherents in his ten years of ministry in Mecca. Yet the more Muhammad's tribe, the Quraish, persecuted him, the more Arabs converted to Islam. The very core belief of Islam is fed on war and violence. Jihad is the very essence of the Islamic faith. The more we fight them, the more of them with whom we must exchange blows.

A great example of this fact is the recent Palestinian uprising (*Intifada*) in the nation of Israel. Since the *Intifada* began in 1987, radical Islam has gained momentum. If you study Palestinian history, you will know that the Palestinian leadership, for the most part, including the Palestine Liberation Organization (PLO), was more of a secular leftist group than a zealous Islamic movement. Even today, the PLO's membership is made up by separate paramilitary and political organizations, often referred to as factions. The PLO has no central decision-making or mechanism that enables it to directly control these factions, but they are supposed to follow the PLO charter and Executive Committee decisions.[7]

The *Intifada* began on December 6, 1987, with the stabbing death of one Israeli person. One day later, four residents of the Jabalya refugee camp in Gaza were killed in a traffic accident, and rumors spread that the four had been killed by Israelis as a deliberate act of revenge.[8] By the end of four years of fighting, more than forty-three hundred attacks had been reported, and more than fourteen hundred Israeli civilians and seventeen hundred Israeli soldiers were injured.[9] The heavier a hand Israel showed to the Palestinian *Intifada*, the more radical Islam grew among the Palestinian populace.

The radical Islamic group Hamas (which is the Arabic acronym of *Harakat al-Muqawwamah al-Islamiyya*, meaning the Islamic Resistance Movement) emerged with the outbreak of the *Intifada* in 1987. In his book *Hamas: Political Thought and Practice*, Khaled Hroub, a Palestinian academic and commentator, examines Hamas political ideologies. According to Hroub, the Muslim Brotherhood, an Islamic radical group that originated in Egypt, from which Hamas branched out, was already active in Palestine prior to the statehood of Israel in 1948.[10]

The question is: Why wasn't the Muslim Brotherhood on the scene of the Palestinian political apparatus? Why, all of a sudden, does a group like Hamas rise up with violent Islamic ideologies and become a dominant force in the political arena of the world?

The landslide victory of Hamas in the Palestinian election proves that Israel gave birth and strengthened Hamas and has lost the battle of defeating the radical Islamic group. Israel now has to contend with an archenemy within her own soil! Could anyone ever imagine that Hamas, which until a few years ago was an unknown group even among the Palestinians, would today dominate the Palestinian parliament? Yet on January 26, 2006, *BBC News* reported: "Preliminary results give Hamas 76 of the 132 seats in the chamber, with the ruling Fatah party trailing on 43."[11]

This characteristic of radical Islam to become progressively stronger with progressive resistance is why I believe that our two wars in Afghanistan and Iraq, and now our dealings with Iran, have, and are, paving the way for a long, long warfare with radical Islam. We are giving birth to many groups such as Hamas without even being aware of it. Because we lack the wisdom and understanding to deal with radical Islam, we will not be in peace for many years to come until we better understand this enemy.

The question you may ask then is: "What must we do? If Iran is attacked, it will become a power factor within the Islamic world. But if it is left alone, it will threaten Israel's existence and the world's peace." I believe that God is raising a force against the Islamic faith *within the boundaries of that country.* God is moving in Iran like I have never seen, heard, or read about in any other nation of the earth in our modern history (with the possible exception of the Welsh revival).

Let us look, then, at this nation of Iran—its history, its people, and its church. And let us see a lot more light than what the news media and others are portraying. As the Shakespearean adage goes: "The evil that men do lives after them; the good is oft interred with their bones."[12] Although Shakespeare meant this concerning Caesar, I believe that it is applicable for the nation of Iran. Iran has had thirty-five hundred years of written history and has deposited much in our world in the fields of science, poetry, art, and philosophy. The country's political standards became the foundation of the political platforms of the Greek and Roman empires. Yet what we see, hear, and remember today about Iran are the crazy slogans coming out of a small, extreme, radical group of people within its current government.

In this book, I also want to examine our political policies in the Middle East. We will look at the Truman and Eisenhower administrations and their actions in Iran. If you believe that America's government is incapable of making any mistakes, I hope that you will please be patient with some portions of my book. Remember that I am not examining situations with a critical spirit, but rather with constructive observations. I am on no one's side, except the side of truth. It is the knowledge of the truth that will set us free. We must admit our wrongdoings and enhance our stance. Only fools close their eyes to their mistakes and do not seek restoration.

America will prevail because we have a noble cause. We love freedom, and we value human souls. We must win. I pray and believe that we will take heed and act upon the truth. If not, we will follow the same path as that taken by the old empires of Persia, Greece, and Rome.

Concerning the church's role, I believe that the church must rise up to carry a heavier load in this warfare than she has been willing to carry. This fight against radical Islam is *spiritual warfare*, and we cannot expect the politicians and governments to carry the load alone.

God is raising up a standard against the spirit of Islam. Isaiah 59:19 says, "When the enemy comes like a flood, the Spirit of the LORD will lift up a standard against him." I believe that Iran is that standard against the spirit of radical Islam. The nationwide revival that is taking place in Iran today is God's provision for this age of radicalism. These new believers in Iran have paid a high price for their faith. They have lived under the domain of an Islamic republic with all its fearsome rules against the church. These are the ones that are being tried in fire and storms. If the church in America will pray and watch over this great harvest in Iran, we will have an army of God that can invade the Muslim world. Iran is the firstfruits of the Islamic world in fifteen hundred years. The firstfruits are holy, and they must be consecrated unto the Lord. So let us watch and pray, and take care of this great harvest of souls in Iran.

They cannot succeed alone. I admonish you to be alert and to be awake. I believe that America is facing its God-ordained mission for this world— here and now. Therefore with hope, faith, and knowledge I write. May God bless this great nation and grant us wisdom in these last days.

For His Glory,
Reza F. Safa

1

God at Work in Iran

In spite of religious persecution—indeed, at times because of it—Iranians are coming to the Lord in droves. God is touching the people of Iran, and they are being won to God through the simple sharing of friendship, through miraculous dreams and visions, because of Christian satellite TV, and in other supernatural circumstances.

Christianity is not new in Iran. It has been in Iran since the beginning of the church. Elamites (Persians), Medes, and Parthians were present during Peter's speech on Pentecost. According to some historians, the Church of St. Mary in northwestern Iran is the second oldest church, after the Church of Bethlehem. The Armenian Apostolic Church, Assyrian Church of the East, and the Chaldean Catholic Church trace their roots to the early centuries of the church.

Modern missionary work in Iran began in earnest as a result of the Haystack Movement and the establishment by the American Board of Commissioners for Foreign Missions of its first mission station in Urumiah (Rezaiyeh) near Tabriz. Rev. Justin Perkins and his wife, Charlotte, arrived at their post in 1834 and opened the first missions school in 1836.[1] In 1869 the British Church Missionary Society also began work in Iran. Much of the work by these early missionaries and those who followed was dedicated to education and health care. They did, however, begin interaction with the Persian Muslim community. The building of a church, though, was a very slow work.

By the time of the Islamic Revolution in 1979, various Protestant denominations had been established, including Presbyterians, the Iranian Assemblies of God (*Jamiat-e Rabbani*), and the Anglican Church of Iran. The total number of Iranian believers in 1979 was estimated to be just fewer than three thousand, although exact numbers are difficult to ascertain.[2]

Dr. William M. Miller was a statesman-missionary to Iran from 1919–1962.

He wrote a book titled *Ten Muslims Meet Christ*, first published in 1969.[3] It was long considered a miraculous story. During these early, struggling years for the church work in Iran, it would have been miraculous to see ten converts come to Christ at any one time. But in June 2004, Lazarus Yeghnazar, a leader of the Elam Iranian churches, now based in Great Britain, stated, "In the last twenty years, more Iranians have come to Christ compared to the last fourteen centuries. We've never seen such a phenomenal thirst."[4] By the grace of God, Dr. Miller lived to see the beginnings of this great influx of believers.

Iran's Turning Point

The turning point in the history of the church in Iran and among Iranians was the Islamic Revolution of 1979. The implementation of Islamic law has led to this phenomenal thirst and to an unprecedented exodus from the Muslim faith. The openness of Iranians to the gospel is primarily due to the oppression they have suffered at the hands of Islamic clergymen who rule the nation with an ironfisted regime. Tens of thousands of former Shi'ite Muslims are now Bible-believing Christians.

The Islamic Revolution of 1979 was also another turning point of sorts. While religious persecution has long existed in Iran against believers of any religion other than Islam, the rise of Islamic fanaticism also gave rise to increasing persecution against Christians or Muslims converting to Christianity in Iran. And with the election of Iran's new president, Mahmoud Ahmadinejad, Christians in Iran, especially converts from Islam, have experienced growing persecution from the government.

Christian Today, an independent, interdenominational Christian media company that provides direct and current news information to the general Christian public, reported on December 2, 2005:

> The recent wave of persecution traces back to the kidnapping and stabbing of an Iranian convert to Christianity named Ghorban Tori on November 22. Since Tori's death, not only was the church to which he belonged raided, but ten other Christians were arrested in other cities, including the Iranian capital, Tehran.[5]

Tori had converted to Christianity more than ten years ago while in Turkmenistan. He began to share his faith with friends and relatives in Iran in 1998 and had formed a meeting of believers in his home.[6]

The government in Iran vigilantly enforces a governmental prohibition against "proselytizing" and forces some evangelical leaders to sign pledges that "they will not evangelize Muslims or allow Muslims to attend church services." The *Christian Today* article quoted a religious freedom report as stating: "Conversion of a Muslim to a non-Muslim religion is considered apostasy under the law and is punishable by the death penalty."[7]

According to an Iranian source, the new Iranian president has openly declared his opposition to house church movement and Christianity during a meeting with the nation's thirty provincial governors. Ahmadinejad was quoted as saying, "I will stop Christianity in this country."[8]

Determining exact numbers of believers inside Iran is difficult. According to Iranian Christians International, a Persian ministry based in Colorado: "In 1979 there were less than three hundred Iranian MBBs (Muslim Background Believers, i.e. Christians from Muslim families) and only about a dozen Afghan MBBs. Now the numbers are estimated to be seventy thousand (excluding the secret believers) and five thousand respectively."[9]

"Half of the population would desert Islam if they had the freedom to do so," said Abe Ghaffari, the director of Iranian Christians International (ICI).[10]

A majority of these new converts have been introduced to Christ via Christian satellite television programs beamed to Iran in the Farsi (Persian) language from the United States.

International Antioch Ministries (IAM) of San Jose, California, founded by Pastor Hormoz Shariat, PhD, claims that through their ministry's satellite TV broadcasts, they have won over fifty thousand Iranian Muslims to Christ since it first aired in 2002.[11] IAM's ICTV (Iranian Christian TVTM) offers ten hours of programming each week, including a live, call-in pastoral show. In an e-mail letter to his supporters, Pastor Shariat wrote:

> We are continuing our daily Christian satellite TV broadcasts into the Middle East and are seeing numerous salvations every week. In terms of statistics, for the month of May we received 184 emails and 775 phone calls.[12]

This in spite of the fact that the ministry does not encourage people to e-mail or call because the ministry staff knows that it cannot respond properly to all of the people. Many times as many as ten to twenty messages are left while the one person responsible for answering the phones is talking to one caller. Many others just hang up and do not leave a message.

But the television ministry of Dr. Hormoz Shariat is making a difference in Iran. This one example sent by a twenty-year-old girl who is a house church leader in Tehran shows the impact of the gospel of God reaching into the homes of Iranian people.

> I really love your programs and watch them regularly with my family. I have been a believer for two years now and have been praying for my dad to become a believer also. He was angry at first, and he beat me up several times for my faith in Jesus. One time he even broke my arm. He started watching your program several months ago. Recently I have seen him soften up and watch your programs faithfully and with interest. So several weeks ago, I started playing your evangelistic video called "God Is Love," segment by segment, and then discussing each segment with him. It took several weeks to go through that video with my dad. Last week after he watched the last segment, he knelt down with Pastor Hormoz in the video and prayed with him and gave his heart to Jesus. We are so happy and thankful for what God is doing through you in our lives.[13]

Programs such as *God Is Love* are recorded, duplicated, and distributed by many viewers. They are tools in the hands of underground house church leaders in Iran.

Other ministries also give evidence that numerous Iranians are reached through TV broadcasts. One of these ministries is Bridging the Gap Ministries, founded by Donald Fareed, a former Iranian Muslim, based now in San Jose, California.[14]

As a result of these unparalleled numbers of conversions, hundreds of home groups have been springing up everywhere in Iran and also abroad. In a report by *CNS (Cybercast News Service)*, Tom White, director of the Voice of the Martyrs, an Oklahoma-based ministry to persecuted Christians worldwide, states:

> "In the past eight years, there has been a dramatic increase in the number of converts from Islam." He notes that "the courage and spiritual passion of Iranian believers is a key factor in the 'spontaneous growth' of Iran's house-church movement." Driven under-

ground by persecution, thousands of Iranian Christians—as many as thirty thousand, according to White—meet in homes. They switch locations to avoid detection. The Iranians are hungry to learn, eager to discuss the Bible and, in particular, Jesus.[15]

White states, "They're searching for the truth," indicating that "much of the evangelism goes on inside people's homes."[16]

Iranians Around the World

The growth of churches among Iranians is not exclusively within Iran. Iranians who have converted have fled to Germany, England, the United States, and throughout the world. There is a great move of God among the diaspora of nearly eight to nine million Iranians throughout the world. According to ICI, before the revolution, "the number of Iranian churches and fellowship groups outside of Iran was two; it has now grown to over one hundred. In the meantime ICI has also helped over one thousand persecuted Iranian and Afghan families as well as MBBs from other countries with their resettlement in their new homelands where they worship God free from fear."[17]

New churches are beginning everywhere all the time. There are thirty-five Iranian churches in the United States alone, according to ICI. In almost every major city where this author has traveled in Europe, there is at least one Iranian church. In Stockholm, the capital city of Sweden, there are five Iranian churches, plus many others throughout the country. In Germany there are at least thirty-five Iranian churches scattered throughout the country.

The second largest gathering of Iranians outside of Iran, besides the United States, is in Great Britain. There is at least one Iranian church in almost every major city in that country. Pastor Matthew and Julie Beemer, American missionaries to Great Britain since 1994, started World Harvest Bible Church in Manchester, England, in April of 1997. During the first five years they saw more than six hundred Iranians come to Christ through their ministry, even though their direct ministry was to the British people. "At one point we were averaging two Iranians coming to the Lord each week. Over the past eight years, we have seen an estimated eight hundred Iranians confess Jesus as Savior, with hundreds of these being water baptized," Pastor Beemer wrote to me in a recent communication.

Since the majority of these new believers were asylum seekers, many have been relocated to other parts of England by the government. Throughout the country, small groups who were "birthed" out of the Beemers' church in Manchester meet and fellowship together. Each group is winning people to the Lord, and the Beemers have no way of knowing exactly how many have been reached. One group has, by itself, reached many dozens. Pastor Beemer notes: "Their hearts are so open. Especially those who have come to the UK, because for many it means they've decided that the Iranian government is not good, and because it is led by Muslim clerics, they've turned their backs on Islam to some degree—sometimes without realizing they have. However, many just don't know where to turn until they come in contact with born-again, Spirit-filled Christians."

In Canada also there is quite a large number of Persian churches. According to the 2003 census, an estimated eighty-five thousand Iranians live in Canada, many in the Toronto area. Many outreaches have been conducted among the Iranians in the Toronto area. Pastor Kourosh Barani immigrated to Canada in 1989. He was a member of Pastor Soodmand's church in Mashhad, Iran. (Pastor Soodmand was later charged with apostasy and sentenced to death by hanging on December 3, 1990, by the Iranian government.)

Pastor Kourosh began the Toronto Iranian Christian Church in 1992, reaching out to thousands of Iranians living in Toronto. Through his ministry in Canada, he has baptized four hundred fifty former Iranian Muslims who have come to Christ.[18]

The majority of these churches began with one convert from a Muslim background, who then began witnessing among his countrymen. Nader Mohajer is an example. In 1997, Nader left Iran for Turkey. There he met Khosrou Kodadadi, an Iranian pastor from a Muslim background. After hearing the gospel on November 22, 1998, Nader gave his heart to Christ and became a Christian. Shortly after his conversion, he left Turkey and went to Greece with a group of believers from the church.

In Greece, they saw the need for a church among the Iranian refugees. They organized a three-day seminar with two missionaries from England and the United States. Then, on May 14, 2000, they started the Persian Christian Fellowship in Athens with five believers who had come from Turkey. Pastor Nader, in a letter to the author, writes:

The church where we meet for Sunday services is the place where we minister to the refugees. We have Greek language class before the church service at 7:00 in the evening. We serve food after the service. Every Monday, we have prayer night and Bible study. We have more than twenty nationalities coming to the centre.

About five hundred to six hundred people visit the center, bringing various needs. They come for food, clothing, language classes, ministry to women, children's ministry, and medical needs. Since Greece is more of a temporary stop for the majority of the Iranian refugees, many of them are transferred to other parts of Europe, Canada, or the United States. In his letter, Pastor Nader continues, "We have many testimonies from refugees who came to know the Lord through this ministry."

In the remaining pages of this first chapter, and throughout this book, you will read miraculous stories that show God's amazing love for Iranian people and their responses to Him when they hear the gospel message. Each story represents many more who have given their lives to Christ and have come out of Islam into the freedom and liberty of Christ's love for them.

Here are some of their stories:

"Hallelujah! What Does It Mean?"

Born in a Muslim family and a closed Islamic society, for as long as he could remember Amir had hated himself and hated life. Bitterness had filled his heart, and the only way he could find peace was to take refuge in alcohol and cigarettes. An unsuccessful marriage led to an addiction to opium, for which he spent time in prison. He blamed his unhappiness on the political condition in Iran and decided to leave the country. He moved to Japan and started to work there.

Although Amir's economic situation improved due to a good paying job, his inner condition worsened day by day. Once again he retreated to drugs, this time to heroin and other more serious drugs. His addiction led to his participation in criminal activities in Japan. Amir despised his life. Often he would get involved in fights, and several times he stabbed people with a knife, eventually ending up in a Japanese prison. After his release he returned to Iran.

Back in Iran, he sought the help of many medical doctors for the anxiety he felt in his heart. None offered any lasting results. His addiction to heroin led to other addictions—alcohol, opium, hashish, and sleeping pills. Day by day the addictions grew stronger.

One morning while driving while under the influence of drugs, Amir ran over a man riding a bicycle. "I was so high on drugs I didn't know where I was going," Amir admits. He tried to flee from the scene of the accident, but found he couldn't. Amir took the injured man to the hospital, where his victim died a few hours later. The police arrested Amir and put him in prison.

That night in jail he decided to kill himself. He took many sleeping pills. But he didn't die—instead, he fell asleep for two days. "I hadn't had a good night's sleep for two years," recalls Amir. "Those two days I was completely knocked out. When I woke up, it was the first time I had felt rested in my body in twenty years." While in prison, he attempted suicide several other times, but with no success. *Why can't I die?* he wondered.

When his prison term was completed, a friend took him to see a Muslim prayer man. The man told him, in detail, some of the experiences of his past. This meeting with the Muslim fortuneteller spiked an interest in Amir to find out more about the Quran, Islam's holy book. He began reading the Quran.

Reading the Quran was a strange experience for him, even though he was born a Muslim. The violence that filled the pages of the Quran brought stinging fear to his heart that he had never felt before. He was afraid to ask anyone about these verses of the Quran that preached violence.

Amir's mother was a very religious woman and often told Amir that Hazrat-e-Ali (the first Imam of Shi'ite Islam) had given him to her. She had even called his name *Abd-al-Amir*, meaning "a slave of the prophet." She had told him that he must do his daily prayer and his thirty days of Ramadan fasting in order for God to save him. (All Muslims are commanded to pray their daily prayer in the Arabic language and to learn the five sets of prayers by heart in the Arabic language.)

Amir began praying and fasting. Many times while he prayed, he was doubtful and confused because he didn't understand what he was saying in Arabic. He felt like his thoughts were not in conjunction with his words. After a while he quit praying and fasting. *All of these religious deeds are a lie; there is no God*, he thought to himself. *If there was a God who created me, He would be willing to help me and people like me who live in misery.* Islam could not help Amir.

The darkness that Amir felt within isolated him. He had minimal contact with other people. He lived in his parents' house and continued with his daily drug habit.

One night he turned on the TV in his room to watch some programs from the satellite stations from America. While he was surfing through the stations he came across a program called *Roz-e-Nejat* (*Day of Salvation*—the name of my TV ministry) and heard me say: "I have good news for all of you who are drug addicts!" During the program Amir saw TV footage of the healing crusades our ministry holds around the world.

Amir says, "When I saw deaf and blind and paralyzed people getting healed, I thought to myself, *This is a new scheme, and Reza Safa is a charlatan.*" He believed that all the healings were staged so that our ministry could get people to give us some money.

"For several weeks I watched this program and wondered why Reza Safa wasn't talking about money and taking an offering," Amir says. "I also realized that there were multitudes of people getting healed, and that the healings were not being taped in a studio. And every time someone got healed, Reza Safa repeatedly cried out, 'Hallelujah!' over and over again." Amir was puzzled at that word because he had never heard it in the Farsi language. "I wondered what that word meant," Amir says. He was very curious, so he looked it up in the dictionary, but he couldn't find any word similar to it.

Amir explains, "That day I had such an urge to make a call to Reza Safa's office in America and find out what that word meant. I left the house, which was a rare event for me during those days, and bought a long distance phone card and called America. I was surprised to hear the phone being answered by Mr. Reza Safa himself. I asked him, 'What does the word *hallelujah* mean?'"

I told Amir that *hallelujah* means "praise the Lord." Then I asked Amir if he wanted to pray the prayer of salvation.

Amir tells the rest of the story: "'Would you like me to pray for you?' Mr. Safa asked me. At that time I felt like I had lost all my hope, so I couldn't lose anything else by him praying for me. 'Sure,' I said to him. When he started to pray for me I began to weep uncontrollably, without any reason. I was so embarrassed that I hung up the phone on him. Somehow a peace entered into my heart, and that was the beginning of my interest in Christianity. That was the first spark of faith in my heart."

One day as Amir was going through his brother's books, to his surprise he found an old Bible. The Bible is rarely in people's homes in Iran since Muslims believe that it is not the original Bible that Jesus wrote. Amir began to read the Bible every night. He recalls, "It was very interesting to read about a man who prayed for forgiveness for those who crucified Him. I wondered why Christians called Christ *God* although He was only a prophet. It must be because they have a great respect for him!" Reading the Bible brought great peace to Amir's heart, but he could not understand why.

A few months passed, and Amir decided to leave Iran again. He traveled to several countries—Russia, Ukraine, the Czech Republic, Austria, Germany, Holland, and Norway. "I was confused and didn't know what to do or where to go," Amir says.

In Norway Amir applied for a refugee status and was sent to a refugee camp. There he met a man by the name of Daniel, an Iranian preacher who invited him to church. Amir accepted his invitation.

"Every time I went to their meetings I felt peace in my heart," Amir remembers. He stayed in that refugee camp for a few weeks. Then he was transferred to the northern part of Norway. There were no Christians in the new refugee camp, and the unrest returned.

With the unrest came Amir's old feelings of depression and hopelessness. He told the camp director that he was suicidal, and the authorities at the camp sent him to a psychiatrist to help him with some medication. "After a few months I realized my condition was no better," Amir explains. "So I thought to myself, *The skies have the same color everywhere.* I decided to return to Iran again. I went back to my old life and forgot all about Christianity and Christ."

One night Amir had a visitation from the Lord. He describes the vision:

> I saw a very strange sight. I don't know if I was asleep or if I was awake. I saw Jesus in a vision. He stood at the bottom of my bed. He had a very white robe on. It was as though His hands and face were of light. He didn't say a word and didn't move. I saw Him so vividly and clearly that I could even tell you how tall He was. Without moving He removed something like a cover from me, as though someone was pulling a sheet away from me, uncovering me slowly. It was very strange. I was asleep, yet I could see Jesus right in front of me. It was as though my body was still lying on the bed, but I was in between my body and Jesus. I was both asleep and awake.

When Amir came to himself after the vision, he experienced a tremendous joy. "Have you ever been awakened by joy? That's how I felt. I couldn't compare that joy with anything I have ever experienced. I was filled with overflowing joy," Amir says.

The following morning while Amir was meditating on the vision, he heard a voice within saying, "Now you can leave the drugs." He says, "The voice was so comforting that without hesitation I began to look for all the drugs in my house, whether it was opium, hashish, or pills. I bagged them all up and took them to my brother." He told his brother that he didn't need the drugs anymore.

"My brother was shocked. My mother thought that I had lost my mind from using too many drugs," Amir says laughingly.

That evening Amir's brother called him and assured him that he would take Amir to the hospital to be treated for the overdose. He was worried about Amir's mental condition! Amir was so joyful that he kept laughing heartily. "I had such an extreme joy that I couldn't settle down," he says. "I told my brother that every cell in my body was celebrating." Amir had finally experienced freedom, and it had come to him as a result of the salvation of Jesus Christ.

Since that first vision of Jesus, Amir has had other supernatural experiences. He explains: "One day I saw Reza Safa's program again. As he prayed at the end of his program, I also prayed with him for my heart condition. For ten years I had been suffering from a heart condition. That day during the prayer, I felt as though something came out from behind my chest and out of my body. I was instantly healed. On another day, I was in prayer when I saw an open vision, which I will never forget. In the vision I saw my body was laid down on the floor. My skin was like a bag and all of my bones were jumbled disorderly in that bag. After that vision I lost my desire for things like money, cars, gold, and the like. With gladness, I returned the money I had taken unrighteously and by force from people.

"After that vision I began thinking about Islam. The same comforting voice that had spoken to me earlier told me that Islam was of Satan. I started searching in my room for everything that was from Islam—prayers, the Quran, fetishes, and such things—and I burned as much of it as I could. What I couldn't burn, I threw in the trash bin."

Amir had yet another vision. He relays the following vision:

One day as I was in prayer I had another vision. In this vision I was flying over a valley where I saw multitudes of people who were dressed in white robes. Their numbers were so great that the ground had become invisible. Everyone was so still and silent. There was a voice heard over the entire valley. It was the voice of a woman singing songs of praise unto God. I did not understand the meaning of the words she sang. But her voice was so joyful and peaceful that I would give my life to hear that sound again. After the vision I felt a heat in the palm of my hands. Whenever I pray, I feel the intensity of the heat in my hands.

That day I felt that I could pray for the sick. I tested it on my mother first. She had been suffering for many years from type 2 diabetes. I laid my hands on her head, and I prayed just like I had seen Mr. Reza Safa lay hands on the sick and pray. My mother was instantly healed. But she lost her healing after ten days because she kept saying that without Imam Abolfarz (one of the Shi'ite Imams) her healing would not be possible.

The second person I prayed for was my brother, who was also an opium addict. Even though he had seen the change in my life, still he would not believe. But one night as he was asleep, I prayed for him, quietly laying hands on him. I praise God that He heard my prayer and healed my brother from addiction. He is now a believer also in Christ Jesus.

God changed Amir and brought him out of darkness into His marvelous light. "After all these great miracles that I have experienced in my life, I am no longer the old person. I do not have any hate in my life toward anybody. I have a great compassion for people. They are like prisoners who must be freed. The prison doors are wide open. They must be willing to come out of the prisons. Jesus Christ said, 'Come to Me, all you who labor and are heavy laden, and I will give you rest' (Matt. 11:28)." Quoting the Scripture, Amir finishes his testimony.[19]

The hunger in Amir's heart led him to try everything that was available to him—to no avail. He was not free until the day he heard the message of the gospel of Jesus Christ. And of all the words he heard that day through the program *Roz-e-Nejat*, the word *hallelujah* struck a chord with him. Thank God for this great door of opportunity that He has opened to the Middle East through satellite TV.

There are hundreds and hundreds of great testimonies like Amir's. The pages of this book and ten more could be filled with one testimony after another of the many Iranians who have recently come to the knowledge of the Son of God, Jesus Christ.

Here are just a few more stories to show you the intensity of the move of God's Spirit in Iran.

"I Feel Like I Just Got Born!"

"I feel like I just got born!...like a baby...I feel like I weigh two kilograms! So light!"

These were the words that floated over the phone. After Homa and her family emigrated from Iran, they opened a family restaurant in their German town. The restaurant was located directly across from a Lutheran church. Hearing the sound of the church's bell ringing every day, Homa asked the "Prophet Jesus" to help her son, Farid, who was very rebellious.

One night her son had a dream about Jesus. In his dream, he wanted to lift up a heavy load but couldn't. He then asked his mother for help. In his dream he saw Jesus telling him that his mother could not help him! Then Jesus tapped the left side of his shoulder, entered into his body, and came out the other side! Farid woke up sweating and in tears and told his mother what he had seen in his dream. "Oh, Mom, it was so good, Jesus is so good."

From that day on, Farid was a changed man. He forsook his lifestyle of immoral behavior and became more serious about his studies at the local medical school.

In tears, Homa continued her long distance phone conversation with a *Roz-e-Nejat* counselor: "I just called you to tell you about my son's dream. Jesus truly changed my son. He is so different now. He is like a new son! So kind, so attentive, so loving...this Jesus.

"When I was very young, my husband and I visited Germany. It was during the Christmas time. I wasn't able to have children, and my husband's family wasn't nice to me. A Christian lady told me that if I were to pray to Jesus, He would grant me my desire! So, I asked Him for children, and the next Christmas my first child was born."

When they moved to Germany years later, Homa was more drawn to the church than to the mosque, and so she often visited the church.

That day, over the phone, Homa heard the message of salvation. She was totally filled with awe over all she heard about Jesus. Suddenly she cried out, "I feel Jesus is calling me. His Holy Spirit is calling me."

Homa gave her heart to Jesus as her Lord and Savior. Her voice shaking, crying, and full of emotion, she said, "How I lived in ignorance, not knowing these truths about Jesus!" That was a new day for Homa, a woman who had labored in hardship for many years.[20]

Mostafa Walks for the First Time

One day the parents of a young, seven-year-old boy named Mostafa watched the *Roz-e-Nejat* TV program and heard the testimonies of people who had been physically healed after watching the program. They needed prayer for Mostafa, who had been born with the umbilical cord wrapped around his neck, nearly killing him. The birth complication left Mostafa with paralysis and seizures. Doctors told the parents that they were not able to do anything for him.

Mostafa's family had taken their child to *mullahs* (Islamic clergymen) and asked for help with no results. But after watching the healing testimonies on the satellite program, the hope for Mostafa's healing was ignited in their hearts again. Now they wanted to see if Jesus would be able to help them!

When they called the telephone number given on the program, they were unable to make direct contact with a counselor, so they left a message on the *Roz-e-Nejat* answering machine—just one of many messages left daily. There are too few Persian-speaking workers to answer the overwhelming volume of calls. When a phone counselor reviewed the message, she returned their call. During the conversation, Mostafa's parents gave their hearts to Jesus. Then the phone counselor prayed for Mostafa. It was difficult to talk to him, because he was screaming and couldn't be still. Nevertheless, the phone counselor prayed for him.

A week later Mostafa's parents called again to give a great, joyful report. A few days earlier, Jesus had touched Mostafa, and he began to walk for the first time in his life.

After calling the first time, Fatemeh (Mostafa's mother) had a dream. In the dream, she saw herself giving birth to Mostafa again! According to her word, "It was as if he was born again." She told the dream to her husband, Abrahim, and he told her that Jesus wanted to heal Mostafa! Then a few days later Abrahim had a dream. In his dream he saw me come to their front door and pray for Mostafa. One day after that dream, Mostafa began to walk. They experienced an unspeakable joy as they witnessed their child walking for the first time, going around the house by himself. They were so thankful to the Lord.

Not only were their prayers answered for the healing of Mostafa, but the Lord also blessed them with a car! "We haven't had a car for twenty-two years. Truly Jesus' light is shining all over our home," Abrahim said.[21]

New Life in Manchester, England

Pastor Matt Beemer from World Harvest Bible Church in Manchester, England, tells of two Iranian conversions. (Please note that only initials are used for their names for security reasons.)[22]

Mr. C

Mr. C is a thirty-year-old man from south of Iran who was totally against God. A Persian member of World Harvest Bible Church (WHBC) tried several times to witness to him and his friend and to pray for them, but each time he would interrupt the conversations by arguing with the church member.

One day he phoned the man from WHBC and said, "Can you come to my home? I need to tell you something good that happened to me."

The man thought, *Probably his visa has been approved by the home office or something similar.* He decided to go and find out.

When he arrived at Mr. C's house, the normally disgruntled man welcomed him joyfully and began to apologize to him. "I am sorry for all the things that I have said against you and God," he said humbly.

He had become a changed person! He looked very peaceful. The Christian man wanted to know why he had changed. Mr. C responded by telling him that he had seen Jesus in his dream the previous night. "Jesus Christ is real and very kind," he said.

In Mr. C's dream, Jesus knocked on his door. When he opened the door, Jesus stood at the door and called him by his name and told him, "Follow Me." Jesus took him to World Harvest Bible Church where the other man attended. He took him to Pastor Matt Beemer's office, put his hand into the pastor's hand, and said to him, "Listen and follow Pastor Matt, and you will be fine." That day he became a born-again Christian. God changed him from an atheist to a believer in Christ. Glory to Jesus.

The man with cancer

During a meeting at World Harvest Bible Church, a forty-five-year-old man from Sheffield, originally from Iran, came with a diagnosis of cancer on both kidneys. Two women held his hands as they brought him to WHBC for healing.

At the front door of the church, one of the women explained to a Persian worker that the man had been told he had only a short time to live. The worker looked at him and noticed that he was skinny, sickly, and yellow. He did not even have enough strength to walk on his own. The Persian believer told him, "Jesus will heal you today," to which he replied, "I hope so." Mr. M., an Iranian member of the church who was standing next to him, told him loudly, "Jesus is the only healer, and He shall heal you today!"

When he came forward for prayer at the end of the service, he fell to the floor under the power and anointing of the Holy Spirit. While on the floor he said he saw Jesus, who told him, "You are healed." When he got up he said, "Cancer is finished." He did not even look sickly anymore—he looked strong and healthy.

Two weeks later he phoned the Persian worker and said, "I am healed. I want to testify to this in my church, but some brothers wouldn't believe me. But I know I am healed. What can I do?" The Persian worker told him, "Thank God for your healing. You are healed in Jesus' name. Be bold, trust God, and testify in the church." At the first opportunity, he did exactly that.

The government of Iran may be intimidating the world with its fanatical Islamic rhetoric and terrorist actions. But the people of Iran are hearing the truth of God's Word and are experiencing the warmth of God's love, causing them to reject the oppression of Islam to live in the freedom and liberty of Christ.

2

The Spirit of Islam

Many **Christians view** Islam through the same spectacles that the world uses. Yet the analysis of Islam that we often hear from the news media is far different from the reality of the true Islam. Most of these news stories come from in-the-field journalists who are covering a current event story for their magazines or newspapers. How can journalists who spend only a few weeks interviewing people in a foreign country with their cameras and lights explain the truth of a religion that is dominating 1.3 billion people and covers fifteen hundred years of history?

Islam extends from Africa to Asia and encompasses many cultures and people groups. The Islam practiced in Kenya is different from the Islam practiced in Indonesia or the Islam in the Middle East. Therefore, even someone with some experience in scholarly studies and degrees cannot paint the true picture of Islam. To really understand the religion of Islam, one must be born into it and spend time practicing the laws and ordinances of the religion. To be honest with you, I am hesitant to read books on Islam written by authors who were not born into a truly radical Muslim family. Anything less than that is like Barbara Walters' report on heaven where she attempted to tell us whether there is a heaven and where it is!

In the same way, you should not believe the commonly accepted notions that "Islam is a peaceful religion, and the radicals or 'extremists' have 'hijacked' that religion." As a former radical Shi'ite Muslim, I can tell you that nothing could be further from the truth.

Therefore, it is vital for us to put on our spiritual glasses and analyze Islam from a spiritual standpoint and not from a politically correct point of view. How do we do that? The Lord Jesus said, "Do not judge according to appearance, but judge with righteous judgment" (John 7:24). What is "righteous judgment"? Righteous judgment is that which is right before God, the way

God sees it. How then do we know what God says about Islam? In order for us to know what God says about Islam, we must first know what the Word of God says about other religions, and then we must know the teaching of Islam so that we can compare it with the words of Jesus. The scale we use is not based upon other people's understandings or points of view but rather upon the everlasting, eternal, and incorruptible Word of God.

In the Epistle of 1 John, we have been given a scale by which we can judge all prophecies and those who call themselves prophets. Every revelation received by man throughout history has come from one of three different sources—God's Spirit, the human spirit, or a demonic spirit.

The Bible says, "Do not believe every spirit, but test the spirits, whether they are of God; because many false prophets have gone out into the world" (1 John 4:1). The apostle then gives a condition by which these spirits should be judged:

> By this you know the Spirit of God: Every spirit that confesses that Jesus Christ has come in the flesh is of God, and every spirit that does not confess that Jesus Christ has come in the flesh is not of God. And this is the spirit of the Antichrist, which you have heard was coming, and is now already in the world.
>
> —1 JOHN 4:2–3

The condition by which we can judge a spirit rests on the point of whether or not that spirit confesses and acknowledges the deity of Jesus and the fact that Jesus, as God, became flesh.

If a spirit does not confess the deity and divinity of the resurrected Christ, that spirit is an *antichrist spirit*. The word *anti* (*an-tee* in Greek) means "opposite, i.e. instead or because of, for, in the room of." This word is often used in composition to denote contrast, requital, substitution, correspondence, and so forth. In other words, an *antichrist spirit* is the spirit that wants to take the place of Jesus. It is a revelation that claims supersession over Jesus. It therefore must deny the deity of Jesus; if it accepts the deity of Jesus, then it must acknowledge that every word of Jesus in the Bible is the truth.

Now we are getting somewhere. So now, with that understanding, let's judge Islam. What does Islam say about the person of Jesus, especially about His *deity*?

In the Quran we read:

> O People of the Book! commit no excesses in your religion: nor say
> of Allah anything but the truth. Christ Jesus the son of Mary was
> (*no more than*) a Messenger of Allah.... *Christ the son of Mary was no
> more than a Messenger;* many were the Messengers that passed away
> before him. His mother was a woman of truth. They had both to eat
> their (daily) food. See how Allah makes His Signs clear to them; yet
> see in what ways they are deluded away from the truth.
> —SURAH 4:171; 5:75, EMPHASIS ADDED

Not only does the Quran deny the deity of Jesus, but it also puts a curse
on all who believe in it.

> The Jews call 'Uzair a son of Allah, and the Christians call Christ
> the Son of Allah. That is a saying from their mouth; (in this) they
> but imitate what the Unbelievers of old used to say. *Allah's curse be
> on them:* how they are deluded away from the Truth!
> —SURAH 9:30, EMPHASIS ADDED

Islam denies the death and resurrection of Jesus, as well as His deity.

> That they said (in boast), "We killed Christ Jesus, the son of Mary,
> the Messenger of Allah";—but they did not kill him, nor crucified
> him, but so it was made to appear to them, and those who differ
> therein are full of doubts, with no (certain) knowledge, but only
> conjecture to follow, *for of a surety they did not kill him.*
> —SURAH 4:157, EMPHASIS ADDED

Islam denies the deity of Jesus and despises His cross. It denies the redemption and the forgiveness that were wrought for mankind through the shed
blood of Jesus. It denies the death and resurrection of Jesus.

I am not talking about the Antichrist, the person who will be manifested
before the return of Christ. I am speaking of the spirit of antichrist. John
says, "Test the spirits" (1 John 4:1). The word *spirits* is plural, meaning there
is more than one antichrist spirit. These are, of course, the demonic spirits
who are fallen beings.

An antichrist spirit works mainly through false prophets. John acknowledges, "Many false prophets have gone out into the world." I believe that every
person who calls himself a prophet must be tested. The Bible says, "Let two

or three prophets speak, and let the others judge" (1 Cor. 14:29). We must judge every revelation according to the Word of God. If the revelation does not align itself with the Word of God, it is not from God—no matter how it was given. I don't care if a host of angels came and manifested themselves and brought that revelation. The Bible warns us that Satan can appear as an angel of light (2 Cor. 11:14).

Islam denies the deity, death, and resurrection of Jesus; therefore, it is an antichrist religion. Islam denies the shed blood of Jesus and the redemption and forgiveness of sins through that blood, which makes Muhammad a false prophet and Islam a false religion.

In addition, Islam contradicts many facts and truths of the Bible. The Quran gives numerous revelations that totally contradict the Bible and the God of the Bible. Islam also produces a religious spirit in its followers that results in violence, bloodshed, and vengeance.

That Islam is an antichrist and anti-Christian religion is well known to all people around the world. There are not enough pages in a book to record all the atrocities that the followers of Islam have committed against Christians throughout the world. Iran today is a great example. The Islamic regime of the Ayatollah Khomeini has inflicted much pain and hardship upon the body of Christ in Iran.

Because of its violent nature and its opposition against Christ and Christianity, Islam reveals itself as a spiritual principality that will usher in the person of the Antichrist. I believe that Islam is spared for the End Time and will embody the wrath of Satan upon Planet Earth during the seven-year tribulation period. Islam will pave the way for the Antichrist through the tumult that it will cause in the years to come. I also believe that Islam will be an instrument in the hand of God in the same way Pharaoh was. Its purpose is twofold: to punish God's enemy, and to bring about obedience in God's people.

Two Different Ways of Thinking!

We in America and the West have come up short in our relations with the Muslim world because we have no understanding of the way Muslims think. It is important to recognize that a people's faith forms their thought world and their culture. The teachings of Islam and the traditions of Muhammad have formed a culture that is in grave contradiction to the way of life in the West, whose thinking and reasoning are founded on a Christian belief system.

Christianity gave birth to a culture characterized by love, forgiveness, justice, compassion, and freedom for the individual. These characteristics of a Christian ethos have formed the basis upon which most European societies and the New World were founded. Even though there is great opposition today against Christianity and its values in the Western Hemisphere, in reality its foundation was laid centuries ago, and the benefits derived from that foundation continue to be felt throughout society today.

In Western culture, the life of an individual has great value. For instance, in a country like Sweden, where I lived for eight years, there are many laws and ordinances that the Swedish government enforces to protect its citizens. This can be seen throughout Europe as well as in the United States, which is known for its protection of the rights of individuals and its system of justice.

In non-Christian countries like Afghanistan, India, Pakistan, and the nations of the Middle East, the life of an individual is not as important. In these countries, families routinely go without basic needs and die of simple diseases, while those in power live lavishly and fight for control. Children are forced to provide for their families, and young boys are often conscripted to fight. Justice does not prevail. In Saudi Arabia, for instance, you can lose a hand for stealing. In Afghanistan and other Muslim nations, you can lose your life for changing religions.

Human life is cheap in these countries. Is this because they are not educated? Is it because they are poor? Is it because they have no democracy? No, a country can lack all of these things, yet still honor human life. Why, then, don't they? It is due to the root problem—that the foundation upon which the culture is formed has not established the value of human life.

In the West, the way we look at politics, economics, relationships, and many other aspects of life differs vastly from the way a Muslim looks at them. This is simply because our religion constitutes our way of thinking, and our thinking generates our perceptions. Since our thinking is very different from that of a Muslim person, so will our understanding be dissimilar. It is imperative, in my opinion, that we realize this distinction, or else we will not be able to understand why the militant Muslims hate us and the ordinary Muslims dislike us.

Consequently, we cannot promote our values to Muslims and expect them to understand. What is holy to us is unholy to them, and that which is clean to them is unclean to us. Our freedom is a blasphemy to their religion, and their practices are abominations to us.

I grew up in a strong Muslim family in Iran. I was a devout Muslim who practiced all the laws and commandments of the Islamic faith. I understand the mind-set of Islam and the radical Muslims because I was one. So what I share with you is more than just book knowledge.

I have also spent over half of my life in the West. Comparison of the two cultures and mind-sets is imperative with us. The more we understand their ways of thinking, the less conflict we will have with them.

To understand the Islamic mind-set, we must first study the formation of the philosophy of Islam and its warfare.

Basis for War

Islam was founded in a seventh-century Arabian tribal society where the strong ruled. In the time of Muhammad, there were several influential tribes in Arabia who opposed Muhammad and the revelation of his new religion.

Arabia was dominated by powerful merchant families, among whom the men of Quraish were preeminent. They rejected Muhammad harshly in Mecca. The Quraish, the tribe to which Muhammad himself belonged, had charge of the Ka'aba, the cubic shrine upon which different tribes hung their idol gods. Because of their spiritual position in Mecca, the Quraish enjoyed a secure position free from all danger. They were prosperous merchants and travelers whose trade caravans drew people from neighboring countries to visit Mecca.

The Quraish resisted Muhammad and his revelation. They asked him for signs, such as bringing people back from the dead, to show he was Allah's prophet (Surah 44:34–36). They mocked Muhammad and his followers. They persecuted and oppressed the small Muslim community in Mecca. As a result, a concept of justification for warfare (authorized by Allah) developed within the Islamic philosophy. This concept forms the basis of Muslim thinking and the ideology of the Islamic jihad organizations all around the world.

Among Muslims, the primary grounds for confrontation are displayed arrogance, oppression against the weak, and *kofr*, or "blasphemy," toward Allah. These traits were all reputed to be characteristic of the tribe of

Quraish, which resisted Muhammad.

As a result, Allah warned Muhammad about the Quraish. These warnings against the infidel Quraish are important for us to note.

> To the People of Pharaoh, too, aforetime, came Warners (from Allah). The (people) rejected all Our Signs; but We seized them with such penalty (as comes) from One Exalted in Power, able to carry out His Will. Are you Unbelievers, (O Quraish), better than they? Or do you have an immunity in the Sacred Books?
>
> —SURAH 54:41–43

The warning became reality when revelation came to Muhammad to fight against the infidel Quraish.

> And why should you not fight in the cause of Allah and of those who, being weak, are ill-treated (and oppressed)?—men, women, and children, whose cry is: "Our Lord! rescue us from this town, whose people are oppressors; and raise for us from You one who will protect; and raise for us from You one who will help!"
>
> —SURAH 4:75

Yusuf Ali, in his commentary of the above verse writes:

> Even from the human point of view the cause of Allah is the cause of justice, the cause of the oppressed. In the great persecution, before Mekkah was won again, what sorrows, threats, tortures, and oppression were suffered by those whose faith was unshaken? Muhammad's life and that of his adherents was threatened: they were mocked, assaulted, insulted and beaten; those within the power of the enemy were put into chains and cast into prisons; others were boycotted, and shut out of trade, business, and social intercourse; they could not even buy food they wanted, or perform their religious duties. The persecution was redoubled for the believing slaves, women, and children after the Hijrah. Their cry for a protector and helper from Allah was answered when Muhammad, the chosen one, brought freedom and peace to Mekkah again.[1]

Thus Muhammad received permission from Allah to fight against the infidel Quraish. With an army of about three hundred men, Muhammad raided the Quraish caravan, which was protected by an army of one thousand men at Badr, a plain fifty miles southwest of Medina. Though outnumbered, the Muslim army won an impressive victory over the Meccan Quraish. This was a sign for the Muslim community that Allah's hand was upon them.

> There has already been for you a Sign in the two armies that met (in combat): one was fighting in the Cause of Allah, the other resisting Allah; these saw with their own eyes twice their number. But Allah supports with His aid whom He pleases. In this is a warning for such as have eyes to see.
>
> —SURAH 3:13

Thus began the ideology of Islam: righteous warfare in the cause of justice against the infidels and those who resist Allah and his prophet Muhammad.

Divisions and Warfare Within Islam

Violence became the norm of life for Muhammad's expansion throughout the Arabian Peninsula and also the neighboring kingdoms. By the time of Muhammad's death in A.D. 632, Islam had become the dominant power in the Arabian Peninsula. However, the Muslim community was faced with the problem of succession. Who would be the next Islamic leader? Muhammad's successors (caliphs) were appointed by the Muslim community to carry out the leadership and rule of Islam throughout the Arabian Peninsula and other parts of the world.

Four persons were recognized for their ability for leadership. Their role would be to lead the Islamic community according to the Quran and the tradition of Muhammad. These four caliphs in succession were: Abu Bakr, who ruled two years (632–634); Omar, who ruled the Islamic communities for ten years (634–644); Othman, who reigned thirteen years; and finally, Ali, the cousin and son-in-law of Muhammad, who reigned for a period of four years (656–661). The caliphs were political as well as spiritual leaders for the Muslim communities.

From its start, Islam gave birth to many tribal rivalries. The two major influential tribes in Arabia, Banu Hashem and Banu Umayyad, continued their feuds after the death of Muhammad. Banu Hashem accepted Abu Bakr and Omar as caliphs.

The rule of Abu Bakr, who was chosen to be the first caliph, was short lived but successful. After Muhammad's death, some tribes in Arabia renounced Islam and were divided. In a hefty effort, Abu Bakr swiftly disciplined them by military force and brought all the tribes in the Arabian Peninsula under the rule of Islam. He was able to divert the Arabs' tribal energies from internal division to warfare against the powerful empires of the East: the Sassanians in Persia, and the Byzantines in Syria, Palestine, and Egypt. In a short period of time, Abu Bakr was able to demonstrate the viability of the Muslim state.

Abu Bakr appointed Omar, known as the Amir al-Momineen ("Commander of the Believers"), as the second caliph. Under Omar's rulership a phenomenal expansion began, which continued for about a hundred years. The Muslim armies defeated the armies of the Sassanians (Persian) and Byzantine empires. They then swept through the area that is present-day Iraq and Iran to Central Asia (Bukhara and Samarkand) and the Punjab. They conquered all the Asiatic territories of the Roman Empire except Anatolia (modern Turkey). Northward they occupied Syria, and Damascus became the capital during the Umayyad Dynasty (661–750). They conquered Egypt and moved across North Africa and into Europe, ruling most of Spain.

Their move into the West was finally stopped in 732 by Charles Martel at the Battle of Tours in France. Thus Islam was established in Africa, the Middle East, and Asia. Within a hundred years after Muhammad's death, Islam had become an empire in which Allah and the laws of Islam ruled from the Punjab to the Pyrenees, and from Samarkand to the Sahara.

Omar served as caliph for ten years and ended his rule with a notable victory over the Persian Empire. His caliphate was a high point in early Islamic history. He was noted for his social ideals, administration, and statesmanship.

After the death of Omar, an advisory council composed of companions of Muhammad selected Othman as the third caliph. Othman, a wealthy man, helped Islam's march forward. He continued the Islamic invasion into Persia and the Byzantine empires. He moved into Africa and conquered what is now Libya and also Armenia. One of his notable achievements for Muslims was the compilation of the Quran, Islam's most holy book.

Othman became caliph in 644. Coming from the Umayyads tribe, he appointed his tribesmen to all key posts of the state, utterly excluding the Banu Hashem tribe. The feuds between these two tribes continued as Mu'awyah, an Umayyad, was appointed the governor of Syria. Merwan,

Othman's cousin and his chief minister, appointed Umayyads everywhere.

Hashemites, unhappy with the political positioning of the Umayyads, supported a man by the name of Abdullah ibn Saba, who gathered groups of people to march on Medina in 656, kill Othman, and appoint Ali, the cousin and son-in-law of Muhammad, as the rightful caliph. This move led to a civil war within the Muslim community.

In Medina, the city of their prophet Muhammad, death and chaos continued. Ali took control of the caliphate and dismissed all the Umayyad political positions, leading to discontentment among the Umayyads. Mu'awyah, the governor of Syria, refused to submit or recognize Ali as caliph. He was a strong opposer of Ali's election. (This is why Mu'awyah is greatly hated by the Shi'ite Muslims, the party of Ali.) He believed that Ali's caliphate was not valid because it had been supported by those responsible for Othman's assassination. The dissension between these two Muslim groups led to another war called *Siffin*, in which ninety thousand Muslims were killed on both sides.

The conflict between these Muslim groups eventually resulted in a major separation between the *Sunnis* or Sunnites, and the *Shi'ites* (also called Shi'ah), the party of Ali. Shi'ite, meaning a section, or schism, was developed based on the person of Ali, the fourth caliph. The essential tenet of Shi'ism is Imamat, which is the belief in the twelve Imams (Pontiff), who call themselves *Ithna-ashriyah*, or "the Twelvers."

The Shi'ites became strong opposers of the Umayyads. The power struggle between these two Muslim groups continued after Ali's assassination in 661 by his former followers, called *Kharijites*. Ali's son Hossein was the next in line for the caliphate according to Shi'ite belief. The Sunnis, however, appointed Mu'awyah as caliph.

The killing, hatred, and division went on as Yazid, the son of Mu'awyah of the Umayyad Dynasty, massacred Hossein, the son of Ali, along with his family in 680 at Karbala in Iraq. This event is celebrated by Shi'ites every year as a time of mourning during the Islamic month of Moharram. Moharram is the first month of *Hijra* (the migration of Muhammad and his followers from Mecca to Medina). The Shi'ites devote this month, especially the first ten days, to mourning by reenacting events of the battle of Karbala. They hold thousands upon thousands of passion plays and penitential processions, crying and weeping bitterly, beating their chests with their hands and their backs with chains, and chanting love songs in commemoration of Imam Hossein and his family.

The Shi'ites' dispute over the caliphate took a strong hold in Persia, some parts of Iraq, and also Yemen. In Iran (Persia), the Shi'ites are especially ardent about Ali's caliphate. They believe that the caliphate must remain within the family of the Prophet Muhammad. To the Shi'ites, Ali, the cousin and son-in-law of Muhammad, is the first valid caliph. He is an *Imam* or *Pontiff*, a rightful spiritual heir of Muhammad. The Shi'ites comprise about 10 percent of the Muslim population of the world.

According to the demographics of Islam as of mid-year 2005, the majority of Muslims are Sunnis, approximately 88.7 percent.[2] They believe in the process by which the caliphate was chosen. They are known as *ahl-al-sunnah wa-al-jama'ah*, meaning "the people of tradition and community," or "Sunnis." The Sunnis consider the caliph to be the guardian of the *sharia*, or Islamic law. The Shi'ites believe the Imams are the trustees of the law, inheriting Muhammad's spiritual position and knowledge. To the Shi'ites, Ali is a holy man, spiritually in the same rank as Muhammad. In Iran, for example, any blasphemy against Ali is punished with death. This view, according to the Sunnis, is considered an extremely exaggerated and distorted image of the person of Ali.

The Sunnis and the Shi'ites, however, believe and practice nearly all the same basic tenets of Islam. They both believe in the Quran. They both observe the same religious rituals, including praying five times a day, fasting, giving of alms, *hajj*, and so on.

Shi'ism

The Shi'ite creed consists of:

- Belief in the Imamat of Ali and his posterity

- The love of *Ahl-e-Bait*, the posterity of Muhammad through Ali, Fatima, Hassan, and Hossein

- Belief that the first three caliphs were usurpers, and therefore are considered to be unbelievers and renegades

- Belief that Ali is the uninterrupted caliph

- The cornerstone of Shi'ism is the belief in the Imamat of Ali and his posterity. According to Shi'ite belief, a good Momen (a true believer) is the one who believes in this.[3]

The Shi'ites believe in twelve Imams (Pontiffs): Ali, Hasan, Hossein, Zainul Aabedeen, Muhammad Bin Ali, Jaffer Siddique, Musa Kazim, Ali Sabir, Muhammad Taqi (called Ismailis), Ali Naqi, Hasan Zaki, and Muhammad Mehdi. The Shi'ites believe that the twelfth Imam—also called the "awaited Imam Mehdi"—according to the will of Allah, will remain underground for more than a thousand years and shall appear at the end of the time with Prophet Jesus to judge the world and spread Islam worldwide.

One can recognize a Shi'a from a Sunni Muslim by the way they posture during *namaz* (prayer). The Sunnis fold their arms during their prayer whereas the Shi'ites keep their arms loose. The Shi'ites also keep a piece of clay collected from Karbala in front and place their foreheads on it while prostrating in prayer.

Moharram is the first month of *Hijra* and is a sacred month, as the great Deliverance Day of Ashura falls on the tenth of this month. All Muslims observe Ashura as a day of devotion. On this day the Shi'ites mourn because of the massacre that took place at Karbala when Hossein and his family were slaughtered at the hands of the army of Yazid. During the first ten days of Moharram, the Shi'ites cry and weep, beating their chests with their hands and their backs with chains. Others carry small daggers and cut their shaved heads open as they chant and march throughout the city, replicating the blood that was shed by Imam Hossein and his family.

Islam in the Seventh Through the Nineteenth Centuries

The Umayyad Dynasty lasted for nearly one hundred years (661–750).[4] The successor dynasty, the Abbasid caliphate (750–1258), brought the rule of Islam into a new dimension of political power and wealth. Baghdad, the capital of the Abbasid caliphs, became a major center for the political and economic activity of the empire. During this period, the Islamic community experienced a renaissance in art, craft, education, science, commerce, and law. It was a period of cultural glitter for the Islamic community.

By the end of the tenth century, the caliphs lost their political power, and the empire began to break up into smaller provinces led by governors and warlords. Different political and religious views caused more division within the Islamic community.

In 1258, Baghdad fell to the Mongol army. The Mongol invasion was devastating; however, the Muslims converted their Mongol and Tatar conquerors, and by the fifteenth century the Islamic community had recovered.

From the fifteenth to the eighteenth centuries, Islam expanded into many new territories around the world. The political power of the Islamic community rose again to new heights with the rise of three new empires—the Mughal in India, the Safavieh in Iran, and the Ottoman in Anatolia (Turkey). These three empires controlled most of North Africa, the Middle East, Turkey, India, and central Asia. During the reign of these three empires, Islam spread throughout many new regions in Africa, Asia, and the Middle East, and many people were converted to Islam.

The Ottoman Empire was the most aggressive of them all and was the leading force against the Byzantine Empire. By the end of the thirteenth century, the Ottomans had conquered several Byzantine provinces, including Greece and Bulgaria. Constantinople, long a bulwark of Christendom against the Muslim advance, fell in 1453 and became Istanbul, the capital of the Ottoman Empire.[5]

During the fifteenth and sixteenth centuries, the Ottoman Turkish Empire continued to expand. Under Suleiman the Magnificent (1520–1566), it included all of the Balkan Peninsula, except rugged Montenegro and a strip of the Dalmatian coast. It reached into Hungary, made the Black Sea a Turkish lake, and embraced Asia Minor, Armenia, Georgia, the Euphrates valley, Syria, Palestine, Egypt, and the north coast of Africa as far as Morocco. The Ottoman Empire's advance to the West was stopped at the gates of Vienna in 1529, but it expanded southeastward, occupying Iraq and parts of Arabia.

Many areas where Christianity had been the faith of the majority now became predominantly Muslim. Christian communities survived but mainly in the historic Greek cities on the coast and among the Armenians. Systematic and compulsory conversion to Islam was common. Many Christian slaves whose masters were Muslims conformed to the faith of their owners. In the Balkan Peninsula, some of the Bogomils became Muslims to escape persecution by Orthodox and Catholic Christians. Thousands of Christian boys were torn from their parents, reared as Muslims, and enrolled in the armies. Many churches were transformed into mosques.

As we can clearly see by the history of the peoples it has ruled, from its inception Islam has been a religion of bloodshed, warfare, and division. Assassinations, betrayal, murders, and slaughter have been recorded on almost every page of this religion, both among its own communities as well as in its efforts to expand to other parts of the world.

A Bloodthirsty Spirit

In the following surah we read of a dreadful Allah who punishes harshly those who oppose him. Those who claim that Islam is a peaceful religion should note these verses.

> Remember your Lord inspired the angels (with the message): "I am with you: give firmness to the Believers: I will instill terror into the hearts of the Unbelievers: you smite above their necks and smite all their finger-tips off them." This because they contended against Allah and His Messenger: if any contend against Allah and His Messenger, Allah is strict in punishment. Thus (will it be said): "You taste then of the (punishment): for those who resist Allah, is the penalty of the Fire."
>
> —SURAH 8:12–14

Note how violent verse 12 is. This is not some extremist group declaration. This is the *Quran*, the highest authority in Islam. This verse is the reason the punishment of beheading has been practiced by Muslim governments and radical Islamic groups.

In a rally in Baalbek a week after the bombing of the U.S. Marines battalion headquarters in Lebanon in 1983, Sheikh Mohammed Yazbeck stated: "Let America, Israel and the world know that we have a lust for martyrdom and our motto is being translated into reality."[6]

Islam has left a fingerprint of blood through every page of its history, beginning with *Hijra* up to this very day. The spirit that promoted Islam is a bloodthirsty spirit that rages war and division. It is a spirit of revenge and retaliation. Its purpose is to create hate, sorrow, mourning, confusion, and fear. The following statement by Hussein Musawi, the leader of the Islamic Amal movement, illustrates such a spirit:

> This path is the path of blood, the path of martyrdom. For us death is easier than smoking a cigarette if it comes while fighting for the cause of God and while defending the oppressed.[7]

Where this spirit is permitted, there is terror and fear. It feeds on fear and death. Though Muslim scholars try to justify the acts, teachings, and laws of Islam, they cannot deny the history of bloodshed that Islam has left upon the pages of human history.

All of these beliefs come together in the Islamic practice of jihad, or holy war. Let us look in greater depth at what the Quran and other writings say about jihad and at modern-day examples of it in practice.

Jihad, the True Nature of Islam

The word *jihad* in Arabic means, "to strive for the cause of Islam." The Arabic word *taghala* also has the same meaning; jihad has a more militant connotation to it. Jihad has different meanings at different times within the life of an Islamic community. It can mean to protect the religion of Islam from an invading force; to spread the Islamic faith, values, and precepts in the time of peace; to make the word of Allah supreme; or to fight for the cause of Allah or Islam in the time of war. It is an obligation upon every Muslim who is capable of fighting, giving, or striving.

Jihad is the pinnacle of the Muslim faith and is the responsibility of Muslim rulers to initiate. If jihad is proclaimed, Muslims must be mobilized, and everyone who is able should answer the call to jihad.

Jihad in the Quran

Islam's holy writings have much to say about jihad. Dr. Mark Gabriel, former professor at the Islamic University of Al-Azhar in Egypt, estimates that approximately 60 percent of Islamic teachings are about jihad.[8]

The focus of jihad is fourfold:

- Fighting against the enemy of Islam—Surahs 2:190–191; 4:89; 5:33; 8:12–13, 65–67

- Fighting against the oppressors—Surahs 2:193, 217; 4:75; 8:30

- Fighting against the infidels—Surahs 4:71–104; 8:12, 24–65; 9:5; 47:4

- Fighting for the expansion of Islam—Surahs 8:39; 9:29, 41

There are hundreds and hundreds of other verses for the above points. It is also noteworthy that Yusuf Ali translates the word *ghatalo*, which in Arabic means "to kill," as meaning "to fight." Yusuf Ali was educated in the West and realized that the language of the Quran is too violent for the Western mind. Thus he tones down the translation of the Quran to be more suitable for the people in the West.

Since the September 11 attacks on the World Trade Center and the Pentagon, many Muslims in the West and abroad have given us their version of the meaning of jihad to keep Islam from being further defamed. Let's look at the actual meaning of jihad in light of what the Quran and other Islamic writings say.

> But when the forbidden months are past, then fight and *slay the Pagans* wherever ye find them, and seize them, beleaguer them, and lie in wait for them in every stratagem (of war); but if they repent, and establish regular prayers and practise regular charity, then open the way for them: for Allah is Oft-Forgiving, Most Merciful.
> —SURAH 9:5, EMPHASIS ADDED

> You go forth, (whether equipped) lightly or heavily, and *strive and struggle,* with your goods and your persons, in the Cause of Allah. That is best for you, if you (but) knew.
> —SURAH 9:41, EMPHASIS ADDED

> Allah hath purchased of the Believers their persons and their goods; for theirs (in return) is the Garden (of Paradise): *they fight*

in His Cause, and slay and are slain: a promise binding on Him in Truth, through the Law, the Gospel, and the Qur'an: and who is more faithful to his Covenant than Allah? Then rejoice in the bargain which you have concluded: that is the supreme achievement.

—SURAH 9:111, EMPHASIS ADDED

O Prophet! Strive hard against the Unbelievers and the Hypocrites, and be firm against them. Their abode is Hell,—an evil refuge (indeed).

—SURAH 66:9

Did you think that you would enter Heaven without Allah testing those of you who *fought hard (in His Cause)* and remained steadfast?

—SURAH 3:142, EMPHASIS ADDED

And if you are slain, or die, in the Way of Allah, forgiveness and mercy from Allah are far better than all they could amass. *And if you die, or are slain,* lo! it is unto Allah that you are brought together.

—SURAH 3:157–158, EMPHASIS ADDED

Those who *believe fight in the cause of Allah,* and those who reject Faith fight in the cause of Evil: so you fight against the friends of Satan: feeble indeed is the cunning of Satan. Have you not turned your vision to those who were told to hold back their hands (from fight) but establish regular prayers and spend in regular Charity? When (at length) the order for fighting was issued to them, behold! a section of them feared men as—or even more than—they should have feared Allah: they said: "Our Lord! why have you ordered us to fight? Would You not grant us respite to our (natural) term, near (enough)?" Say: "Short is the enjoyment of this world: the Hereafter is the best for those who do right; never will you be dealt with unjustly in the very least!"

—SURAH 4:76–77

O you who believe! when ye go abroad in the cause of Allah, investigate carefully, and do not say to any one who offers you a salutation: "You are not a Believer!" coveting the perishable goods of this life: with Allah are profits and spoils abundant. Even thus were you yourselves before, till Allah conferred on you His favors: therefore carefully investigate. For Allah is well aware of all that you do. Not equal are those believers who sit (at home) and receive no hurt, and those who

strive and fight in the cause of Allah with their goods and their persons. Allah has granted a grade higher to those who strive and fight with their goods and persons than to those who sit (at home). To all (in Faith) Allah has promised good: *but those who strive and fight He has distinguished above those who sit (at home) by a special reward.*
—SURAH 4:94–95, EMPHASIS ADDED

Surah 8 was the surah that Muhammad Atta ordered his group to read before they began hijacking the planes on September 11. In that surah we read:

Against them make ready your strength to the utmost of your power, including steeds of war, *to strike terror into (the hearts of) the enemies, of Allah and your enemies*, and others besides, whom you may not know, but whom Allah knows. Whatever you shall spend in the Cause of Allah, shall be repaid to you, and you shall not be treated unjustly.
—SURAH 8:60, EMPHASIS ADDED

O Messenger! rouse the Believers to the fight. If there are twenty amongst you, patient and persevering, they will vanquish two hundred: if a hundred, *they will vanquish a thousand of the Unbelievers*: for these are a people without understanding.
—SURAH 8:65, EMPHASIS ADDED

Those who believe, and adopt exile, *and fight for the Faith*, in the cause of Allah, as well as those who give (them) asylum and aid,— these are (all) in very truth the Believers: for them is the forgiveness of sins and a provision most generous.
—SURAH 8:74, EMPHASIS ADDED

We can also read in Surah 2:

And fight them on until there is no more tumult or oppression, and there prevail justice and faith in Allah; but if they cease, let there be no hostility except to those who practise oppression.
—SURAH 2:193, EMPHASIS ADDED

Fighting is prescribed for you, and you dislike it. But it is possible that you dislike a thing which is good for you, and that you love a

thing which is bad for you. But Allah knows, and you know not.
—SURAH 2: 216, EMPHASIS ADDED

Jihad in the Hadith

After the Quran, the hadith is the second most important source of Islamic theology. The hadith are the sayings, deeds, and traditions of Muhammad, the prophet of Islam. The Quran was revealed to Muhammad by various means within a period of twenty-two years. Since Muhammad was illiterate, the verses of the Quran were recorded by Muhammad's companions as he received them and recited them. While he was reciting these verses of the Quran, his companions wrote them down on various materials that were later compiled into a book called the Quran (Recital). There are 114 surahs, or chapters, in the Quran. These chapters are organized according to their length and are not historically ordered. Since there is no chronological order, it is difficult to interpret it in accordance to a commandment or an ordinance. There are also many controversies within the Quran. For instance, Surah 2:256 states, "Let there be no compulsion in religion." Yet in Surah 9:5 Muhammad was commanded to kill the pagans:

> But when the forbidden months are past, then fight and slay the Pagans wherever you find them, and seize them, beleaguer them, and lie in wait for them in every stratagem (of war); but if they repent, and establish regular prayers and practise regular charity, then open the way for them: for Allah is Oft-forgiving, Most Merciful.

To justify the many controversies of the Quran and present a more comprehensive understanding of it, Muslim scholars refer to the hadith, which records how Muhammad reacted and what he said and did in every situation during his ministry as a prophet of Allah.

There are unlimited numbers of hadith, most of them fabricated. However, the majority of the Islamic world agrees on the authenticity of the hadith recorded by Sahih Bukhari, or actually known as Muhammad al-Bukhari. *Sahih* is an Arabic word that means "correct" or "authentic," so "Sahih Bukhari" could be translated as "Bukhari's Authentic (correct) Sources." Sahih Bukhari is one of the six Sunni major hadith collections. Muhammad al-Bukhari chose 9,082 hadiths to be authentic among 300,000 hadith that he had collected. It took him six years to write the nine volumes of hadiths. It is the most famous hadith collection among the Sunni Muslims.[9]

The following stories are some hadith, which are the sayings and deeds of Muhammad. Abu Hurairah reports a hadith:

> The Messenger of Allah (may peace be upon him) was asked: What deed could be an equivalent to Jihad in the way of Allah, the Almighty and Exalted? He answered: You do not have the strength to do that deed. They repeated the question twice or thrice. Every time he answered: You do not have the strength to do it. When the question was asked for the third time, he said: One who goes out for Jihad is like a person who keeps Fast, stands in the Prayer (constantly), (obeying) Allah's (behests contained in) the verses (of the Qur'an), and does not exhibit any lassitude in Fasting and the Prayer until the Mujahid returns from Jihad in the way of Allah, the Exalted.[10]

A hadith reported by Abu Sa'id Al-Khudri:

> A man came to the Holy Prophet (may peace be upon him) and said: Who is the best of men? He replied: A man who fights in the way of Allah spending his wealth and staking his life. The man then asked: Who is next to him (in excellence)? He said: Next to him is a believer who lives in a mountain gorge worshipping his Lord and sparing men from his mischief.[11]

A hadith reported by Al-Bara:

> A man from Banu Al-Nabit (one of the Ansar tribes) came to the Holy Prophet (may peace be upon him) and said: I testify that there is no god except Allah and that you are His servant and Messenger. Then he went forward and fought until he was killed. The Holy Prophet (may peace be upon him) said: He has done little but will be given a great reward.[12]

Abu Hurairah reported:

> The Messenger of Allah (may peace be upon him) said: I have been commanded to fight against people until they testify that there is no god but Allah, and he who professes it is guaranteed the protec-

tion of his property and life on my behalf except for a right warrant, and his affairs rest with Allah.[13]

Abdullah bin Umar reported:

Allah's Messenger said: I have been commanded to fight against people till they testify that there is no god but Allah, and that Muhammad is the Messenger of Allah, perform the Prayer, and pay Zakah. If they do that, their blood and property are guaranteed protection on my behalf except when justified by law, and their affairs rest with Allah.[14]

Usamah bin Zaid narrated:

Allah's Messenger (may peace be upon him) sent us in military detachment. We raided Al-Huraqat of the Juhainah in the morning. I caught hold of a man and he said La Ilaha Illal Allah (There is no god but Allah), I attacked him with a spear. It once occurred to me and I talked about it to the Messenger (may peace be upon him). The Messenger of Allah (may peace be upon him) asked: Did he profess "There is no god but Allah," and even then you killed him? I said: Messenger of Allah, he made a profession of it out of the fear of the weapon. He (the Holy Prophet) observed: Did you check inside his heart to find out whether he said it (out of fear) or not?" And he went on repeating it to me till I wished I had embraced Islam only that day. Sa'd said: By Allah, I would never kill any Muslim so long as the person with a heavy belly, i.e. Usamah, would not kill. Upon this a person remarked: Did Allah not say this: "And fight them until there is no more mischief and religion is wholly for Allah"? Sa'd said: We fought so that there should be no mischief, but you and your companions wish to fight so that there should be mischief.[15]

True Islam Is Militant

Hundreds upon hundreds of hadith and Quranic verses speak of warfare, violence, killing, and bloodshed. How could one with a decent intelligence declare that Islam is a peaceful religion?

When Khomeini rose to power in Iran, the experts on Islam in the West believed that his version of Islam was different from the true Islam. "They are

Shi'ite," they said. "Shi'ites are militant." This was how they justified these violent acts, by saying that they did not represent true Islam, or that a true Muslim is not militant. And in the aftermath of September 11, the phrase "Islam is peaceful" has been proclaimed from nearly every newsroom in the country as well as from Washington. We are being politically correct, but we are very wrong in our conception of the true Islam.

In like manner, the Islamic communities in America have distanced themselves from the grim and merciless acts of Al-Qaeda and Osama bin Laden. "They are not true Muslims," they say. "*Islam* comes from the word *Salaam*, which means 'peace.'" But bin Laden is a Sunni Muslim, as are the majority of the radical militant groups. And, actually, the word *Islam* comes from the root word *Tasleem*, which means "surrender."

Out of ignorance, deception, self-defense, or political correctness, many are endorsing their own versions of Islam. But their assertions are no truer than if I were to declare that I have been to the moon. Islam's history reveals that the ideology and way of warfare of bin Laden, Khomeini, Hamas, Hezbollah, and many other Islamic groups were born in seventh-century Arabia with the institution of the religion.

In his book *Hokumat-e-Islami* [Islamic Rule], Khomeini clearly identifies his ideologies, claims, and views as a revival of a tradition he traces to Muhammad, the prophet and founder of Islam. A scholar commented regarding Khomeini, "[He] defines Islamic identity in terms of paradigm or an archetype provided by the activity of the Prophet Muhammad, Imam Ali and Imam Hossein."[16]

The Muslim Brotherhood in Egypt and Syria is another example. This organization is not related to bin Laden, the Taliban, or Khomeini, yet it possesses the same spirit of death and violence. The organization was founded by Hassan al-Banna (1904–1949) in 1928 in Egypt with the goal of returning to the fundamentals of true Islam. The movement expanded in membership as persecution from the Egyptian government increased. The Brotherhood became more and more militant; they trained their young members for jihad against British colonialists. They also prepared to help the Palestinians against the Israelis. Their slogan was, "The Koran is our constitution, the Prophet is our guide; death for the glory of Allah is our greatest ambition."[17]

The following, recorded by Robin Wright in her book *Sacred Rage*, explains the spirit of hate and bloodshed in the Muslim Brotherhood:

A former Egyptian Interior Minister, Ahmed Mortada al Maraghi, wrote about how the young militants were recruited:

A small room lit with candle light and smoky with incense is chosen. . . . Once the likely young man is selected, he is brought to this room . . . where he will find a sheikh repeating verses from the Koran. . . . The Sheikh [*sic*], with eyes like magnets, stares at the young man who is paralyzed with awe. . . . They will then pray, and the sheikh will recite verses from the Koran about those fighting for the sake of Allah and are therefore promised to go to heaven. "Are you ready for martyrdom?" the young man is asked. "Yes, yes," he repeats. He is then given the oath on the Koran. These young men leave the meeting with one determination: to kill.[18]

Out of the Muslim Brotherhood organization many other radical groups sprouted in Egypt, groups like *Al Jihad* ("The Jihad Organization") and *Al Taqfir Wal Higrah* ("Repentance and Migration"), a group responsible for the assassination of many innocent people. The nature of these groups is truly demonstrated in how they kill their victims. Sheikh Muhammad al Dhahabi, the minister of religious endowment of Egypt, was among the victims assassinated by *Al Taqfir Wal Higrah*. He was first strangled, and then a bullet was fired into his left eye.[19]

Al Jihad is known as the organization responsible for the 1981 assassination of Egyptian President Anwar Sadat and seven others. Sheikh Omar Abdel Rahman, one of the recognized spiritual leaders of *Al Jihad*, was arrested, imprisoned, and then acquitted for encouraging the assassination. Today he sits in a prison cell in the United States for masterminding the 1993 bombing of the World Trade Center.

TIME magazine says of Abdel Rahman:

U.S. and Egyptian officials suspect him of issuing "fatwas," or religious decrees, in the 1990 Manhattan slaying of Jewish militant Rabbi Meir Kahane and the 1992 Brooklyn murder of an Egyptian named Mustafa Shalabi. . . . Cairo officials also blame Sheik Omar and his 10,000 hardcore disciples in Egypt for 20 attacks against tourist targets. Islamic groups, of which Sheik Omar's is just one of many, have accelerated their attacks on security forces and Coptic Christians, as well as tourist sites. Last year 80 people were killed and 130 wounded.[20]

In the same article Sheikh Omar explained his view:

> I just want to serve Islam by all my strength and power. Khomeini led a revolution and beautified his country, made it clean of Shah, who was so unjust. What Khomeini did was a real success.[21]

Islamic organizations like Al-Qaeda, Mojahedin, Hamas, Hezbollah, Amal, the Palestine Liberation Organization (PLO), and others have proven that war and bloodshed are distinct patterns for a true Islam.

Mohammed Taki Moudarrissi, another leader of the Islamic Amal movement, has stated, "I can in one week assemble five hundred faithful ready to throw themselves into suicide operations. No frontier will stop them."[22]

Dying to Please Allah

To a radical Muslim, dying and killing for the cause of Islam is not only an honor but also a way of pleasing Allah. The only way a Muslim can have assurance of salvation and eternal life is by becoming a martyr for the cause of Islam.

> Those who believe, and suffer exile and strive with might and main, in the cause of Allah, with their goods and their persons, have the highest rank in the sight of Allah: they are the people who will achieve (salvation). Their Lord gives them glad tidings of a Mercy from Himself, of His good pleasure, and of Gardens for them, wherein are delights that endure: They will dwell therein forever. Verily in Allah's presence is a reward, the greatest (of all).
> —Surah 9:20–22

> And their Lord has accepted of them, and answered them: "Never will I suffer to be lost the work of any of you, be he male or female: you are members, one of another: those who have left their homes, or been driven out therefrom, or suffered harm in My Cause, or fought or been slain,—verily, I will blot out from them their iniquities, and admit them into Gardens with rivers flowing beneath;—a reward from the Presence of Allah, and from His Presence is the best of rewards."
> —Surah 3:195

A handwritten letter found in the luggage of Muhammad Atta, the young well-educated Egyptian suspected to be the ringleader of the September 11 attacks, reads:

> Purify your heart and forget something called life, for the time of play is gone and the time of the truth has come.... God will absolve you of your sins, and be assured that it will be only moments and then you will attain the ultimate and greatest reward.... Check your bag, clothes, knives, tools, ID, passport, all your papers, inspect all your weapons before departure. Let each find his blade for the prey to be slaughtered.... As soon as you put your feet in and before you enter [the plane] start praying and realize that this is a battle for the sake of Allah, and when you sit in your seat say these prayers that we had mentioned before. When the plane starts moving, then you are traveling toward Allah and what a blessing that travel is.[23]

Assurance of salvation is why so many young boys in Iran volunteered to become a *basiji* ("the mobilized") during the Iran-Iraq war. Khomeini would one night appear on Iranian national television asking for volunteers to fight in the war. The following day, thousands of young boys, ages twelve to eighteen, would be recruited from local schools and the streets. These young, brainwashed volunteers would be given a red or green band that was to be worn on their foreheads, reading *Shahid,* or "the martyrs." Their task would be to die for the cause of Islam.

A *basiji* was committed to death, not just the possibility of death. These young boys volunteered to clear the minefields with their bodies. Military leaders would send out as many as five thousand boys at once to run through the fields and trip the mines. Sometimes they asked the boys to clear high-voltage border fences by throwing their bodies against the fences. Thousands of young bodies were shattered and electrocuted in this manner. Many of these young boys were only twelve or thirteen years old. To them, Khomeini gave the promise of *behesht* ("paradise"). To symbolize this false promise, he gave them a key that they hung around their neck—a key with which they could open the gate of heaven.

A note left by one young Iranian soldier, Mohsen Naeemi, who died in the war with Iraq, reflects the mind of Islam and the deception of this religion.

My wedding is at the front and my bride is martyrdom. The sermon will be uttered by the roar of guns. I shall attire myself in my blood for this ceremony. My bride, martyrdom, shall give birth to my son, freedom. I leave this son in your safekeeping. Keep him well.[24]

One Western official remarked:

As we are learning, these are not the odd men out. Whatever hardship stories come out of Iran, it remains a source of pride to the Shia. They truly live in a different world, their thinking totally alien and incomprehensible to the Western mind. We keep thinking they will come to their senses and realize this foolhardiness will cost them their one and only life. What is hard for us to fathom is that this is what life is all about to them, a gateway to heaven that must be earned.[25]

For Khomeini, the death of these young people of Iran was not a loss but an asset. Khomeini's message to Saddam Hussein was, "We should sacrifice all our loved ones for the sake of Islam. If we are killed, we have performed our duty."[26]

Khomeini truly fulfilled this proclamation during the eight-year war with Iraq. Many Iranians told me that finding a husband in Iran after the war was a miracle, because there weren't many young men left alive.

I believe that the spirits that gave birth to Islam are the spirits of hatred, bloodshed, warfare, and death. The history of Islam will prove that wherever and whenever Islam has trod, it has created an atmosphere of fear, death, bloodshed, and hatred.

I believe that the same spirit that introduced Baal worship in Israel birthed Islam. Islam's spirit is a demon spirit, a spirit of death and destruction. This is why I believe that we can never win the battle against radical (true) Islam with physical and military warfare. The more you fight it, the stronger it will become, because that spirit is fed by bloodshed and hatred.

Let us now see how it resurged in the twentieth century.

3

America and Iran at Odds

The Islamic Revolution of 1979 and the years that led up to it are vital parts of the history and future of America. It is of utmost importance to have an understanding of what actually took place in Iran to cause the revolution. If we do not learn the process that led to the revolution, we will see it repeated again in other parts of the Islamic world in a not too distant future. The potential for a radical Islamic Revolution of Khomeini's type is more of a reality today in countries such as Pakistan, Saudi Arabia, Algeria, and Egypt than ever before in the modern history of the world. If we do not want Iran's Revolution to be repeated, we must study the conditions that gave birth to it.

Studying the past and present policies of the United States regarding the Middle Eastern nations such as Iran will reveal that we have not always been effective in our interactions with people of the Muslim faith. As Gary Sick, former national Security Council staff during the Carter administration, puts it, "The evidence suggests that we are poorly equipped to deal with revolutionary societies, and when religion is added to revolution, we are paralyzed."[1] In other words, I believe that we do not know how to deal with the Muslim faith. A study of the past and present policies of the United States regarding Middle Eastern nations demonstrates that our dealings with these nations are based upon *our strengths* and not *their weaknesses*. And that, I believe, is our weakness.

For example, the current conflict in the Middle East in Afghanistan and Iraq is a demonstration of American strength. Overpowering someone with a strong hand leads to a quick success (relatively speaking) and brings a great sense of accomplishment in the eyes of patriotism. But ten years from now, what will be the consequences of our military forces pounding the Taliban in Afghanistan and Saddam's regime in Iraq?

In the case of Iran, we already know the answer. I believe, as do many scholars and well-versed politicians, that the Islamic Revolution of Ayatollah

Khomeini was a direct result of our policies with the shah of Iran. In this chapter we will develop the history of American and Iranian relations and help you to see the impact that the actions of the American government in the past has had on that nation, helping to create the climate of hostility and hatred that exists between America and Iran today.

This may sound like a harsh judgment to the ears of those who have no knowledge of the events that led to the revolution of 1979. Perhaps you remember the days when the shah of Iran gained American support to prevent nationalization of Iran's oil industry. In return for assuring the United States a steady supply of oil, the shah received economic and military aid from eight American presidents.

But can you answer this question: "Why has Iran been harboring such a fierce rage against the United States for the past twenty-six years?" It couldn't just be because of a few bad policies, could it? If that were the case, we should have been able to mend our relationship with Iran during the past twenty-six years. But it seems that the sore is deeper, and we need to find out why and how we can fix it. For if we do not, the times ahead will be harder than these past two and a half decades.

The current climate in the Middle East is filled with fear and uncertainties. You cannot watch the morning news today or read a national newspaper without becoming more and more aware of Iran's race to acquire nuclear ability. The possibility of an Iran armed with nukes to force its hard-line policies upon Israel and the infidel West is becoming an ominous reality. Iran should be the greatest concern of the Western politicians, and also of the Christians.

In his best-selling book *Jerusalem Countdown,* John Hagee cited information from confidential sources in Israel to expose this reality: "Unless the entire world—including America, Israel, and the Middle East—reach soon a diplomatic and peaceful solution to Iran's nuclear threat, Israel and America will be on a nuclear collision course with Iran."[2] Hagee continued by saying:

> Iran's hatred for America and Israel is without limit. Iran's nuclear program is designed to make Islam a global force and, in my judgment, is as great a threat to democracy as Hitler's Nazis and Lenin's Communism.[3]

Iran and America

Prior to the Islamic Revolution of the Ayatollah Khomeini and the taking of the American hostages in 1979, where they were held for 444 days, Iran was an exotic name to many, if not all, Americans. Even though Iran (Persia) was one of the major ancient empires with great influence in the fields of architecture and medicine, there is little mention of Persian culture and history in American textbooks, other than the story of Cyrus the Great and his defeat at the hands of the Greeks.

Let me tell you why I believe I can help you to understand what has brought us to such a climate of hatred between America and Iran. I was born into a Muslim family in Iran and became a devout and practicing Shi'ite, observing the laws and regulations of Islam. I lived eighteen years in Iran. I have the strong personality of a Persian, and, even after eighteen years with the great American diet, I still prefer Persian food above all others. I have also, at the time of this writing, lived eighteen years in the United States. I am married to a pure Yankee from Philadelphia, and I live and minister as a pastor among the American people. I can boldly claim that I know as much about the American culture and people as I do about Iran and the Iranian people.

I do not consider myself a pure Persian, due to the fact that I have lived over half of my life in three countries outside of Iran. I think I am three nationalities in one—Iranian, Swedish, and American. It was in Sweden that I was born again, and part of that culture was instilled in me. I am proud of carrying a dual citizenship with Sweden.

As an American, I have traveled extensively to fifty countries around the world, yet nowhere do I feel more at home than in the United States. Not because of all the comfort of life in this country (although I am sure that helps the matter), but I love America because of what America is—its people, its laws, and its possibilities. It fits who I am.

The 1979 Iranian Revolution resulted in one of the largest migrations in Iran's history. Among these émigrés were many who left Iran for political and religious reasons. Many others escaped the country to seek refuge from the eight-year Iran-Iraq War (1980–1988). The largest number of these immigrants, refugees, or exiles chose the United States as their new home.[4] According to current statistics, nearly 4.2 million Iranians live outside Iran, with nearly 1.7 million Iranians living in the United States.[5]

In spite of the fact that the Iranian regime remains the most resolute in confronting the United States, Iran itself suffers from internal contradictions that the mullahs wish did not exist. The Iranian people love America, and there is very little the government in Tehran can do to cool pro-Americanism on the streets.[6]

Iran and America are two completely different cultures, yet, in many ways, they possess the same zeal and personality characteristics. Let me illustrate this by telling you about Bob Nelson, a friend of mine who is a successful businessman in Tulsa, Oklahoma. Bobby, as we call him, is almost a spitting image of my personality. Although we come from two completely different backgrounds and cultures—mine as an Iranian, and his as a native "Okie," an American through and through—we couldn't be more similar in person-alities. We are rivals on the golf course, but aside from my pastor, Bror Spetz, from Sweden, I consider Bobby to be my closest friend and brother.

I believe that Americans and Iranians carry the same zeal for life and also a similar passion for conquest. As people, Americans and Iranians are similar by nature, yet so distant by culture and lifestyle. I believe that people of the same character and essence must meet each other on the same level. One cannot stand on a higher ground than the other. That would create competition and rivalries. And if the relationship is hurt, competition will turn into animosity and hatred.

Our human nature dictates that we do not so much mind being beaten by someone who is better and bigger than us, but we cannot tolerate defeat by our equal. This is why there are so many sibling rivalries. And I believe that part of our problem with Iran is that we have not met them as equals but have taken the higher ground of exerting our strength and authority over them.

The Missing Piece of the Puzzle

To understand the current Iranian hostility toward America, we need to go back a few decades in history and look at some key points.

The first American-Iranian interaction took place in 1856 when the Treaty of Friendship and Commerce was signed between Washington and the Qajar Shah of Iran. And in 1883 the United States opened its first dip-lomatic office in Tehran.[7]

In 1925 the Iranian Parliament (Majles) deposed the corrupt Qajar dynasty and amended the constitution to confer the monarchy on Reza Khan and his descendants, and he became Reza Shah Pahlavi, the shah (king) of Iran. In 1928, a new commerce treaty was signed between Reza Khan (also known as Reza Shah) and the United States.

Reza Shah emerged at a time when the Iranian people were wary of the corrupt rule of the Qajar dynasty. Qajar's corrupt reign had given way to several decades of relentless foreign interventions in Iranian affairs. The Russians and the British were two main foreign powers who had their eyes fixed on Iran. Great Britain had especially caused much affliction and damage to the Iranian economy by usurping their national resources such as oil.

After World War I, Iran became a battleground for the foreign forces who left Iran in economic disaster. It is believed that as many as two million Iranians may have died as a result of the famine caused by the fighting of foreign forces in northern Iran.[8]

After the war Iran became, for the most part, another territorial colony for the British. A few years before World War I, the British-born Australian William D. Arcy had discovered the black gold—oil—in Masjed-e-Soleyman in southwestern Iran. Oil became a vital part of the British war engines. And almost all of that oil came from Iran.

The Anglo-Persian Oil Company (APOC), also known as Anglo-Iranian Oil Company (AIOC), was founded in 1909. Fifty-one percent of the company's share went to the British. From 1914 to 1945 the export of oil from Iran grew from 300,000 tons to 16.5 million tons. Most of the profit from it ended up in British pockets. In 1950, Iran earned only 37 million pounds from the sale of oil. If Iran had had full control of their own oil, that amount would have been almost ten times more.[9]

The British fleecing of the Iranians of their national resources has led to much distrust among the Iranians toward the foreign powers, especially toward the Englishmen. Even today much of the political misfortunes in Iran are blamed on the English people. As a matter of fact, the majority of Iranians believe that the Islamic Revolution of the Ayatollah Khomeini in 1979 was plotted and planned by the British. This sentiment was aptly expressed by a Tehran taxi driver's knowing remark to his passenger: "The British are behind everything in Iran."[10]

This sentiment is so strong that even the shah of Iran had a strong conviction and mistrust toward the British government. In his memoir, *Answer to History*, he writes:

> The attempt on my life on February 4, 1949, convinced me once more that I was protected. That day, in the early afternoon, I was to attend the annual ceremony to commemorate the founding of Teheran University. I was dressed in uniform and was going to preside over the presentation of diplomas.
>
> I took my place at the head of the official procession just after 3 p.m. Photographers had lined up to take pictures when a man broke away from the group and rushed at me. Not ten feet away from me he pulled a gun and fired at point-blank range. Three bullets whizzed through my hat and knocked it off but did not burn a hair. A fourth bullet went through my cheek and came out under my nose without doing much damage. He fired a fifth time and I knew instinctively that the shot was aimed at my heart. In a fraction of a second, I moved slightly and the bullet hit my shoulder. One bullet remained. Then the assassin's gun jammed. Despite the blood dripping from my face, my enemies would say afterwards that he had used cotton bullets.
>
> Unfortunately my assailant, a certain Fakhr Arai, was killed immediately. Perhaps it was in someone's interest that he not be questioned. What little we discovered about him was strange enough to motivate efforts to silence him. Arai was involved with an ultraconservative religious group that was comprised of the most backward religious fanatics. We also found Communist literature and brochures in his home relating to the Tudeh, the Iranian Communist party. Significantly or not, the Tudeh happened to be holding its national congress at the time of the attempted assassination. And there was a third connection: Arai's mistress was the daughter of the British embassy's gardener.
>
> The British had their fingers in strange pies. They were always interested in forging links with diverse groups in nations they wished to control, and they had long exercised a good deal of control over Iran. There is little doubt that London was involved with the Tudeh in various ways and of course the British had ties to the most reactionary clergy in the country.[11]

The AIOC affairs planted a great seed of mistrust and frustration in the hearts of Iranians against the English and the Western political apparatus in general.

Reza Shah, the Pahlavi Dynasty

Reza Khan moved into the forefront of Iranian politics when, as a colonel of the Cossack Brigade from Qazvin, he led the coup of February 21, 1921, marching into Tehran and taking control of government offices, declaring martial law and ousting the cabinet officials.[12] Five days after the coup, the Soviet-Iranian Friendship Treaty was signed, and in the months following the coup, Reza Khan successfully consolidated all military forces under his command, enhancing his prestige and standing in the eyes of the Iranian public.[13] Just five years later, the Majles (elected parliament) conferred on Reza Khan and his descendants the monarchy of Iran. On April 25, 1926, the newly appointed Reza Shah Pahlavi (Reza Khan) crowned himself in an impressive ceremony at Golestan Palace in Tehran.

One of Reza Shah's first priorities after being crowned as the Shah Pahlavi was to reunite the country from various factions influenced by the foreign powers. He wanted to eliminate the foreign control over Iranian politics and economy. From his military background as the commander of the Persian Cossack Division, he knew that in order for Iran to become a sovereign nation, he must possess a capable army. Thus he set out to build an army that would subdue various separatists supported by the Russians in the north and the British in the south. And the revenues from the oil made it possible for him to organize a sizable army.

After dealing with these various separatist factions, Reza Shah began some incredible domestic social reforms. In a short time he was able to modernize the country by building the infrastructure. He built roads, railroads that stretched from the north to the south, power plants, telephone lines, and so forth. His reforms in the areas of education, finances, infrastructure, and health are monumental and well acknowledged by all Iranians, even those who opposed the Pahlavi dynasty.

One of Reza Shah's greatest achievements in terms of social change was his move toward the emancipation of women. Prior to the Reza Shah's era, the status of women in Iran was one of the worst among all the Muslim nations.

Reza Shah changed that by opening the way for women to be received and respected in educational institutions and work places. It was his specific insistence that female as well as male students were admitted to the University of Tehran when it opened in 1936.[14] Reza Shah resisted some of the Islamic religious practices such as women's *chadors*, the covering that veiled Iranian women all around except their faces. He had long attempted to set an example by having his own wife and daughters appear unveiled and in mixed company. In some areas the police would grab the chadors off of the women in public places by force and unveil them. In 1934, a law was passed that actually prohibited female students and teachers from wearing the chador, and in 1936 the law was expanded to apply to women in many other public facilities, although the use of the chador was never completely outlawed and remained in common use despite the efforts to discourage it.[15]

On June 22, 1941, Hitler invaded Russia with a massive force. Churchill promised to give aid to Russia against Nazi Germany. The supply routes were few. Iran with its newly opened Trans-Iranian Railroad, which stretched from the Persian Gulf in the south to the Caspian Sea to the north, was the most attractive option for the Allied forces to transport supplies from the Persian Gulf to the Soviet fronts. Reza Shah had declared his neutral position in the war even though he was more of a sympathizer to Nazi Germany.

Britain and Russia demanded that Reza Shah expel the many German nationals who lived in Iran at that time, but he refused. And so in August of 1941, Britain and the USSR invaded Iran. Reza Shah's army could not stand against the Allied forces. London took control of Iran's communications and coveted railroad, sent Reza Shah into exile, and installed his young son, Muhammad Reza, as the shah of Iran on September 16, 1941. London hoped that the younger king would be more open to Allied influence. Once again foreign forces interfered in the political affairs of the Iranian people. Iran now had become a major mouthpiece for the British and later for the American aid to the USSR. This massive supply effort became known as the "Persian Corridor" and was the beginning of a major U.S. involvement in Iran.[16]

The new young king had his work cut out for him. To begin with, he was no more than a figurehead. The British and Russians made all major decisions for him. There was little he could do but bide his time. In many ways it was as if Reza Shah had accomplished nothing. Foreign troops were again on Iranian soil, the country was divided into British and Soviet zones, foreign ambassadors dictated essential policies, the tribes had reasserted their autonomy, and the economy was in shambles.[17]

Just like his father, the young shah knew that in order to have an independent Iran, he must have a strong military. This seems to have been his main priority during his thirty-eight-year reign on the Peacock Throne.

The young inexperienced shah feared that Great Britain and their counterpart Russia might desire more of a permanent abode in Iran, but Iranians saw the United States as a superpower that did not have the colonial lust of the British. It was, therefore, logical to be drawn more toward the United States as a political force that could stop the British and Russian governments from dividing Iran like a pie. This was a legitimate fear since Russia had already annexed the northern part of Persia, which came to be known as Tajikistan in the beginning of the nineteenth century.

The assurance came in the form of a conference in Tehran at the end of November 1943 between the Allied forces, Joseph Stalin, Franklin D. Roosevelt, and Winston Churchill. The three powers pledged to recognize Iran's sovereignty and independence:

> The Three Governments realize that the war has caused special economic difficulties for Iran, and they are agreed that they will continue to make available to the Government of Iran such economic assistance as may be possible, having regard to the heavy demands made upon them by their world-wide military operations, and to the world-wide shortage of transport, raw materials, and supplies for civilian consumption.[18]

Muhammad Mosaddeq

Muhammad Mosaddeq, one of the four Majles delegates who spoke against Reza Khan becoming the shah, had pulled together a number of liberal, antiroyalist, and nationalist factions, and in 1949, he formed the National Front (*Jebhe-ye-Melli*), a nationalistic party, after the war, becoming one of the main political figures in the history of Iran.[19] Muhammad Mosaddeq emerged, giving strength to nationalistic sentiments that had been weakened by decades of foreign influence. The party's main goal was to nationalize the oil industry that was mainly controlled by the British Anglo-Iranian Oil Company.

In the spring of 1951, Mosaddeq led the Iranian Parliament (Majles) to pass the Oil Nationalization Act, which nationalized the oil assets and expelled Western companies from the Iranian oil refineries. This led to rioting and violent protests that broke out at oil refineries, known as the "Abadan Crisis," over the grossly unequal terms under which the AIOC had operated under British control. In his book *The Persian Puzzle*, Kenneth M. Pollack says this about the conditions at the Abadan refinery: "The working conditions of AIOC's Iranian employees were unconscionable: they were paid 50 cents per day and lived in a shantytown...without running water or electricity....Each family occupied the space of one blanket."[20]

The British government, furious over the Oil Nationalization Act, decided to invade Iran. However, that plan was soon to be called off due to opposition from the U.S. government. The Truman administration feared that the British invasion of Iran would lead Iran into the arms of the Soviets. Mosaddeq tried to strike a deal with the British through Truman's mediation. The British were not willing to agree to a concession in which the AIOC profits would be equally split between the two parties, Tehran and London.

In Britain, the newly reelected Conservative Party with its head, Winston Churchill, took some drastic economic measures against Iran. They enforced an embargo against the Iranian oil and froze all the Iranian assets in the British banks, putting a massive economic strain on the Mosaddeq government and the Iranian people. The economic pressure took its toll on the Mosaddeq government. Mosaddeq tried to take more control of the government, recognizing that his failure in the oil negotiation might give way to the defeat of the National Front's leadership in the Majles. He suspended the election for the Majles and also chose his own minister of war, which, traditionally, was a post to be elected entirely by the shah being the Commander of the Armed Forces. The shah refused to accept Mosaddeq's nominee, and so Mosaddeq resigned.

After Mosaddeq's resignation, the shah selected Ahmad Qavam as the prime minister. Qavam was a pro-British politician and decided to reverse Mosaddeq's Oil Nationalization Act. This was, of course, a foolish move by Qavam that triggered violent opposition from the Iranian people. Demonstrations were organized by the National Front and the Communist Tudeh (Masses) Party in support of Mosaddeq. The shah had no choice but to yield to people's demands to reinstate Mosaddeq as the prime minister and also name him the minister of war.[21]

It seems that Mosaddeq's new power and position went to his head. He took several measures that were discouraging and dictatorial in nature. These actions were criticized by some members of the Majles (Parliament), and others refused to attend sessions. Some claim this was an orchestration by Mosaddeq in order to deprive Majles of a quorum. He dissolved the Supreme Court, suspended the elections for the Majles, and asked for a national referendum in order to dissolve the Majles. According to some accounts, the votes were rigged, and Mosaddeq won unanimously by over 99 percent of all votes. Mosaddeq's goal was to abolish the monarchy.

Mosaddeq's hatred toward British colonialism and their treatment of the Iranian people hindered him from coming to an agreement with the British government. The British had accepted the Iranian oil nationalization and were willing to compromise on a fifty-fifty profit split deal with Mosaddeq's government, but he refused.

The British tried to oust Mosaddeq by a coup. Once Mosaddeq found out about the British plot, he broke diplomatic ties with London and closed their embassy in Tehran. This is when the British sought help from Eisenhower's administration. The new U.S. administration under Dwight Eisenhower and the British government under Winston Churchill agreed to work together to remove Mosaddeq from office.[22] In my opinion, this was the beginning of the fall of U.S. diplomacy in the Middle East even before the United States had its foot in the door.

Again, this is where I believe that our trouble in the Middle East began. You must understand that Britain, at that time, was a dying imperialist nation. Much of its then postwar economy depended upon the oil tax revenue and the dividends from the AIOC. Add to that a century of imperialistic pride. What else can you expect?

This wasn't the case with the United States. After the war, the United States was emerging as a world power with a great standard politically and also spiritually. Here was a fresh nation with a great spiritual and moral stance, raising up a standard against Soviet Communism. There was no need of walking the paths that nations such as Great Britain had walked earlier with a disastrous Middle Ages political philosophy.

America was founded on a system of government that is "for the people" and "by the people." The minute we begin to create policies—whether nationally or internationally—that cross the line of our belief in a government for the people and by the people, we begin to move away from the foundation that has made this nation great. If what I believe is solid, it must be applicable everywhere—home or abroad. In my opinion, we display our political weakness when we try to operate under one system here in America and from a different political paradigm in other parts of the world!

In the next section, we will see this weakness demonstrated in America's actions in Iran just prior to the coup of 1953. This will help you to understand why most Muslim nations hate American policies and political figures. I believe it is the hypocrisy of our politics—in 1953 and even today—that instills the hatred of many Muslim nations. In our dealings with these Muslim nations, we have failed to act according to the foundational principles that made America great, just as the British failed and were hated by the people in Iran and other oppressed nations.

Collapsing Democracy With a Coup D'etat

In February 1953, an agreement was struck between the Americans and the British for a covert operation, code-named *Ajax*, to topple the Mosaddeq government. The CIA sent Kermit Roosevelt, grandson of Theodore Roosevelt, as an agent to Iran to oversee the operation. On April 4, 1953, CIA director Allen W. Dulles approved $1 million to be used in any way that would bring about the fall of Mosaddeq.[23]

Elton Daniel, in his book *The History of Iran*, notes:

> The basic strategy was to create an atmosphere conducive to a coup by spreading propaganda about Mosaddeq, stirring up more public disorder and tribal unrest, and using fear of the Tudeh to induce Kashani and others to turn completely against Mosaddeq. One of the most effective tactics was reportedly hiring thugs to pose as Tudeh demonstrators and act in an incendiary manor to frighten the non communist public.[24]

CIA and MI6 covert operations strategy was clear—sow division and then reign. One of the plots was to sow discord among the religious groups such as Fadaian-e-Islam, an Islamic radical group, against Mosaddeq. The CIA had secured the support of Islamic leaders such as Ayatollah Kashani, Ayatollah Behbahani, and Hojatolislam Falsafi. The Muslim mobs under the directions of these ayatollahs crowded the streets in protest against Mosaddeq. The popular uprisings were to give the notion that Mosaddeq was unfit to rule.

The British did not wait for the Americans to move forward with this plot. They were provoking fights with the government of Iran and working to convince key Iranian politicians and tribes to turn against Mosaddeq.[25] When the American CIA arrived with huge amounts of cash to spend, the British welcomed the reinforcements. Six new newspapers suddenly appeared on the streets of Tehran in the summer of 1953, all of them spewing venom against Mosaddeq. Richard Cottam, a leading scholar of Iran and, at the time, one of the CIA's leading Iran propagandists, estimated that by the end of the summer four-fifths of the newspapers in Tehran were under the influence of the CIA.[26]

Mosaddeq's desperation to deal with these growing hostilities caused him to fear he was losing control of the Majles Parliament. Therefore, he called for a popular referendum to dissolve the Parliament, gambling on the support of the one group that still backed him—the Iranian people. On August 3, Mosaddeq "won" the referendum with more than 99 percent of the vote.[27] The CIA also tried to convince the young shah that he had to use his constitutional power to depose Mosaddeq and replace him with General Zahedi as the prime minister. This was provided by an amendment to the constitution in 1950 that gave the shah the power to dissolve the Parliament and order new elections, written on the night of August 15.[28]

Mosaddeq was tipped off to the plot to depose him as prime minister, and the plot failed when he reported to the nation that there had been an attempted coup and that those responsible were being rounded up. The young shah, afraid of the consequences, fled to Baghdad and then onward to Rome, and General Zahedi went into hiding.

However, Kermit Roosevelt, the chief of the operation, refused to give up. CIA headquarters ordered Roosevelt to leave Tehran, but he remained and organized a second coup on August 19, 1953.[29]

Mobs of people paid by Roosevelt and posing as Tudeh (the Communist Party) together with the followers of the Shi'a ayatollahs began violent demonstrations in the streets. Army units were called in to control the demonstrators. About three hundred people were killed in the violence.[30] The chaos ended with the arrest of Mosaddeq by the shah's Imperial Guard units. Roosevelt had finally, with the help of Shi'a clerics and the military forces loyal to the shah, accomplished the coup d'etat of 1953.

The shah returned to Iran, and Mosaddeq was tried for treason and sentenced to three years in prison. Following his release he remained under house arrest until his death on March 5, 1967.

With the fall of the democratic government of Mosaddeq, a tyrant was on the rise in Iran with the strong backing of the United States. This was the beginning of a troublesome process in the Middle East. The shah's dictatorial reign would eventually give birth to one of the most violent forces the earth had ever seen—radical Islam. Stephen Kinzer, in his well-documented book *All the Shah's Men*, defines the result of the coup d'etat of 1953 as follows:

> The world has paid a heavy price for the lack of democracy in most of the Middle East. Operation Ajax [CIA code for the August 1953 coup] taught tyrants and aspiring tyrants there that the world's most powerful governments were willing to tolerate limitless oppression as long as oppressive regimes were friendly to the West and to Western oil companies. That helped tilt the political balance in a vast region away from freedom and toward dictatorship.[31]

The importance of the events of 1953 in shaping Iranian perceptions of American involvement in Iranian affairs can hardly be exaggerated. American involvement in the coup is cited by most historians as a prime example of its harmful meddling in the affairs of other countries. It is an illustration of how we stepped far away from the foundational principle of government "of the people" and "for the people." Although there were other factors contributing to the disastrous events of 1953—including Mosaddeq's own actions and the British exploitation of Iran through the AIOC—these events paved the way to the hostility and hatred of Iran toward America today.

America's Confession

For decades after the coup of 1953, angry Iranians had demanded an admission of guilt from America for its part not only in the 1953 events, but also, more importantly, for its involvement in the revolution of 1979. On March 17, 2000, the U.S. administration under President Clinton, for the first time in forty-seven years, acknowledged the role of the U.S. government in the 1953 coup in Iran. Secretary of State Madeleine Albright in her speech from a conference in Washington on United States relations with Iran announced:

In 1953, the United States played a significant role in orchestrating the overthrow of Iran's popular Prime Minister, Muhammad Mosaddeq. The Eisenhower administration believed its actions were justified for strategic reasons; but the coup was clearly a setback for Iran's political development. And it is easy to see now why many Iranians continue to resent this intervention by America in their internal affairs. Moreover, during the next quarter century, the United States and the West gave sustained backing to the Shah's regime. Although it did much to develop the country economically, the Shah's government also brutally repressed the political dissent. As President Clinton has said, the United States must bear its fair share of responsibility for the problems that have arisen in the U.S.-Iranian relations.[32]

Yet, today, America is facing even greater challenges in its attempt to de-escalate the hatred and hostility of Iranians toward our country. In his best-selling book *The Persian Puzzle,* author Kenneth Pollack makes this poignant assessment of the future:

> We must sort through the myriad pieces of our own relationship with this troubled and troubling nation, while also sorting out our equally difficult relations with the rest of the world. For this reason, perhaps more than the invasion of Iraq, the war on terror, or any of the other conflicts we have waged since the fall of the Berlin Wall, the problem of Iran may be the ultimate test of America's leadership in the new era that is dawning. How we handle the problem of Iran will tell us a great deal about whether we are up to its challenges.[33]

Conclusion

It is truly hard to justly evaluate a major political event in which so many human elements are involved. To be impartial in our judgment of a great political event such as the 1953 coup, one must be either part of the event or in close association to it. The historical books that I have read on this subject are, for the most part, written by outsiders who are not well versed in the vibes of the Iranian culture and psyche. Their assessments, therefore, are mainly from an historical point of view, which has some value and demands respect, but they miss the essence of the reality of the life of the Persian people.

It is one thing to sit outside of a boxing ring and shout, "Knock him down!" Being in the ring and trying to "knock him down," however, is something totally different. We must analyze this major event so that we can see the dark spots and the points upon which they failed. Then we can pave the way for the future generations not to walk in the same path of destruction—for the Iranian people, as well as the American and the British policy makers. I do not believe that the Iranian people were the only ones who lost in the coup d'etat of 1953. America has also lost tremendous amounts of interests. Looking at it from an economic angle, since the Islamic Revolution of the Ayatollah Khomeini in 1979, billions of dollars in trade are being directed to the European markets instead of to the Americans. Thus, it is vital for all of us to have a sound judgment on this whole event. Here, then, is my examination of this major event.

First of all, Iran was at that time in the baby stages of democracy. The concept of democracy is a relatively new concept for most of the world. This is especially true for those nations and cultures such as Iran who have survived under the rulership of kings and tribal warlords for endless centuries, and, in the case of Iran, for six millennia of kingdom dynasties.

Mosaddeq came to the political scene of the Iranian society during a time of great religious blindness and mass ignorance. The rate of literacy in rural areas in Iran was almost nonexistent. Mosaddeq could not raise a strong coalition of support among the people even though most Iranians will argue otherwise. The fact of the matter is that his party, the National Front, had less than 10 percent of the seats in the sixteenth Majles.[34] Mosaddeq was popular on the grounds of his nationalistic sentiments. Since his party was mainly composed of the secularists and the elitist of the Iranian society, it would have been hard for him to raise mass support among the religious Shi'a populace.

Second, Mosaddeq must not have been a seasoned politician because of the way he dealt with the British. Even though Great Britain and the AIOC were exploiting the Iranian people ruthlessly, and, as Mosaddeq put it, they were the *enemies*, one cannot fight an enemy on emotional grounds alone, especially a bulldog like Churchill.

Mosaddeq's hatred toward the AIOC and the British policy makers blinded him to the point of taking drastic measures that had in effect crippled the Iranian economy. He left himself no margin for error.

Third, he trusted a friend of his enemy, the United States. Mosaddeq expected that economic aid would come from the United States after Great

Britain had placed an embargo on the Iranian oil. When it comes to politics and politicians, everyone watches out for their own interests. Your friend today can be your enemy tomorrow. One cannot base his relationship in the political arena on friendship—not in today's political bull pit. That is an Iranian weakness—trusting friendship above policies.

Mosaddeq wanted to rid Iran of foreign influence, yet he sought help from another foreign power! That does not equate.

The United States administrations, at the time, were hugely concerned about the Soviet expansion. Immediately after World War II, Russia showed its appetite for world dominance. The cold war was being set in place with the Russian army invasion of the northern province of Azerbaijan in Iran. Stalin had agreed in a conference in London that they would leave Iran by March of 1946. It wasn't until May of that year that the Red Army left Iran following a major battle between the pro-Communist rebels and the shah's army.

It is said that the *Azerbaijan Affair*, as it is known, was one of the precipitating events of the emerging cold war, the postwar rivalry between the United States and the Soviet Union.[35]

With this political condition in mind, America would never have chosen a new guy on the block such as Mosaddeq whose supporters were the Communist Tudeh. Mosaddeq with the measures that he had taken destabilized the Iranian economy and politics. He would definitely give way to the expansion of the Tudeh influence, which in turn would mean Soviet invasion of Iran. That would be a "no-no" to Eisenhower or Truman.

The problem that I have with this whole scenario, even though my Persian blood is kicking in and I want to justify the cause of Mosaddeq, is this: How could a man, by the name of Kermit Roosevelt, within a short time cause a whole government to fall? Sure, he had unlimited amounts of cash to buy out thugs and cause riots and civil unrest, but then again what kind of political influence did Mosaddeq, as the head of the government, have over his people? It couldn't have been much. Not more than Kermit Roosevelt!

The popular notion among the Iranians has always been that they see the CIA or SAVAK (Iranian intelligence agency) or any other intimidating agency as gods. That is the lack of maturity of democracy that I was speaking about. They believe that governments have more power than people. I wonder, how many regime changes must take place in Iran before the Iranian people realize that these governments and agencies are no more powerful than we, the people, make them to be?

The Mosaddeq epic is a great lesson on many fronts. It shows us the weakness of American policies with Muslim nations or third world countries. The fact that we have the power to manipulate and control the people and circumstances doesn't necessarily mean that we are the winners. Look at where we are with Iran and the Muslim nations. I wouldn't say we have won! The powerful don't always rule if they do not rule in wisdom.

In his book *Answer to History*, the late shah of Iran criticizes Mosaddeq for usurping power in 1952 by trying to dissolve the Majles and abolishing the monarchy. Yet he himself did much worse for a longer period of time than Mosaddeq. The shah's idea of the constitution of 1906 and freedom was one party completely under his control. His ruthless reign was proven to be worse in nature than Mosaddeq's short-lived theatrical government. The lesson is that a human being to whom too much power has been entrusted is untrustworthy. No human being should have too much power over others, other than what the majority of the people grant him.

The economic lesson of this event is that any big corporation that fleeces people will lose at the end. The behavior of AIOC was so unethical that after fifty years the people of Iran are still holding grudges against them and the British government. By reading the account of the conditions the Iranians found at the oil refineries after the British were expelled, you will understand the reasons Iranians feel this way.[36]

As I have said before, the Iranians are still blaming their misfortune on the British government and the CIA. Wow! What an incredible reputation to have as a politician and as a nation!

My prayer is that the Iranian people may see the whole picture, forgive the past, and see a bright and glorious future. I also pray that America may show its greatness not only to the American people but also to the world.

I believe that in order for the world to experience the greatness of this great nation, America needs to side with the majority of the Iranian people and not their oppressive government. America, its people, its Congress, and the White House need to support the cause of the oppressed and become an advocate for them. This may sound a bit poetic to the ears of a political world that only bites at what's most profitable, but remember that only "righteousness exalts a nation" (Prov. 14:34).

Here is an example: The United States supports the government of President Hosni Mubarak in Egypt. President Mubarak's prisons are packed with political dissidents and radical Muslims. The more President Mubarak stifles the voices of these political and religious dissidents, the more of them he has to deal with. We can prevent the growth of radical Islam by defending human rights in countries such as Egypt, Saudi Arabia, and Algeria.

Here is another practical point for our government. In one of President Bush's State of the Union addresses, he called Iran an "axis of evil." In such a public addressing of the nation, we must separate the Iranian government from the Iranian people, otherwise we will only isolate Iran into more radical resolve. One of the greatest dangers with the radical Islamic movement is isolating the forceful elements within the movement. This was the greatest mistake that the shah of Iran made, isolating an ayatollah and sending him into exile. The result was an Islamic revolution led by the one isolated. The United States policy of isolating countries such as Iran and groups such as Hamas and Hezbollah is a major political mistake, in my opinion. That is how Islam became a radical movement. The more Muhammad's tribe, the Quraish, enforced isolation and persecution on Muhammad and his three hundred followers, the more violent revelation Muhammad received from Allah. The more violent they became, the greater they grew.

Islam carries a poison from within. If we leave it by itself, it will destroy itself from within. The recent violent acts of Muslims against Muslims are a great example of this fact: the massacre of the Shi'ite community by the Taliban Islamic government in the Nezare-Sharif region in Afghanistan, the eight-year war between Iraq and Iran that left more than one million Muslims dead and handicapped, the daily suicide bombings of Sunni Muslims against the Shi'ite Muslims, and visa versa, in Iraq, leaving hundreds dead on a weekly basis, and the most recent shoot-out that took place between the Hamas and Fatah followers in Gaza Strip. According to a report by Greg Myre of the *International Herald Tribune*, three people died and ten people were wounded in the shoot-out between these two rival political groups in the Palestinian territory.[37] Palestinian Muslims killing Palestinian Muslims! That is the nature of Islam. Islam's spirit is a spirit of death and destruction. It will eventually destroy itself and its adherents.

I also would like to recommend the following steps to the United States government:

First, realize that the battle with radical Islam (terrorist groups) is primarily a battle of ideology. It is good versus evil. In the eyes of radical Muslims, America, with its political, social, and economical system, personifies evil. It is the great Satan that permits and promotes abominable behaviors such as pornography, homosexuality, the drug culture, racism, greed, and the usurpation of the resources of the third-world nations. The United States government must create a means to combat these stereotypes with the truth and a righteous ideology. Let me explain what I mean.

The platform of radical Islam is the teaching and traditions of Muhammad, their prophet, in whom they impute the great values of valor, holiness, righteousness, and truth. For instance, in Surah 9:5 Muhammad commands the Muslims to slay infidels. Killing innocent people who are infidels is permitted and commanded by Islam. Thus a radical Muslim has no problem walking into a bus full of kids in Jerusalem or New York City and blowing himself up in order to kill infidels. What has been the reaction of the Israeli government or the U.S. government to these attacks? They strike back with killing or by bringing to justice the group responsible for such violent acts! Have they solved the problem with the suicide bombers? No; there are more of them day by day. Why? Because we have dealt with the problem's aftermath, not with its root.

The root of the problem is Surah 9:5, so we must challenge that commandment. The question is, how? Our government is definitely not doing that by proclaiming that Islam is a "peaceful religion." What we need to do is have a means of public information such as TV debate programs and tackle the commandment in the Quran. The evilness of that commandment must be exposed by means of documentation, theology, discussion, and debate. The enemy is not the suicide bomber; the enemy is the ideology that created such hatred and murder in the suicide bomber's heart.

I believe an entire ideological ministry must be created within the U.S. government to combat this very issue. I believe that the teaching of the Bible is the antidote against the teaching of the Quran.

There are two simple ways we can stop a murderer from committing a murder. One, lock him up. But this is impossible since he or she has not yet committed the act of murder. Two, change his heart. Can we lock up or fight 1.3 billion Muslims, the majority of whom have the potential to obey Surah 9:5? No. But can we change their hearts with the message of love? Yes.

I was a hateful Muslim, but Jesus changed my heart. I used to hate America, but today I am willing to lay my life down to protect it! What changed my heart? Jesus Christ. And once my heart was changed, my eyes were opened to see the truth.

Isn't it ironic that the very thing that so many liberal organizations such as the ACLU are trying to eliminate from America is the very thing that will save this great nation from destruction? Jesus Christ is the only hope.

Recently we received a call from a suicide bomber in Iran who was a member of a brigade of suicide bombers organized and sponsored by the Iranian government. According to the information we received from him, there are ten thousand strong members in this organization who have already signed their death warrant. He told us that his mission was already scheduled to be in Iraq. His targets: American troops. He told us that he kept watching our TV program *Day of Salvation.* One day he was so overwhelmed and convicted that he fell prostrate before the TV weeping and praying the prayer of salvation. He then decided to abandon his mission. Knowing that the penalty for rejecting his mission means death, he chose not to hate any longer. Unfortunately we lost contact with him after a week and do not know the outcome of his escape from Iran.

So far we have had two suicide bombers who have seen our program and have repented and turned away from their missions. The United States must realize that our efforts through the preaching of the gospel are the most effective tool in combating the hatred in the hearts of these radicals.

Second, the right and just deeds of the United States must become public knowledge in the Muslim world. For instance, despite its faults, the judicial process in this country is the finest in the world. The Muslim world needs to see and know it through various documentary programs. This is a generation of sound and sight. We must expose the greatness of the freedom and the value system of America to the Islamic world.

I lived in Sweden for eight years. I often saw documentary programs on Swedish TV made by the Swedish government about life in the United States. The Swedish government social democrats wanted to show the negative side of capitalism. So these documentaries were often about the violence, poverty, and life of the people in the ghettoes. As a result of these documentaries, the majority of people in Sweden had a negative impression of the life of Americans. The common notion among the Swedes was that Americans are shallow, greedy, and violent. Even though the majority of people in the world are envious of the American dream, they detest America because of all the negative propaganda against this great nation.

I strongly believe that we are losing this battle, the great battle of ideology in the world. I firmly believe that a well-funded organization within our government must be created to combat mass (world) opinion about the United States.

Third, I believe that a scholarly foundation must be formed, a think tank if you will, of men and women who come from the Middle East and understand both cultures. They must be those who know the evil of Islam and also love freedom. I would highly recommend men and women who come from an Islamic background. I am willing to initiate such a process. There are many such people whose knowledge of how to combat radical Islam would be priceless for our government. The purpose of this foundation would be to become a think tank for our government in their efforts to combat radical Islam.

In order to win the battle against a formidable enemy, one must be able to read their mind, to know how they think. A Harvard graduate cannot do that, no matter how much he has studied Islam. I recently heard on the radio one of the highly educated think-tank members from Washington DC speak on the struggle in Iraq. His analysis of the warfare between the various groups in Iraq was incredibly naïve. He simply didn't understand the mind-set of these radical factions in Iraq.

Again, much could be discussed on these three points. The key is that the United States must consider that 50 percent of its battle against the growth and threats of radical Islam must be fought on an ideological platform, because radical Islam's sole reason for its hatred against the United States is firmly based upon an ideology.

Within her bosom, the United States of America has planted some of the greatest human laws that have ever been known to man, aside from the Mosaic law. I believe that freedom is the greatest cry of man's soul, and America has been given a banner of freedom to carry. Let's be great, and let's carry that banner, not only for us here in America, but also for the world.

4

The Formation of the Islamic Revolution

The coup of 1953 and the fall of Mosaddeq were the beginning of a long series of events that would eventually give birth to the Islamic Revolution of 1979.

Within a few years after the coup, the shah had bolstered his throne in Iran. The shah, just like his father, saw the security and integrity of Iran in building a massive military. As part of that plan, in the early 1970s the shah attached himself enthusiastically to the Nixon Doctrine, which proposed that the United States, in the wake of the Vietnam fiasco, deal with regional crises through proxies rather than direct military involvement. The United States, particularly during the Nixon and Ford administrations, viewed the shah as an ally against the Soviets and readily endorsed the shah taking on the task of maintaining security in the Persian Gulf area.[1] The United States provided the shah with billions of dollars worth of arms, and by 1976, Iran's military force was the fifth or sixth largest armed forces in the world. From 1972 to 1977, Iran spent a whopping $16 billion purchasing American weaponry alone.[2] These weapons included tanks, helicopter gunships, artillery, fighter aircraft F-14s, F-16s, and F-18s, and a host of other weapons. (A list of the shah's American military equipment is printed at the back of his memoir, *Answer to History*.)

Securing his throne against the internal threats such as the Communist Tudeh party and other anti-monarchy groups, the shah established the national intelligence and security organization SAVAK (*Sazemane Eatelaat Va Amniate Keshvar*). It became known for its cruel torture of the shah's dissidents, and the mention of its name brought dread and horror to the minds of the Iranian people. SAVAK was believed, among the Iranians, to be the creation of the CIA. To what extent the CIA was involved in the operation and training of SAVAK, we do not really know. We know that Colonel Stephen J. Meade was sent to Iran to help the shah with the establishment of an intelligence organization that would focus on the Soviet's activities in Iran.[3] SAVAK's mishandling and torture of the political and the religious prisoners planted a strong seed of hatred in the hearts of Iranians toward the shah and his backup force, the United States.

The shah began his social and infrastructure reforms known as the "White Revolution." This revolution was based on six reform measures submitted to a referendum in January 1963. One of these reforms was to divide up the large estates that were owned by the private landowners into smaller tracts and give them to the farmers who worked on them. Some of these owners, who were tribal khans, owned as many as forty villages. In January of 1963 the shah passed a law that would limit private ownership of Iran's arable land. The shah faced a violent reaction from the landowners and the religious clergymen. Riots were organized by the landowners, and also by a religious leader called Ruhollah Khomeini. Khomeini was arrested and sent to exile, first in Turkey and then to Iraq.

To push his White Revolution reforms, the shah assumed more power. The Majles (parliament) had become just a *Yes, sir* group of people to all the wishes of the shah. There was only one active political party allowed—the party of the shah. With the SAVAK growing and becoming a fearful agency, no voice of opposition was allowed. The shah had become a full-fledged dictator.

The shah was fixed on the idea of bringing Iran up to par with other modern states, such as European countries. I often used to hear him on national TV proclaiming that Iran is moving toward the "*Darvazehaye Tamadon*," or the "gates of civilization." It seems as though he was not in touch with the reality of the life of the Iranian people. It had taken five centuries to bring Europe from the Middle Ages to where they are now. The shah wanted to have that same process in the matter of a few decades. Would it be possible? Yes, but at what price? While the shah was spending billions of petrodollars in purchasing American weaponry, and also wallowing in millions himself and with his cohorts, the Iranian people were suffering great economic setbacks. The poor were getting poorer, and the shah and his gangs were getting richer. This was the same scenario under the Qajar dynasty, something the Iranian people hated with a passion.

We must acknowledge that Reza Shah and his son, the shah, brought great developments to the Iranian society. But we must also recognize that was done at too fast a pace. It is similar to the building of an athlete by growth hormones. One cannot take a backward religious Muslim society into a secular modern one in a short time. The result can be disastrous.

I believe that the shah was trying to duplicate his father's work without having his father's character and his father's time. The Iranian people were introduced to all the courses of the West except the main dish—freedom!

The Fermentation of a Revolution

One of the characteristics of the Persian people is that the harder you hit them, the more resolved they become. The stronger the shah's SAVAK became, the more dissent emerged. By and by Iran was becoming a police state, and more groups were forming underground to fight the shah's totalitarian regime. By the beginning of the 1970s, the horrific tortures and executions of the political prisoners in the legendary Evin Prison were widely known among the people. The fear of reprisal by the regime made the opposition stronger and the weak weaker. The shah was no longer a king, but now he was exalted as the "Shan-an-Shah," meaning the king of kings. The pride in his heart had blinded him from seeing and feeling the pain and the hardship of his people. I think, as a teenager growing up in Iran, I was more in touch with the political, economical, and the spiritual condition of Iran than the shah was. To be honest with you, it was very discouraging for me to read the shah's memoir, *Answer to History*. It amazes me that even after his fall, he still didn't see what was going on in his country. I don't believe he ever saw it.

As the dissension grew stronger, the regime became harsher and more intolerant of the opposition. The resistance against the shah's regime evolved into three major groups: the religious right with several ayatollahs in the leadership (the head of which was Khomeini, living in exile in Iraq), the religious Marxists known as the Mojahedine Khalgh, and the Tudeh Party. The most violent and active of these three groups was the Mojahedin, a group of Marxist revolutionary ideologists with a hint of the Shi'ite Islam. The group led several major terrorist assassinations and bomb attacks against the shah's regime. Many of the Mojahedin were tortured and executed. SAVAK was relentless in its tactics and tortures of even the religious leaders. Touching the religious clerics of a strong Shi'ite society is a major political suicide. During the 1970s, SAVAK imprisoned, tortured, exiled, and executed some six hundred Shi'ite clergymen.[4]

None of the U.S. administration realized or paid much attention to the internal political condition of the Iranian people. Economically Iran was growing rapidly, and the shah had become a great ally of the United States. The lack of knowledge of the internal upheaval in Iran among the U.S. administration is well evident in the statement that President Carter made in his visit to Iran in January of 1978, a year before the Islamic Revolution. In a formal toast at a state dinner in Tehran, President Carter claimed that, "Iran is an island of stability in a turbulent corner of the world," a statement that couldn't be any further from the truth.[5]

The United States was so sure of the shah that by 1978 there were forty-five thousand American military and civilians working in Iran.[6]

On one side of the coin, the United States saw Iran as a vital front against the expansions of the Soviet Union. And on the other hand, the Iranians saw America as the evil force imposing and supporting a tyrant. There was ignorance on the side of the shah and Washington as to the way that they should be dealing with the underlying discontent and hatred that grew stronger against the shah and his backup force, Washington, day by day. The shah was obsessed with his White Revolution. His idea was that social reform, which included land reform, nationalization of forests, the public sale of state-owned factories, electoral power for women, industry privatization, rural literacy, and modernization of the private sectors, would propitiate the murmuring sound within the camp. A prosperous Iran would leave behind the idea of a revolution.

People desired freedom, which became an impossible goal for them under the shah. The promise of freedom came only from one source—an Islamic revivalist of the seventh-century Islam, such as Khomeini. The shah's ideology was reformation instead of freedom! This is total blindness to a culture that has been a dominant force on the earth for many centuries.

Ruhollah Khomeini was one of the few religious mullahs who, thirty years earlier, had refused to join the coalition with Mosaddeq. Now he emerged in the 1970s as Muhammad Reza Shah's most potent enemy. Though the shah sent him into exile in 1964, he continued preaching his fundamentalist message and became a powerful religious leader.[7]

Right after President Carter's visit to Iran, an article was printed in an official paper in Tehran that attacked Khomeini and claimed that he was a homosexual, which is an abomination in the religious culture of the Iranian people. By 1979 Khomeini had become a national hero in Iran even though at the time he was still in exile in France. His fiery messages against the shah and his regime were taped on audiocassette and smuggled into Iran, where they were then duplicated and spread among the people. The smearing of Khomeini's name, who by now had become a holy Imam, was the boiling point, or the critical mass that set in motion a series of demonstrations, strikes, and mass riots that would eventually bring about the fall of the shah and his government.

On September 8, 1978, known as the Black Friday, thousands of people were demonstrating in a square near my house called *Meidan-e Jalleh*. A military unit was called in to disperse the demonstrators since the shah had decreed martial law. I myself saw the horrible video of this bloody event. The demonstrators were all locking hands and sitting down on the pavement in the massive square. The soldiers began firing on the crowds. The young people, mainly students, were falling down on the ground like leaves. The official records state that as many as four hundred people died in that massacre, and the news of it spread all over the country. The majority of Iranians believe as many as three thousand died. It was a heart-wrenching incident that, in my opinion, sealed the fall of the shah.

Violent riots and demonstrations erupted all over the country. Official buildings were ransacked, and banks were broken into and looted. The shah was losing his iron-fisted control of the country. The steps that he took to calm people down were as foolish as ever. Again he proved that he was not in touch with the reality of the life of the people. He placed in position a military government and jailed the head of SAVAK and his faithful prime minister, Hoveida. He also released many political prisoners. Yet all of his actions signified that he was defeated and no longer could manipulate the country. On January 16, 1979, the shah left Iran in fear that his life was endangered. He never returned. Two weeks later, Ayatollah Khomeini arrived in Iran from Paris and began the process of an Islamic revolution that, in a short time, would be more costly in terms of human lives than the combined reigns since 1925 of the shah and his father.

The Islamic Revolution of 1979

Even though the 1979 revolution is always called *the Islamic Revolution*, in actuality it was the people's revolution. Mullahs were not the only ones who opposed the shah, although the main fire was lit by the Ayatollahs Shariatmadari and Taleghani. But because Khomeini had become a violent voice without any compromise against the shah, the Iranian people received him as the leader of the revolution and named it the Islamic Revolution.

At the beginning, the direction of the revolution was not clear—what was the political path to be? An Islamic state? A moderate democracy? To begin with, an interim government was established, headed by Mehdi Bazargan as the first prime minister. Bazargan was one of the cofounders of the Liberation Movement of Iran. He had served as the first Iranian head of the National Iranian Oil Company under Prime Minister Mosaddeq.

Bazargan's government faced constant conflict with the religious clerics and the Islamic Revolutionary Council (IRC). Iran at this time had become a hodgepodge of ideologists, including many Marxists and Leninists. This was a time of conflict of ideologies, the beginning of violence and bloodshed.

It was at this time that I returned to Iran from my studies in the United States. I had left the country in 1978, a year before the revolution, for higher studies in the States.

Growing up in a society where one was under the reign of an oppressive regime had left a sense of emptiness and void in my heart. I was looking for a change and a new perspective in my life. So in 1978, I decided to leave Iran and study for a few years in the United States. As a radical Muslim, I was part of an Islamic organization led by Ibrahim Yazdi in Houston, Texas. After the revolution, Yazdi moved back to Iran and became Khomeini's Revolutionary Court's special prosecutor. This court was responsible for the execution of some of the shah's generals.

Once the Islamic Revolution took place, my perspective on life changed dramatically. I wanted to be a part of "God's government," the Islamic government of Ayatollah Khomeini. So I ended my educational ambitions and returned to Iran.

Coming back to Iran was as much of a culture shock to me as when I had first arrived in New York City. I was in the land of my forefathers, but I could not recognize the people. Even my family had been changed. Almost everyone had become self-righteous and demanded their own rights. It was as though a violent spirit had been released over the people. Everyone was agitated and easily aggravated.

The day following my arrival in Tehran, I had to go back to the airport to claim my luggage since my bags had not made it with my flight. My brother-in-law who had accompanied me to the airport got into a fistfight with the customs official. When I tried to separate the two men, I received a bunch of punches! I wondered what had happened to the kind and hospitable people I had known over a year ago.

The spirit of Islam had brought into the land a spirit of hatred, bloodshed, violence, and division. That was not what I had dreamed of.

I personally saw the division and groupings that had taken place right after the revolution. Everybody and their cousins had become an ideologist, especially the young people, many of whom were supporters of Communist ideology. I remember the day I went to the University of Tehran. There were possibly several hundred thousand people gathered in formation inside the fences of the university and outside. On the inside there were tens of thousands of students locking hands and singing songs of freedom. On the outside, there were multitudes of radical Muslims lined up with clubs and chains cursing the students and shouting back at them. There was such hatred in that crowd. I wondered to myself, *What has happened to the people?* Even among my friends there were groupings and animosity. It was as though a spirit of chaos, bloodshed, and violence had been loosed over the country.

It is normal, I guess, for a postrevolutionary society to face a period of anarchy where everyone feels that they have had a part in the revolution and therefore must have a piece of it. This was definitely the case with the Iranian revolution. Almost everywhere around the country, the weak took over the strong in the name of the revolution.

Those who were oppressed wanted to take justice into their own hands against their oppressors. It is important to note that the word *justice* is a massive concept in Islamic societies, especially in Iran. The formation of Islam was built upon the fact that Muhammad and his small group of followers were oppressed for many years at the hands of their own tribe, the Quraish. Out of that oppression came forth the idea of justice, revenge, and warfare. In an Islamic society, blood is not washed with water but with blood. And that was the course of events in Iran immediately after the revolution.

Bazargan's government faced constant frictions with the Islamic clerics and their newly found factions that did whatever they deemed to be right. Soon all the judicial, police, law enforcements, and other important government posts were controlled by the radical Muslim factions and not the interim government of Bazargan. He was no more than a temporary puppet.

One of the breaking points for Bazargan's government was the seizure of the American embassy on November 4, 1979, by a group of radical Muslim students, which was directed and supported by Khomeini himself. This action was a protest over the United States admitting the former shah into the country on October 22 for medical treatment for his terminal cancer. The group that seized the embassy pledged not to relinquish the embassy or release its personnel until the shah was returned to Iran for trial.[8]

The sixty-three staff members at the embassy, and three others, were held hostage for four hundred forty-four days (thirteen hostages were released on November 20 in an effort to manipulate American political opinion).[9] One of the Muslim student leaders told a hostage that the embassy had been taken over, "To teach the American government and the CIA a lesson, so it will keep its hands off other countries, and particularly Iran!"[10] Colonel Charles Scott, one of the hostages, found the same in talking to his captors:

> It was a situation where truth didn't matter. Perceptions were much more important. A large portion of the Iranian people believed that the United States had the ability to pull strings and return the Shah to power. Iranians believed that we were about 1,000 times more powerful in directing their internal affairs than we ever were. The truth is that at this time we had practically no influence in Iran.... But when the Shah was admitted to the United States, we opened Pandora's box for the hardline revolutionaries. They could say, "Look what America did in 1953! They're getting ready to do it again! Another coup is in the wind! They're going to return the Shah to power!" It's hard for many Americans to understand that the entire Iranian population felt wronged by the Shah, and by America's support of the Shah. After he was admitted to the United States, they wanted to strike out at something American. You could search the entire country over, and there was only one target that they could attack. That was the American embassy in Tehran.[11]

In his book *The Persian Puzzle*, Kenneth Pollack states that the taking of the embassy was a response to the 1953 coup against Mosaddeq. He says, "It was an act of vengeance...designed to humiliate the United States, to cause pain to the American people, and to assuage the angry psychological scars that the Iranian people still bore from that event."[12]

Bazargan resigned from his position after failing to reconcile with Khomeini and bring the hostage crisis to an end. It is noteworthy to mention that the current Iranian president, Mahmood Ahmadinejad, is identified by six of the fifty-two hostages as a ringleader of the embassy takeover. Even though Ahmadinejad denies his involvement with the embassy takeover, the first Iranian elected president after the revolution, Abol-Hasan Bani Sadr, has steadfastly confirmed that Ahmadinejad was the student leader throughout the whole hostage crisis. "Ayatollah Khomeini's deputy, Ayatollah Khamenai, demanded of him a constant report on what is happening in the embassy," Bani Sadr said.[13]

Within a short time Khomeini and his clerical factions had completely taken over all aspects of the economy and the social and political apparatus of the Iranian society. Everyone looked up to Khomeini and answered to him. Khomeini was becoming a god in Iran. No one even dared to challenge his authority, not even other ayatollahs in his rank such as Ayatollah Shariatmadari or Taleghani who profoundly disagreed with Khomeini's version of government. They believed that clerics should not be involved in national politics. As a matter of fact, many Iranians believe that Ayatollah Taleghani died in a mysterious way a few days after he had criticized the Khomeini's regime for conducting itself as a religious authoritarianism, although his death was said to have been caused by a heart attack.[14] Ayatollah Shariatmadari was put under house arrest until his death.[15] The government had discovered a plot to assassinate Khomeini by the son-in-law of Ayatollah Shariatmadari and Ghotbzadeh.

Sadeq Ghotbzadeh was the Iranian foreign minister for one year during the Iranian hostage crisis. He was actually an aide to Ayatollah Khomeini while he was in exile in France. In April 1982, Ghotbzadeh was arrested along with a group of army officers and clerics, including the son-in-law of Ayatollah Shariatmadari, accused of plotting against the Islamic Republic and the Islamic Revolution and plotting the assassination of Khomeini. Ghotbzadeh was executed on September 15, 1982.[16]

The hostage crisis brought a great deal of pressure to Carter's administration. All political mediation to release the hostages failed. America was now involved in a game with radical Islam and did not know what to do. As Gary Sick, former National Security Council staff during the Carter administration, puts it: "The evidence suggests that we are poorly equipped to deal with revolutionary societies, and when religion is added to revolution, we are paralyzed."[17]

On April 24, 1980, the Carter Administration, out of sheer despair, planned a military rescue operation. An exceedingly complex plan relying on total secrecy and surprise rather than massive military force was developed. The operation was designed as a series of independent stages, capable of being terminated at any point if the mission was compromised.[18] However, in my opinion, any mission, even one executed in total secrecy, was outrageous. There was no way any highly skilled military unit could barge into the center of Iran's capital, surrounded by extreme fanatical Muslims, and rescue the hostages without risking all of their lives. What would be the outcome of such an action? World War III!

As a matter of fact, the Lord spoke to Lester Sumrall, a great man of God, that if the rescuers had reached the capital, world war was what exactly would have taken place. The risks were undeniable. Technical difficulties with the rescue helicopters, thick swirling dust clouds, malfunction of flight instruments, and, finally, a need to refuel hindered the progress of the rescue team. During a refueling operation, there was a fatal collision, and eight American servicemen died. The mission was a failure.[19] The failed effort strengthened Khomeini's stand against the United States and prolonged the captivity of the fifty-two Americans for four hundred forty-four days.

Velayat-e Faghih

Khomeini, from the start of the revolution, knew the precise format of the new government. He allowed freedom of opinion in the beginning so that every element and every existing ideologist would be exposed. He needed to know who was where!

The political concept of Khomeini was that of the Islamic Ummat (community) of Muhammad's seventh century in Arabia. Muhammad was the leader of the Muslim community in all its spheres—political, social, and economical. This is the core belief of the *velayat-e faghih* (the reign of jurisprudence) and the very religious stance of Khomeini. Some will argue that this concept was a creation of Khomeini's political master plan. But one who knows the history of Islam will admit that this concept was born in Medina after the Hijrat in A.D. 622. Khomeini is the first one who dared to practice it in the twentieth century.

In *velayat-e faghih*, the *faghih* (jurisprudence) must exercise his authority above every law and institution of the government. Actually, the *faghih* is the law. He is the ultimate authority. He is Allah's instrument in enforcing Allah's will practiced on the earth. It is theocracy in its fullest meaning. I would, however, call it *Allah-ocracy*, because the reign of Allah as a supreme leader differs vastly from the theocracy that we know in the Scripture from the time of Moses through the judges in the Old Testament.

In his book *Islam and Revolution I: Writings and Declaration of Imam Khomeini (1941–1980)*, Khomeini writes:

> Islamic government does not correspond to any of the existing forms of government. For example, it is not a tyranny, where the head of state can deal arbitrarily with the property and lives of the people, making use of them as he wills, putting to death anyone he wishes, and enriching anyone he wishes by granting landed estates and distributing the property and holdings of the people. The Most Noble Messenger...the Commander of the Faithful...and the other Caliphs did not have such powers. Islamic government is neither tyrannical nor absolute, but constitutional. It is not constitutional in the current sense of the word, i.e. based on the approval of laws in accordance with the opinion of the majority. It is constitutional in the sense that the rulers are subject to a certain set of conditions in governing and administering the country, conditions that are set forth in the Noble Qur'an and the Sunna of the Most Noble Messenger. It is the laws and ordinances of Islam comprising this set of conditions that must be observed and practiced. Islamic government may therefore be defined as the rule of divine law over men.[20]

This Islamic government needs a jurisprudence, someone who has knowledge of the Islamic law and its interpretation and who also is capable of implementing it. To the Shi'ite philosophy, that is why the Imamate existed. Khomeini writes:

> The Most Noble Messenger...headed the executive and administrative institutions of Muslim society. In addition to conveying the revelation and expounding and interpreting the articles of faith and the ordinances and institutions of Islam, he undertook the implementations of law and the establishment of the ordinances of Islam, thereby bringing into being the Islamic state. He did not content himself with the promulgation of law; rather, he implemented it at

the same time, cutting off hands and administering lashings and stonings. After the Most Noble Messenger, his successor had the same duty and function. When the Prophet appointed a successor, it was not for the purpose of expounding articles of faith and law; it was for the implementation of law and execution of God's ordinances. It was this function—the execution of law and the establishment of Islamic institutions—that made the appointment of a successor such an important matter that the Prophet would have failed to fulfill his mission if he had neglected it.[21]

After the death of Muhammad, the leadership of the Ummat (the Muslim community) was handed down to four caliphs: Abu-Bakr, Omar, Othman, and Ali. According to the Shi'ite belief, the Imamate (the twelve Imams, descendents of Ali) continued with the leadership of the Islamic community. Of course, the majority of Muslims, the Sunnis, reject the ideology of Imamate by the Shi'ite.

Khomeini believed that the law of Islam and its implementation should not be limited only to the time of Muhammad and the caliphate but must continue throughout all ages, since Islam is the last and final revelation of Allah. Islam must be dominant in all ages and in all societies. And how could this be possible without an Islamic state, an Islamic government, and an Islamic executor or jurisprudence? Furthermore, Khomeini saw himself as the one commissioned to do that in Iran to begin with and then onward to other nations of the earth. Studying the history of Islam and its law and philosophy, one must admit that Khomeini was right on target in his philosophy of an Islamic government.

The majority of the people who shouted with joy when Khomeini arrived in Iran on February 1, 1979, and all of those who voted for the Islamic Republic had no clue what was about to take place—not even the clerics, except a few within Khomeini's close circle. In his own mind, Khomeini had mapped it out very clearly: an Islamic state, with him executing every law of the *sharia*. Iran was certainly a religious Shi'ite society, but it was also a society that had been introduced, by the Pahlavi Dynasty, to the goods of the West and the twentieth-century lifestyle with all its glamour and gadgets—Mercedes Benzs, televisions, fancy homes, and so on. Iranians were not educated in the Islamic laws and history. Most people's knowledge of Islam was basically the handed-down fables and fabricated hadiths by the corrupted mullahs. The majority of the Iranians could only quote a few verses in the Quran by heart. Iran was not like Pakistan, where millions of children rock themselves to and fro squatting on their knees on a hard floor in Maddrassas, memorizing the Quran by repetition. Nor was it an Arab nation where the Islamic traditions are engraved in the culture.

Bloodshed

Khomeini wanted to take a semi-modern society from the twentieth century back into seventh-century Islam, with all its dreadful laws. The friction that his movement would cause within the Iranian culture would make it impossible for him to accomplish this task. The only possible way would be to shed so much blood and create a heavy iron-fisted government that would scare the life out of every human being in his sphere. This is exactly what took place in Arabia in the seventh century by Muhammad. And that is exactly what Khomeini did.

Once Khomeini's intentions were known, the population was segmented into three basic categories:

1. Those who followed Khomeini as an Imam and became known as the *Hezbollah* (the party of Allah)

2. Those who resisted Khomeini, which included almost all the intellectuals, the majority of whom were university students and were drawn toward the leftist ideology

3. The common people, who, because of fear of reprisal, did not allow their thoughts and opinions to leave their bedrooms

The Hezbollah became an active part of Khomeini's government. Many groups were formed, such as the Revolutionary *Komiteh* (Committee), which acted as the religious police enforcing the Islamic *sharia*. Another group was the revolutionary tribunals, who were the swords of Allah's judgment in Iran.[22] They began executing ministers and army generals loyal to the shah. Sadeq Khalkhali, the Muslim cleric in charge of tribunals, became known as the *blood drinker*. He began a rampage of executions of people who served the shah's government all across Iran. From February through November of 1979, an average of one hundred people were executed on a monthly basis.[23]

Almost every single one of these people died without any official trial.

Then there was the scary Islamic Revolutionary Guard Corps known as the *Pasdaran*.[24] These were the guardians of the revolution. They became the main paramilitary force that crushed the separatist movements such as the Turkemen, Kurds, and Baluchi people who sought autonomy. They were also a major force against the Iraqis in the eight-year war that was initiated by the Iraqi leader Saddam Hussein. Also, during the war a voluntary group was formed, composed mainly of the young people called *basiji*. These were known as the martyrs of Islam. Thousands of them would run into the minefields to clear the way for the troops.[25] My nephew was one of them. He was fourteen years old when he ran onto a minefield during the war with Iraq. My family assumed that he was dead since they couldn't find his body. He was a prisoner of war in Iraq for four years and almost starved to death. There are also other unofficial groups whose missions were more secretive, such as the Enteharis, who now operate as suicide bombers in Iraq against the American troops.

Little by little Khomeini purged Iran from every opposition against him and the revolution. Prisons began filling up again with tens of thousands of young Mojahedine Khalgh, Tudeh, and Marxist adherents, as well as anyone else who opposed Khomeini. The phrase that became a cliché was "*zede-enghelab*," one who is anti-revolution, which meant they were anti-Islam—the penalty for which was either death or imprisonment with torture. If the shah had created the idea of torture, Khomeini perfected it. The thousands of stories that I have heard from Iranian refugees would bring horror to the mind of anyone. As a witness to the life of these individuals with whom I came into contact during my many years of ministry among them in Europe, I must say that if evil had a name, I would definitely call it the Islamic government of Khomeini.

One of the main opposition groups that suffered the most was the Mojahedin Khalgh, an Islamic political group with a Marxist economical ideology. Mojahedin began an armed struggle against the regime. They planted suicide bombers who infiltrated the government facilities and blew themselves up, killing many of the officials. Among these were many Islamic Republic Party officials, including Ayatollah Beheshti, Ali Rajai, who was the second elected president after Bani-Sadr had escaped for his life from Iran, and Prime Minister Mohammad Javad Bahonar. Rajai and Bahonar served in the presidential office for two weeks before their assassinations.[26]

Khomeini began a campaign of slaughtering the Mojahedin. Scores were arrested and executed immediately. The ruthless crackdown against the Mojahedin started in 1981 by the military and the revolutionary police. Prisons overflowed with men and women ranging in age from twelve to seventy-five. On June 20, 1981, the Islamic government of Ayatollah Khomeini began a reign of terror and executions of the Mojahedin. By December of that year the government had executed some twenty-five hundred Mojahedin followers. Some were hanged; others were put before the firing squads. Sometimes the bodies of these people were left on public gallows.[27]

Robin Wright, an American educator and correspondent journalist for several national and international papers, records the following in her book *In the Name of God:*

> Many times the only way families knew what had happened to their loved ones was by reading newspaper columns listing the latest executions, although not all the names were revealed. The subsequent crackdown was so brutal that it quickly became known as the reign of terror, a term adapted from similar eras under Robespierre in France and Stalin in the Soviet Union.[28]

A well-known Muslim saying states, "One must wash blood with blood." Hatred and bloodshed continued as the Mojahedin countered state terror with its own brand of terror. They carried out daily assassination attacks on high-ranking officials of the government in every major city of the country. Hundreds were blown to pieces by these merciless suicide attacks. The majority of these suicide assassins were young, aged fifteen to twenty-five.

On September 11, 1981, a twenty-two-year-old Mojahed man attended the Friday prayer at Tabriz. He walked up to Ayatollah Baha al-Din Madani and exploded two hand grenades, killing himself, his intended victim, and seventeen *pasdars* (special policemen who enforce Islamic law). Two weeks after this incident, a seventeen-year-old high school student blew up himself and Hojjat al-Islam Hasheminezhad, the Islamic Republic Party leader in the city of Khorasan.[29]

The bloodshed between the Islamic government of Khomeini and the Mojahedin continued for four years, taking the lives of 12,250 political dissidents, three-quarters of who were Mojahedin members or sympathizers.[30]

Bani-Sadr, the first president of the Islamic Republic of Iran and a former strong admirer of Khomeini, was ousted and had to flee to exile in Paris, where he called on Iranians to "rise and resist. Overthrow this regime which has proven more bloodthirsty than the monarchy."[31]

Within two years of the establishment of the Islamic government of the Ayatollah Khomeini, such an atmosphere of terror and fear was created by the Islamic clerics that the first interim prime minister of the Islamic Republic of Iran, Mehdi Bazargan, who resigned after nine months, described the situation of the country in an open letter. In it Bazargan charged the government with creating "an atmosphere of terror, fear, revenge and national disintegration." He continued:

> What has the ruling elite done besides bring death and destruction, pack the prisons and cemeteries in every city, create long queues, shortage, high prices, unemployment, poverty, homeless people, repetitious slogans and a dark future?[32]

Along with the trouble within the country of Iran, a new threat loomed large in the early months of 1980—Saddam Hussein saw opportunities in postrevolution Iran. He coveted the rich oil fields in the Khuzestan province in Iran and resented Khomeini's hard-line Shi'ah stance and desire to declare a jihad against Hussein's Sunni regime. On September 22, 1980, Saddam drove his infantry into Khuzestan with the aim of securing the major cities, major roads, and the mountain passes through which Iranian forces would have to move in defense.[33] The Iranians launched a successful series of limited offensives against the Iraqi forces dug in across Khuzestan. By June of 1981, Saddam magnanimously announced that he was "withdrawing" his units to Iraq. But the radical mullahs of Iran joined with Khomeini to spread the Islamic Revolution beyond Iran and to fight "until the government of heathens in Iraq topples."[34]

Finally, in late 1983, as a last resort to win the war, Iraq launched chemical warfare attacks into Iran, which brought as many as fifty thousand casualties among Iranian people.[35] Iran retaliated with a military strategy to stress a war of attrition and pushed forward to January 1987, when Iran mounted successive attacks against Basra, nearly breaking through to that important city—a battle that became the high point for Iran in the war.[36] In July 1988, Iran accepted a cease-fire with Iraq.

Even before the end of the war, Khomeini recognized that the governmental structure he had created was running into problems. The independent centers of power within his government were competing with one another: the president, the prime minister, the Majles, the army, the Pasdaran, the *bonyads,* the revolutionary tribunals, the *komitehs,* the Council of Guardians, and so on.[37] Each attempt he made to bring order failed. Ill with cancer, Khomeini moved to tie up all of Iran's loose ends in terms of political dissent. He launched a wave of arrests aimed at anyone left with any sort of affiliation with opposition groups. Several thousand were executed by hanging or by firing squad in what Amnesty International called "the biggest wave of secret political executions since the early 1980s."[38]

On June 3, 1989, Khomeini finally died.

Iran After Khomeini

The Islamic government in Iran has been in power for the past twenty-seven years, contrary to many predictions that they would not last long. They have withstood much opposition from within and a major war with Iraq. Even after Khomeini's death, the Islamic government in Iran has been able to hold on to its reign.

Khomeini made sure that his successor was the one who would carry the same line of thoughts of the idea of *velayat-e faghih.* Due to the fact that many of the high-ranking ayatollahs and clerics in Iran did not agree with Khomeini's philosophy on *velayat-e faghih,* Khomeini secured the office of the *faghih* (the Supreme Leader) by declaring that its position was absolute and must precede over all other offices in the land. In other words, a *faghih* was above all the religious and political laws of the land.

Khomeini had his successor in sight, Ayatollah Seyyed Ali Hosseini Khamenei. He became a close associate of Khomeini and one of the key figures in the revolution. He was the leader of Tehran's great Friday prayer. He became known as a "living martyr" after barely escaping an assassination attempt on his life that left him permanently handicapped in his right arm. After Rajai's assassination in 1981, Khamenei became the elected president of the Islamic government by a landslide vote, becoming the first cleric to serve in a political office. Khamenei served two presidency terms before he was appointed as the Supreme Leader (*faghih*) the day after Khomeini's death.

Since his appointment, Khamenei has come into major clashes with the reformist movement within the Majles (Parliament). Many reformist bills have been vetoed by Khamenei, and their candidates were barred from running for the recent presidential and parliamentary elections.

Conclusion

Much could be written about the Islamic government of Khomeini and the Islamic Revolution. There are many well-documented books on the historical events that took place in Iran. Yet we must analyze Iran beyond just the ordinary set of horrible events. Iran has been a main focus of the news since the beginning of the cold war. It has an important geopolitical position, and it carries tremendous spiritual weight in our history today. The Islamic Revolution of the Ayatollah Khomeini gave birth to the notion that the West is evil and that Islam must prevail on all the political scenes of the earth.

The old agenda of the Islamic community has been resurrected—Islam a dominant religion and a power factor on the earth. So far the main body of Islam is fragmented just as it has always been, due to the fact that the teaching of Islam produces hatred, division, and warfare. Therefore when Islam rises, it always carries an internal poison. Throughout the history of Islam, there has always been warfare and bloodshed within the Islamic camp—Muslims massacring Muslims. In other words, that which you sell, you usually eat of it, too. Iran is a great example of the process of an Islamic revolution. The Taliban was another example, except that it didn't live long enough.

Since the fall of Communism, the West, especially the United States, has been in a hot war with the Islamic fundamentalists. Even though the efforts of these groups such as Al-Qaeda, Taliban, Hezbollah, Muslim Brotherhood, and many others are (thankfully) not correlated, they have posed an incredible threat to the peace of the world. Life as we once knew it in America doesn't exist anymore as a result of this fact. The question is this: *What must we—both the Christian community and the political institutions—do to safeguard the future from the annihilation of freedom as we know it?*

The answer is really very simple yet extremely complicated. How can that be? The simplicity of it lies with the knowledge of what we face. I have always stated that knowledge is the key to strength. The difficult part is to apply that simple knowledge. For instance, we Christians, the body of believers, know that the gospel is the answer to the Islamic world. Our Nejat TV has proven this fact beyond any shadow of a doubt. Yet how many Christians see the Islamic world as a threat and are just applying that simple answer?

On the political arena, our politicians are compromising the truth, from our president declaring that "Islam is a peaceful religion" and breaking the *Iftar* (Muslim break-fast in Ramadan) at the White House, to adding the Quran to the White House library, to the European and Western governments that are becoming protectors of the Islamic faith. To be honest with you, I doubt if our government or any other Western government will ever win the war against radical Islam, because they see Islam from a standpoint of political correctness instead of what it actually is.

The burden is laid on the house of God, on the remnant. When Israel had gone into captivity, and Jerusalem had been forsaken and in ruins for seventy years, there weren't many Jews who truly cared for their inheritance except for a few men. The majority had settled their hearts on living in foreign lands apart from a covenant with God. Yet there were a few who loved the gates of Jerusalem. One of these men was Nehemiah, a strong man in the spirit. Because of the efforts of that man and fifty thousand plus others, Israel came together again to become a people and a land so that the Messiah, the Christ of God, could appear in the flesh for the salvation of the world.

Throughout history, God has always been looking for the remnant, men and women who do not compromise with the world system or fear it.

America failed in Iran because they compromised the truth. England failed in Iran because they were unjust and greedy. Russia failed in Iran because they had a corrupt system. Islam has also failed in Iran because it perpetuates more injustice than any other religion or human force. But the truth is prevailing in Iran, the truth that is unchangeable—God's everlasting love and Word through our Lord and Savior, Jesus Christ.

5

Muhammad and God at War

The word *Islam* means submission. It defines a religion in which the follower must completely resign his will and desires to the will and the desires of the god who is called *Allah*. The god of Islam demands submission wholeheartedly to all the laws, statutes, and commandments that were revealed to Muhammad, the prophet of Islam. Within this context, Allah and his mediator are in the absolute control of an entire society in all its aspects—social, cultural, political, and economical. There are no gray areas. Every act from how to wash your hands before prayer to warfare against the infidels is designed and planned out for every member of such society, for Muslims as well as non-Muslims.

Once Islam becomes the dominant physical or political force within a nation, a tribe, or a group, then all the aspects of that community become subject to the Islamic *sharia* and ordinance. And within this parameter no one, not a single human soul, has the power to refute such laws that are ordained by Allah and his prophet, Muhammad. It is a totalitarian system in its fullest meaning.

Islam was a dominant force from the seventh century up to the end of the Ottoman Empire advancement in 1529. In our modern world history, only the Islamic Republic of Iran and the Taliban in Afghanistan are examples of societies where Islam is the dominant force, with all its political, economical, and religious apparatus.

In most Islamic nations, Islam is a dominant force in the practices and culture of the majority of the people but not a dominating factor in the government. An example of this is Pakistan with a population of 240 million people. Islam is the dominant religion with 90 percent of the population claiming to be Muslim. Out of this 90 percent, which is about 215 million people, 10 to 30 percent claim to be radical Muslims. That is anywhere from 20 to 50 million people. Scary! Pakistan's government is a military government led by President Musharaf, who is a nominal or a secular Muslim. Even though the majority of the people in Pakistan are Muslims, the law of Pakistan is not Islamic law (*sharia*), thus the political and economical machineries of Pakistan are based on a secular system rather than a religious ordinance. This is not the case with Iran.

The recent development, or better said, resurgence of the Islamic prototype of governmental rule in accordance to Islamic law and tradition among the radical Muslims such as Al-Qaeda or Khomeini has given rise to much analysis of the Islamic faith and its system of government. For the most part, the majority of these analyses lack solid theological and historical knowledge of Islam. Like most articles written in news magazines about Iran or other Islamic nations, their study is shortsighted and has no firm foundation. An analysis of the philosophy of these Islamic nations, groups, and ideologists must encompass the teaching of the Quran and the lifestyle of Muhammad, known as hadith, because the principles espoused by the Quran and hadith are the sole precepts and imperatives such radical groups are following. Any other form of analysis will lead to a distorted version that is misleading and cannot help us in mapping out the plan of action needed to face the force that is on the rise.

Radical Islam is known by many "tags," including "the hijackers of the religion" and "the terrorists." However, the fact remains that radical Islam obeys the teachings of the Quran and the hadith, and it acts upon the understanding of these writings. Therefore, it is vitally important for us to examine the core of that ideology and not just skim the surface.

Democracy in Islam

Recent developments in Iraq and the possibility of a form of democracy being accepted in countries like Iraq, Iran, Afghanistan, and Saudi Arabia will be discussed further in chapter six, "America and Islam." In the remainder of this chapter, I want to take a look at Iran as an example of freedom within the context of Islam. We will examine the hardship and persecutions facing Christians, Jews, and followers of other religions who have endured at the hand of an Islamic regime.

Iran and Religious Freedom

The Iranian constitution declares that the "official religion of Iran is Islam, and the doctrine followed is that of Ja'fari (Twelver) Shi'ism." On its official Web site, the Iranian government states:

Article 1

The form of government of Iran is that of an Islamic Republic, endorsed by the people of Iran on the basis of their longstanding belief in the sovereignty of truth and Qur'anic justice, in the referendum of Farwardin 9 and 10 in the year 1358 of the solar Islamic calendar, corresponding to Jamadi al-'Awwal 1 and 2 in the year 1399 of the lunar Islamic calendar [March 29 and 30, 1979], through the affirmative vote of a majority of 98.2% of eligible voters, held after the victorious Islamic Revolution led by the eminent marji' al-taqlid, Ayatullah al-Uzma Imam Khumayni.[1]

This clearly informs us that the Islamic government of Iran bases its constitution upon Quranic teachings and beliefs. In article two of the constitution we read:

Article 2

The Islamic Republic is a system based on belief in:

1. the One God (as stated in the phrase "There is no god except Allah"), His exclusive sovereignty and the right to legislate, and the necessity of submission to His commands;

2. Divine revelation and its fundamental role in setting forth the laws;

3. the return to God in the Hereafter, and the constructive role of this belief in the course of man's ascent towards God;

4. the justice of God in creation and legislation;

5. continuous leadership (imamah) and perpetual guidance, and its fundamental role in ensuring the uninterrupted process of the revolution of Islam;

6. the exalted dignity and value of man, and his freedom coupled with responsibility before God; in which equity, justice, politi-

cal, economic, social, and cultural independence, and national
solidarity are secured by recourse to:

1. continuous ijtihad of the fuqaha' possessing necessary qualifica-
   tions, exercised on the basis off the Qur'an and the Sunnah of the
   Ma'sumun, upon all of whom be peace;

2. sciences and arts and the most advanced results of human experience, together with the effort to advance them further;

3. negation of all forms of oppression, both the infliction of and the
   submission to it, and of dominance, both its imposition and its
   acceptance.[2]

At the proclamation of the Islamic Republic of Iran on April 1, 1979,
Ayatollah Khomeini declared, "On this blessed day, the day the Islamic community assumes leadership, the day of victory and triumph of our people, I
declare the Islamic Republic of Iran, the first day of Allah's government."[3]

Since this clearly states that the government of Iran is founded upon the
teachings of Allah as written in the Quran, we must consider this question:
what does Allah say about the rights of other religious minorities? For the
answer to that question, we turn again to the constitution, quoting from
Articles 13 and 14.

Article 13
Zoroastrian, Jewish, and Christian Iranians are the only recognized
religious minorities, who *within the limits of the law*, are free to perform their religious rites and ceremonies, and to act according to
their own canon in matters of personal affairs and religious education (emphasis added).

Article 14
In accordance with the sacred verse; ("God does not forbid you to
deal kindly and justly with those who have not fought against you
because of your religion and who have not expelled you from your
homes" [60:8]), the government of the Islamic Republic of Iran and
all Muslims are duty-bound to treat non-Muslims in conformity
with ethical norms and the principles of Islamic justice and equity,
and to respect their human rights. This principle applies to all who
refrain from engaging in conspiracy or activity against Islam and the
Islamic Republic of Iran.[4]

Notice in Article 13 the wording: "... *within the limits of the law*, are free to perform their religious rites and ceremonies..." In other words, they will give them freedom within the *limits of the Islamic law*. As long as these minorities (Zoroastrian, Jewish, and Christian) and their activities are not in contradiction to the Islamic law, they are OK! Other religious beliefs, such as the Baha'i faith with an estimated 300,000 to 350,000 adherents in Iran, have no freedom to practice their religion at all.[5] As a matter of fact, the Baha'is are considered blasphemers and heretics to the Islamic faith, and they are harshly persecuted.

These religious minorities, including all Christian denominations, are closely monitored by the Ministry of Islamic Culture and Ershad (Guidance) and the Ministry of Intelligence and Security. This includes all the worship services, schools, and every event. Many of the new believers who have come to Christ through our Nejat TV broadcast have told us that they were questioned by the Pasdaran (Revolutionary Guards) at the entrance of the church when they sought to visit a church service. According to the U.S. State Department, "The Government has pressured evangelical Christian groups to compile and submit membership lists for their congregations, but evangelicals have resisted this demand. Non-Muslim owners of grocery shops are required to indicate their religious affiliation on the fronts of their shops."[6]

Christians and Jews have been the target of various discrimination in the areas of housing, education, and employment. In order to be accepted to any higher education institution, for example, one must pass a *sharia* (Islamic law) test. Those of Islamic faith who practice their regular daily prayer and fasting during Ramadan have the greatest chance of being accepted. We know of several examples where a believer has been expelled from the university, and of others who have lost their jobs, as a result of becoming a Christian. This is, of course, the mildest form of persecution that Christians and other religious minorities are enduring at the hands of this Islamic government.

As soon as the Islamic Republic was established, Khomeini and his inner-circle clerics, known as the *Islamic Revolutionary Council (IRC)*, began purging Iran from whatever was un-Islamic and would not subject itself to submission under the Islamic *sharia* and "Allah's government." In his book *The History of Iran*, Elton L. Daniel states:

Khomeini preferred a much tougher approach to dealing with all these problems.... Suspicious of the army, Khomeini... authorized... the formation of... an armed force capable of dealing with any threat to the revolution.... The Guards quickly went to work ruthlessly suppressing the ethnic dissidents.[7]

One of the un-Islamic entities was the Christian community.

Soon after the Islamic Republic began its reign of Islamic terror, all foreign missionaries were forced to leave Iran. In 1988 the Iranian government began a campaign against the Christian churches. Many churches were closed as a result of the government persecution. The church in the city of Mashhad was closed in 1988, Sari church in 1988, Kerman church in the spring of 1992, Shiraz church in 1992, the Gorgan church in October of 1993, Ahwaz church in 1993, and the Kermanshah church for which no date is available.[8]

A majority of these churches were associated with Tehran's Assembly of God mother church, *Jamiat-e Rabbani*. In June of 1993 the Islamic government ordered all Christian churches to sign a statement declaring that they would not evangelize Muslims. The members of these evangelical congregations were required to carry membership cards, and photocopies of these cards had to be sent to the authorities.[9] Bishop Haik Hovsepian Mehr, the president of the Council of Protestant Churches in Iran and the senior pastor of the *Jamiat-e Rabbani* church, refused to abide by the Islamic law of not evangelizing the Muslims. He was ordered by the authorities to disclose a list of all Muslim converts in his congregation. He refused. He loved his Master and considered obeying the Great Commission above the law of the land, even if that cost him his life. As a result, Pastor Haik was assassinated in 1994.[10]

In May of 1993, non-Muslim shopkeepers were forced to put up notices in their shops indicating their religious affiliation. This made it very difficult for Christian businesses to do business in an ordinary manner. Discrimination began at every level toward Christians.[11]

In October 1993, the government passed a law requiring religious affiliation to be stated on all identity cards. Many Iranian converts from Muslim backgrounds who accepted the Lord outside of Iran had a difficult time going back to Iran. Their religious associations also had to be marked on their passport. In one case, one of our friends who returned to Iran was asked about his religion at the passport check-in. When the police found out that he was a Christian, they asked him about his name, which is a Muslim name. "My father loved Muslim names, so he named me after a Muslim!" he explained, which was true, for he comes from a Muslim family.

The main wave of persecution started in 1994 when several of the pastors of major evangelical denominations were murdered by the Islamic regime's death squad, including Bishop Haik Hovsepian Mehr, Mehdi Dibaj, and Tateos Michaelian, who were murdered in Iran, and several Iranian dissidents living outside the country.

On March 21, 1994, *TIME* magazine published an investigative report into the deaths of Iranian dissidents living outside the country and stated: "According to Western intelligence and Iranian dissident sources, decisions to assassinate opponents at home or abroad are made at the highest level of the Iranian government: The Supreme National Security Council. The top political decision-making body is chaired by (President) Rafsanjani and includes, among others, (Minister of Intelligence) Fallahian, (Foreign minister) Velayati and (Supreme Guide) Ali Khamenei."[12]

Other church members and church leaders have been arrested and prosecuted. Pastor Khosro Yusefi is an example of how the Iranian government has been intimidating the law-abiding Christians in Iran. Pastor Khosro Yusefi was arrested and imprisoned along with his wife and their two teenage children in the city of Chalous in the north by the Caspian Sea.

According to Compass Direct, "Dozens of believers from two of Yusefi's church groups were jailed in the first week of May and later released. However, Sunday's arrest marks the first time that the entire family of a Christian leader has been taken into custody. The majority of Christians meeting in secret house-church groups in Iran are former Muslims."[13]

As the persecution intensified, many church members and leaders left the country and sought refugee status in other parts of the world.

One of the hardest hits to the churches was the closing down of the Bible Society in 1990. According to Operation World, in 1988 the supplies of Christian Bibles and literature were banned and distribution outlets were closed. They estimate that some ten million Bibles would be gladly received in Iran if there were such a possibility.[14]

Through our Nejat TV underground workers in Iran, we have distributed several thousand Bibles and other pieces of literature and video CDs and DVDs throughout Iran. One of our main problems has been the shortage of Bibles and Christian literature.

Since 1999, the U.S. Secretary of State has designated Iran as a "Country of Particular Concern" under the International Religious Freedom Act for particularly severe violations of religious freedom.[15] According to Amnesty International in November of 2004, the UN General Assembly passed a resolution condemning the human rights situation in Iran. It drew attention to Iran's "failure to comply with international standards in the administration of justice, the absence of due process of law, the refusal to provide fair and public hearings and right to counsel..." and forms of systematic discrimination. It urged the authorities to appoint an independent and impartial prosecutor in Tehran and to fulfill Iran's international commitments.[16]

The European Union (EU) has repeatedly stated the long-standing human rights concerns in Iran, which include the use of torture, unequal rights for women, the use of the death penalty, religious discrimination, and the lack of an independent judiciary.[17]

No matter how much pressure the European Union or the United States puts on the Iranian government concerning human rights, Iran will continue the path of Islam. According to the Iranian government, there is only one way, and all other ways must be formed according to that way—Islam. Their intention is well documented in the following paragraph in the description of the Iranian constitution:

> With due attention to the Islamic content of the Iranian Revolution, the Constitution provides the necessary basis for ensuring the continuation of the Revolution at home and abroad. In particular, in the development of international relations, the Constitution will strive with other Islamic and popular movements to prepare the way for the formation of a single world community (in accordance with the Koranic verse *"This your community is a single community, and I am your Lord, so worship Me"* [21:92]), and to assure the continuation of the struggle for the liberation of all deprived and oppressed peoples in the world.[18]

6

America and Islam

On September 11, 2001, a gigantic port was opened, a gate that will lead us, eventually, to the end of time. On that day of infamy America faced a new giant unlike any force by which she has ever been challenged. That principality, better known as *Islam*, will be a contending force until it opens the way for its master, the Antichrist. Meanwhile a time is granted to America to shine in its finest hour. I believe that the United States of America was purposed for this very hour and this very task.

In August 23, 686, a great man was born in France by the name of Charles Martel. In 732, Martel won a historical battle, known as the Battle of Tours, against the Arabs. On the *Famous Men of the Middle Ages* Web site, this critically important battle is described as follows:

> After the death of Mohammed the Saracens, as Mohammedans are also called, became great warriors. They conquered many countries and established the Mohammedan religion in them. In 711 the Saracens invaded and conquered a great part of Spain and founded a powerful kingdom there, which lasted about seven hundred years. They intended to conquer the land of the Franks next, and then all Europe....
>
> Their army was led by Abd-er-Rahman (Abd-er-Rah'-man), the Saracen governor of Spain. On his march through the southern districts of the land of the Franks Abd-er-Rahman destroyed many towns and villages, killed a number of the people, and seized all the property he could carry off. He plundered the city of Bordeaux (bor-do'), and, it is said, obtained so many valuable things that every soldier "was loaded with golden vases and cups and emeralds and other precious stones."
>
> But meanwhile Charles Martel was not idle. As quickly as he

could he got together a great army of Franks and Germans and marched against the Saracens. The two armies met between the cities of Tours and Poitiers (pwaw-te-ay) in October, 732. For six days there was nothing but an occasional skirmish between small parties from both sides; but on the seventh day a great battle took place. Both Christians and Mohammedans fought with terrible earnestness. The fight went on all day, and the field was covered with the bodies of the slain. But towards evening, during a resolute charge made by the Franks, Abd-er-Rahman was killed. Then the Saracens gradually retired to their camp.

It was not yet known, however, which side had won; and the Franks expected that the fight would be renewed in the morning. But when Charles Martel, with his Christian warriors, appeared on the field at sunrise there was no enemy to fight. The Mohammedans had fled in the silence and darkness of the night and had left behind them all their valuable spoils. There was now no doubt which side had won.

The battle of Tours, or Poitiers, as it should be called, is regarded as one of the decisive battles of the world. It decided that Christians, and not Moslems, should be the ruling power in Europe.[1]

If it weren't for Charles Martel, Europe would be an Islamic continent today.

That same assignment is set before this great land of America and her people. September 11 was the invitation from the spirit of that religion saying, "Deal with me!" The question is: can America deal with it in accordance with the truth?

America has been given the finest of every thing—constitution, law, prosperity, wisdom, knowledge, understanding, and, greatest of all, *freedom*. No other nation on this earth has the capacity or the possibility of dealing with such a principality other than the United States of America. Grace has been shed upon this land for this very purpose. America carries the rod of judgment for some nations and cities. I believe that cities like Damascus will be judged in the same way that Hiroshima was judged, as awful as this may sound. I believe that only a handful of people in this country foresee the kind of battle that lies ahead of us. If there ever was a battle between right and wrong, evil and good, just and unjust, *it is the battle and warfare between Islam and the United States of America.*

Do we know how to fight this formidable enemy? Most of us don't even consider or dare to call it an *enemy*. Time alone will tell. I know that I know Islam. I was a radical Muslim and well versed in the law and the spirit of this religion. I wish that I was wrong in my conclusions. But again, I have to warn and inform with that with which I am entrusted. The key is knowledge and understanding and also wisdom in its place.

Understanding the Enemy

To understand the ideology of Islam and radical Islamic groups, whose numbers grow day by day, we must understand the birth of Islam. Where did this religion originate? What was the condition at the time of Islam's birth? What kind of opposition did Muhammad and his followers face? What was the revelation? What kinds of mind-sets have been formed within the Islamic philosophy?

To a Muslim, Islam is a complete system that encompasses every aspect of society. Muslims assert that the laws of Islam meet not only the religious and the moral codes of a society, but the political, economical, social, and ethical codes as well.

We must realize that many of the teachings of Islam are based upon the political and economical conditions of the Arabian society of the seventh century. Many rituals and practices enforced by Islam can be traced back to pre-Islamic Arabia. One researcher points out, "Archeological and linguistic work done since the latter part of the nineteenth century has unearthed overwhelming evidence that Mohammad constructed his religion and the Koran from preexisting material in Arabian culture."[2]

Within little more than a decade after the end of the cold war era, the world has taken on an incredible shape and form and has experienced an enormous transition and change, both in the natural and spiritual realms. It has been a period of shifting—politically, economically, and spiritually—from one era to another. The world passed from the cold war era of Communism to an age of new threats from Islamic fundamentalists; from dealing with atheists to an increased concern with religious extremists. The political map of the world took a new shape, and new unpredicted boundaries were drawn.

The events of the earlier era rose in a crescendo to the bankruptcy and fall of the Soviet Union and its Eastern European allies. The walls of that antichrist empire came tumbling down, an oppressive empire that had suppressed the truth and freedom for several decades.

Communism was an ideology that desired justice, at least so it claimed. Its version of justice was "equality for all, enforced by force and terror." Even though its leaders, like Lenin, killed millions of innocent people, Communism did not possess a bloody spirit, not of the type we are facing today with Islamic fundamentalists. The idea of Communism, *justice for all,* was a comfort for millions of young ideologists around the world. Young men and women who desired to eradicate poverty and injustice from their downtrodden and oppressed societies needed an ideology or a force bigger than themselves to fight against tyranny and unjust rulers of their societies. Communism was the only available system and ideology for them. It gave them the hope for equality and freedom from tyrants and dictators.

Once Communism fell and showed its true nature, these young ideologists were left with a huge spiritual vacuum. I grew up with these kinds of kids back in Iran. In those days, Communism was still alive and promising. Islam was not an option for them, because the Islamic leaders were known as the lazy mullahs (Muslim priests) who preached cheap messages at funerals. They were known to be pacified and paid by the repressive regime of the shah. They were not defenders of the oppressed. They were not revolutionaries preaching against injustice and oppression.

On the other hand, the Communists had the zeal, the fire, and the fight against the unjust and the tyrants. When Communism fell and its doors were broken off at their hinges, the world saw that this "ism" was as oppressive as the tyrants, if not more. The fall of Communism left a massive chasm, a gulf of despair in the hearts and souls of millions of young ideologists. How could they fight oppression without the support of an ideology that stands for the needy and the oppressed?

The platform of Communism was social reform, a social reform that would be enforced rather than voted. Even though Communism had become a political apparatus, it was, in its core belief, an ideological system fighting for the human dignity, at least so it believed. In its philosophy, Communism had a starting and an ending point. It was birthed as a result of an idea or a system, and it ended because that system could not be created. It was simply an empty oath. Communism didn't have the ability, in its nature, to produce the utopia for which it fought. Its ending point was reached from within itself, not from without, because it lacked the power of the promise.

Although many political analysts have given credit for the failure of Communism to people like former President Ronald Reagan, Communism fell because it went bankrupt. Its economical system, its main platform, was a balloon full of air. The further it expanded, the more air it collected, to the point where it no longer could hold the air and—it exploded.

The system that Communism fought against—capitalism—is the very ground that is redeeming it from a total annihilation. What an incredible shame! I would conclude that Communism was defeated by the images of capitalism.

Years ago I listened to an interview with Soviet leader Mikhail Gorbachev as he was talking about his first visit to the United States. He was amazed at the amount of goods and food he saw in the supermarkets of America. That trip melted his heart. In June of 1987, Gorbachev introduced the concept of *Perestroika*. Its literal meaning is "structuring," which refers to restructuring of the Soviet economy.

The core belief of Communism was a common economy or, better said, a classless society of common ownership of the means of production. Marxism (the ideology of Karl Marx) was the root of Soviet Communism. Karl Marx, a German Jewish atheist, philosopher, and political economist, believed that "the nature of individuals depends on the material conditions determining their production."[3]

The main thesis of Marx was based upon the class struggle between the high class (bourgeois) capitalist and the working class (proletariat). Marx believed that in order to eliminate the gap and bring the society into a communistic state, a transitional state was required, known as "the revolutionary dictatorship of the proletariat."[4] In other words, the working class would become the ruling elites instead of the bourgeois.

Even though many stubborn communists would still argue that the state of Marxism has never been achieved, in practicality, during the past hundred years we have seen forms of Communism, socialism, and Marxism. In my many years of arguments with Iranian Communists, time and time again I have been told that Albania was the true Marxist state, the Great Utopia. This, of course, was a bold statement by frustrated Communists up until the fall of the Albanian Communist government and the exposure of the terrible condition of the people of Albania.

It is important that you understand the distinctives of Communism, because there is a monumental similarity between Communism and the radical Islam of the seventh century. This is so important for us, and especially our politicians, to understand. It opens our eyes to the mind-set and the environment upon which radical Islam breeds. As a matter of fact, this very point, the economics of the Middle East, is the point of conversion of millions of Muslims from a moderate stand to a radical and hateful position against Western governments. Islam was birthed in repression. Therefore its economic and political perspectives are extremely similar to that of a communistic system.

For example, on the issue of ownership, Islam ratifies the concept into *stewardship*—a demanded stewardship. Here is the definition of personal ownership according to the Islamic scholar Sayyid Qutb:

> But Islam does not establish the right of personal ownership absolutely, without bounds or limitations; it certainly ratifies that right, but along with it are ratified other principles that almost make it theoretical rather than practical. They almost strip a man bare of his right to possession by the time he has met all his essential needs. Islam establishes such limitations and bounds as almost render a man bound rather than free in his disposal of his property, whether he increases, spends, or administers it. But it is consideration for the welfare of society that lies behind all this; it is also consideration for the welfare of the individual himself with regard to the universal objectives by which Islam orders its view of life.
>
> The cardinal principle that Islam ratifies along with that of the right of individual possession is that the individual is in a way a steward of his property on behalf of society; his tenure of property is more of a duty than an actual right of possession. Property in the widest sense is a right than can belong only to society, which in turn receives it as a trust from Allah who is the only true owner of anything.[5]

If I didn't know any better I would say the above text was written in the Kremlin! But it is the teaching of Islam and the practice of Muhammad. The Quran says:

> Believe in Allah and His Messenger, and spend (in charity) out of the (substance) whereof He has made you heirs. For, those of you

who believe and spend (in charity),—for them is a great Reward.

—SURAH 57:7

What Allah has bestowed on His Messenger (and taken away) from the people of the townships,—belongs to Allah,—to His Messenger and to kindred and orphans, the needy and the wayfarer; in order that it may not (merely) make a circuit between the wealthy among you. So take what the Messenger assigns to you, and deny yourselves that which he withholds from you. And fear Allah; for Allah is strict in Punishment.

—SURAH 59:7

To Islam, the access of wealth to some and the lack of it for others create an atmosphere of corruption and evil. Islam disapproves of the system of capitalism where money can be circulated only among the rich. Therefore it must be controlled for the good of all—that is the Islamic justice! This is the mind-set of those Muslims who know anything about the traditions of Muhammad and the teaching of Islam.

Our politicians are wondering why radical Islam is growing so rapidly. Take a look at the Middle East. The wealth of most of the twenty-two nations in the Arab League of Nations is usurped by a minority of the people in those nations—the elites, the sheikhs, and the princes. Why is radical Islam so prevalent in a prosperous nation like Saudi Arabia? This unfair distribution of wealth is the very reason for it. And why do most of the Saudis hate America? Why is bin Laden considered a hero there? Because the Fahd family, the ruling elites, live in luxury, and the majority of their people live in poverty—and America is considered a staunch supporter of the Fahd family! That is why bin Laden is loved by the majority of Muslims in Saudi Arabia. He takes the side of the poor and the oppressed—at least that is what is known to them. And America takes the side of the rich and the oppressors!

Imperialism, a Big Word

There are two important points to the communistic philosophy. The first, out of which the whole concept of Marxism-Leninism was born, is the state of *capitalism*. The second is the state of *the working class*. The highest point of capitalism, according to Marx and Lenin, is the state of *imperialism* where the aristocrats will exploit the developing countries.

The definition of *imperialism* is:

> A policy of extending control or authority over foreign entities as a means of acquisition and or maintenance of empires, either through direct territorial conquest or through indirect methods of exerting control on the politics and/or economy of other countries. The term is often used to describe the policy of a country in maintaining colonies and dominance over distant lands, regardless of whether the country calls itself an empire. Imperialism draws heavy criticism on the grounds that historically it has been frequently employed for economic exploitation in which the imperialist power makes use of other countries as sources of raw materials and cheap labor, shaping their economies to suit its own interests, and keeping their people in poverty. When imperialism is accompanied by overt military conquest, it is also seen as a violation of freedom and human rights.[6]

Think back to the history I covered in chapter three. Doesn't this definition accurately describe the actions of the AIOC and the British government in their dealings in Iran during the Mossaddeq era?

The concept of imperialism is another reason I believe that radical Islam is gaining more and more ground in the Middle East and around the world. This is a key concept. Imperialism is one of the main ideas discussed often by radical revolutionary Islamic leaders such as Khomeini, bin Laden, Sayyid Qutb, and many others. It is a concept greatly hated by Islam.

Social Reform

In order to understand the mind-set of radical Islam, we must understand the point of their frustrations. Social reform is a gigantic concept within the Islamic philosophy. If we do not grasp the ideology of the Islamic social reform, we will never be able to win the battle against radical Islam. We were never able to win the battle against Soviet Communism through an arms race. And we will never defeat Islamic radicalism with military might. We must, and I reiterate strongly, *we must understand the concept of social reform within Islam or we will fail.*

Class struggle plays an equally central role in Islam, as it did in the theory of Marxism. In Marxism there are the two opposite poles, the bourgeois and the proletariat. In Islam these two poles are replaced by the *oppressor* and the *oppressed*.

Islam demands rights—the rights of oppressed people from their oppression and their oppressors. Concerning the rights of an individual, Sayyid Qutb, the Muslim Egyptian scholar, declares that those who abdicate their rights will be severely punished by Allah in the next world. According to Qutb, Islam categorizes this group as "self-oppressors."[7] In other words the oppressed will be punished because they refused to revolt against the oppressor. He quotes Surah 4:97:

> When angels take the souls of those who die in sin against their souls, they say: "In what (plight) were you?" They reply: "Weak and oppressed were we in the earth." They say: "Was not the earth of Allah spacious enough for you to move yourselves away (from evil)?" Such men will find their abode in Hell,—what an evil Refuge!

Thus, Qutb says, Islam urges men to fight for their rights. He concludes by saying, "And he who is killed while attempting to remedy injustice, the same is a martyr."[8]

The Role of an Individual in Islam

The philosophy of Islam concerning human value is not based upon an individual's own worth but rather upon the merit of that person in regard to the unity of his community. In other words, Islam sees and values human life in a group setting rather than by itself. Surah 49:13 states:

> O mankind! We created you from a single (pair) of a male and a female, and made you into nations and tribes, that you may know each other (not that you may despise each other). Verily the most honored of you in the sight of Allah is (he who is) the most righteous of you. And Allah has full knowledge and is well acquainted (with all things).

As we have mentioned before, justice is a monumental concept within Islam, and this justice is defined within the community and not for an individual. Qutb says, "Justice is the greatest of the foundation of Islam; but justice is not always concerned to serve the interests of the individual. Justice is for the individual, but it is for society also, if we are willing to tread the middle way; and so we must have in our life justice in all its shapes and forms."[9]

In such a system, the value of an individual is almost nonexistent. Therefore, one's opinion is worthless unless it is expressed within the sphere of its belonging, within its unit. This, of course, goes back to the formation of Muhammad's community of the seventh century. Islam, from its very beginning, faced much opposition from Muhammad's own tribe, the Quraish. Muhammad had to unify his followers by the enforcement of social order. The tribal society of the seventh century would not allow the survival of individualism.

If you notice, even today there are few single voices within the Islamic communities that contradict Islam. This is why the rights of individuals are almost nonexistent under dictators such as Saddam Hussein of Iraq, the shah as well as Ayatollah Khomeini of Iran, King Fahd of Saudi Arabia, Mubarak of Egypt, and all the other rulers of the Muslim societies. A person can lose his life by just stating his opinion about the governing system. The dealings of Allah are with a community—one that is united and submitted to Allah's will.

> If two parties among the Believers fall into a quarrel, you make peace between them: but if one of them transgresses beyond bounds against the other, then you (all) fight against the one that transgresses until it complies with the command of Allah; but if it complies, then make peace between them with justice, and be fair: for Allah loves those who are fair (and just).
>
> —SURAH 49:9

It is imperative for America to understand this. When we wage war against a radical Muslim group such as Al-Qaeda, for example, according to Islam we are fighting the Muslim community and not that individual group. Our mind-set here in America is based upon the freedom of the individual—not so in an Islamic society. Their identity is in a family unit, a tribe, and a community. Fighting one means we fight them all within their sphere of influence.

The recent outrage of hundreds of thousands of Muslims throughout the world against the depiction of Muhammad in cartoon in a Danish newspaper is another great example of this fact. The publication of the cartoons by the Danish *Jyllands-Posten* in September of 2005 provoked diplomatic sanctions and threats from Islamic militants across the Muslim world. Some of the caricatures included drawings of Muhammad wearing a turban shaped like a bomb, while another showed him saying that paradise was running short of virgins because of the suicide bombers. The trouble all began with Danish writer Kare Bluitgen, who complained that he was unable to find an illustrator for his children's book about the prophet Muhammad because he said no one dared to portray Muhammad's image.[10]

What is important to note here is that the Islamic world blamed the entire nation of Denmark for *Jyllandds-Posten*'s blasphemy. The Danish newspaper received bomb threats, the Saudi Arabian ambassador was pulled out of Copenhagen, armed Palestinians stormed the embassy, and Danish flags went up in flame.[11] According to a CNN report, Islam went so far as the closing down of the EU's office in Gaza City by a group of radical Muslims who demanded an apology from German, French, and Norwegian newspapers for reprinting the cartoons.[12]

Their rage wasn't just toward *Jyllands-Posten*, the Danish newspaper. They were outraged at the nation and the government of Denmark. The Islamic mind-set does not deal with individuals but with the union of the individuals—the group, the congregation, the community, the people, and the nation. So while our government leaders think that they are fighting against a *terrorist group* like Al-Qaeda, the Muslims perceive America as fighting against the Muslim people.

> And, verily, this Brotherhood of yours is a single Brotherhood, and I am your Lord and Cherisher: therefore fear Me (and no other).
> —SURAH 23:52

Freedom Within Islam

To men like Sayyid Qutb, the Islamic social order did not belong to one specific period of history and to a specific group of people, but rather it was an order for mankind in an indefinite time period. He believed that religion *cannot* be divorced from everyday life and the social orders of a society, as the Europeans and the Christians have done. Islam does not support a chasm between religion and the state, as Western societies advocate. Qutb believed that Islam is a perfect value system by which all other social orders and statutes must be framed, both internally within the communities of the Islamic world and externally to the "unhappy, perplexed, and weary world."[13] And that leadership is laid upon the Muslim *Ummat* (Community), as Allah believes:

> You are the best of Peoples, evolved for mankind, enjoining what is right, forbidding what is wrong, and believing in Allah. If only the People of the Book had faith, it were best for them: among them are some who have faith, but most of them are perverted transgressors.
> —SURAH 3:110

The Quran is full of controversies in its doctrines. For example, in Surah 3:110, which we cited above, it declares that Muslims "are the best of Peoples." But in another place it says that, "People are all equal as the teeth of a comb."[14]

In this concept of equality, no superior mentality is tolerated. In Islamic social justice, there must be freedom of conscience within the laws of Allah. Allah is the only entity that can establish justice and the knowledge of justice in this world. What we recognize as freedom of the individual and what Islam calls "the freedom of conscience" are two absolute opposites. To Islam, freedom is defined within the Islamic disposition and not in accordance to the human distinctiveness. That is a Western concept. According to the Islamic scholar Sayyid Qutb, Islamic freedom is a "complete emancipation of the conscience."[15] The question is: emancipation unto what? To our Western mind, freedom doesn't need to have a platform. Its very nature carries its own structure. You do not need to define it, format it, shape it, frame it, or present it. You just have to allow it, or else it will lose its savor.

But to the Islamic mind, "the human mind has come to know all this freedom of conscience; it is free from the least shadow of servility, be it to death or injury, to poverty or weakness, unless what comes by Allah's permission. It is released from the tyranny of the values of social standing and wealth; it is saved from the humiliation of bodily appetites. It can turn towards its One Sole Creator, to Whom all things must turn without exception and without fail; and in addition to all that it is guaranteed a sufficiency of the necessities of life by legal ordinance."[16]

The environment into which Islam was birthed was the class society of the Quraish. The strong ruled the weak. There were the oppressors and the oppressed, the wealthy and the poor, the masters and the slaves. Within this context of the Arabian hierarchies of the seventh century, Muhammad was

born. The profound ignorance among the people of the time could not create an atmosphere of a revolution by the mere proclamation of liberty and
justice for all. Muhammad could not be a liberator aside from a pious platform. Islam became the voice of God for the weak and the oppressed and
for justice. Who could resist a furious God? The fight was a classical fight
between "good" and "evil." The Quraish was the *evil* force—the tyrant,
the oppressor, the infidel, the "great Satan." Muhammad and his gang of
three hundred followers became the *liberators*, the *just*, the *pious*, the *protector of faith* of a totalitarian god. The concept of freedom from the reign of
the Quraish was never meant to be self-sufficient. It was freedom from the
Quraish into the reign and rule of the Islamic ordinances and beliefs.

To this day, Islamic freedom is understood by those terms. During his
exile in Iraq, Khomeini wrote passionate messages against the shah of Iran
and his regime. To Khomeini and radical Muslims, the shah was just like
the Quraish.

In the case of the Shi'ites, the comparison is that of the Mu'awiya. Listen
to the tone of the following message, given by Ayatollah Khomeini against
the shah's regime:

> The Lord of the Martyrs summoned the people to rise in revolt
> by means of sermon, preaching, and correspondence and caused
> them to rebel against a monarch. Imam Hassan struggled against
> the king of his day, Mu'awiya, as far as he was able, and when he was
> betrayed by a group of self-seeking, opportunistic followers and left
> without support, the very peace treaty that he signed with Mu'awiya
> disgraced the monarch, just as Imam Husayn's bloody revolt later
> disgraced Yazid. This struggle and confrontation has continued
> without respite, and the great scholars of Islam have always fought
> against the tyrannical bandits who enslaved their peoples for the
> sake of their passions and squandered their country's wealth on
> trivial amusements. Whenever a vital and alert nation gave them
> support, they were successful in their struggle. If we too are vital
> and alert now, we will be successful. But unfortunately, instead of
> there being unity and harmony among us, each one persists in his
> own individual opinion, and naturally, if 100 million people have
> 100 million different opinions, they will be unable to accomplish
> anything, for "The hand of God is with the group." Solidarity and

unity are essential, and isolated individuals can achieve nothing.... I tell you plainly that a dark, dangerous future lies ahead and it is your duty to resist and to serve Islam and the Muslim peoples. Protest against the pressure exerted upon our oppressed people every day. Purge yourselves of your apathy and selfishness; stop seeking excuses and inventing pretexts for evading your responsibility. You have more forces at your disposal than the Lord of the Martyrs did, who resisted and struggled with his limited forces until he was killed. If (God forbid) he had been a weak, apathetic, and selfish person, he could have come up with some excuse for himself and remained silent. His enemies would have been only too happy for him to remain silent so that they could attain their vile goals, and they were afraid of his rebelling. But he dispatched Muslims to procure the people's allegiance to him so that he might overthrow that corrupt government and set up an Islamic government.[17]

This is the point that our politicians misunderstand: when Muslims cry out for freedom from a tyrant such as Saddam or the shah, they want freedom from a secular tyrant but not freedom from Islam. That is the only concept of freedom they have been taught and even permitted to think. Within the Islamic sphere, freedom outside of Islamic boundaries is blasphemous and nonexistent.

During the whole time of the Muslim outrages against Muhammad's caricature published in a Danish newspaper, even secular Muslims reacted harshly. The idea of them even thinking a thought against Muhammad is alien to their way of life. The fear that is instilled in them, for centuries, toward Islam and its leader will not permit them to think otherwise. Islam made Muhammad the epitome of justice and truth. It secured him to an unshakable position—the position of "The Seal of the Prophets" (Surah 33:40). Even though the Quran and many hadiths talk about Muhammad's sins, to a Muslim Muhammad was almost as holy as God Himself. No one, Muslim or non-Muslim, is permitted to touch him, his person, his character, and his mission. The Danes proved this fact to the Western world by drawing a political caricature of Muhammad.

Justice: A Massive Concept

Studying Islamic philosophy and the cultures of the Islamic world, one could easily define Islam as a concept of "fighting for justice." As Qutb puts it, "Justice is the greatest of the foundation of Islam."

Let's look at a few verses of the Quran on this subject.

> Allah commands justice, the doing of good, and liberality to kith and kin, and He forbids all shameful deeds, and injustice and rebellion: He instructs you, that you may receive admonition.
>
> —Surah 16:90

> If any do that in rancor and injustice,—soon shall We cast them into the Fire: and easy it is for Allah.
>
> —Surah 4:30

> And come not near to the orphan's property, except to improve it, until he attain the age of full strength; give measure and weight with (full) justice;—no burden do We place on any soul, but that which it can bear;—whenever you speak, speak justly, even if a near relative is concerned; and fulfill the covenant of Allah: thus He commands you, that you may remember.
>
> —Surah 6:152

> O you who believe! stand out firmly for Allah, as witnesses to fair dealing, and let not the hatred of others to you make you swerve to wrong and depart from justice. Be just: that is next to Piety: and fear Allah. For Allah is well-acquainted with all that you do.
>
> —Surah 5:8

The injustice that Islam refers to time and time again is the result of what the Islamic community endured at the hand of the Quraish, Muhammad's own tribe, the ruling party in Mecca. Muhammad desired to create a utopia of an impartial and absolute justice where its judgment cannot be swayed and influenced by any social status, wealth, relationship, or any other factors within the society. There are two polar ends to this system—the oppressed who stand at the lower end of it, and then the tyrant at the top of it. Islam judges every society in accordance to this polarization. And thus Islam takes sides, the side of the oppressed, because that is where Muhammad and his adherents were for twelve years in Mecca.

The Islamic radicals have divided American society into the above poles, the oppressed and the tyrants. In this case the tyrants are the American government with its unbeatable military force, and the oppressed are African Americans and Native Americans. Therefore a radical Muslim will love a black man but will kill a white man. When the Iranian Muslim organization under the leadership of Khomeini took over the American embassy in Tehran in 1979, they released the black embassy employees, along with some of the women.[18] Why? Because they are considered the oppressed, and Islam will take the side of the oppressed and fight the tyrant. In such a case, the tyrants must be defeated. According to hadith, "If anyone sees a tyrannical power which is contrary to the will of Allah, which violates the compact of Allah, and which produces evil or enmity among the servants of Allah, and if he does not try to change it by deed or by word, then it is Allah who must supply the initiative."[19]

To the Muslims, America is the strength and the backbone of governments such as Mubarak in Egypt, Abdelaziz in Algeria, Fahd in Saudi Arabia, and other repressive royal families in the Gulf States. The possible reasons for our support of these governments are their allegiance to the West, their antireligious commitment, which is considered stability in the region, and our economical interests such as oil, export of goods, and military equipment. These governments may be in good standing with the U.S. government. They are, however, repressive of freedom over their own people. While they enjoy a lifestyle of luxury and corruption, their people live in poverty and despair. And that is the breeding ground for the growth of the Islamic fundamentalism.

Stephen Zunes, an associate professor of politics and chairman of the Peace and Justice Studies Program at the University of San Francisco, writes in an article in *USA Today*:

> To win the war against terrorism, we need to re-evaluate our definition of security. The more the Untied States militarizes the Middle East, the less secure we become. All of the sophisticated weaponry, all of the brave fighting men and women, all of the talented military leadership we may possess will not stop terrorism as long as our policies cause millions of people to hate us.[20]

He explains further: "President Bush is wrong when he claims we are targeted because we are a 'beacon for freedom.' We are targeted because the support of freedom is not part of our Middle East policy, which instead has been based upon alliances with repressive governments and support for military occupation. If the United States supported a policy based more on human rights, international law and sustainable development, and less on arms transfers, air strikes and punitive sanctions, we would be a lot safer."[21]

Zunes reasons that it is not our values, but the abandonment of our values that made the September 11 attacks possible. He says, "Even if military action eliminated bin Laden, there would be new terrorists to take his place, unless we looked at the underlying grievances that give him power. His methods are evil, but his grievances, such as the oppression of the Palestinians, the humanitarian consequences of the sanctions against Iraq, the U.S. support for Arab dictators, and the ongoing U.S. military presence in the Middle East, have a strong resonance among ordinary Muslims and Arabs."[22]

The Islamic philosophy leaves its adherents with a form of pride that is unlike any other system of belief. Within this frame of mind a Muslim cannot stand oppression by the big and the mighty. "An aggression will be dealt with, and the oppressor will fall" is the center of the Islamic philosophy of the seventh century. As the suicidal attacks from the Palestinian Islamic group Hamas escalated, the political head of Hamas expressed this: "To die in this way [suicidal attacks] is better than to die daily in frustration and humiliation."[23]

Khomeini's Islamic Revolution of 1979 revived the spirit of seventh-century Islam. His uncompromised revolutionary messages and his stance against the "infidels" gave hope to millions of revolutionary ideologists. His revolution brought the Islamic faith of the seventh century to the forefront of twentieth-century society.

Khomeini's political view was: "The governments of the world should know that Islam cannot be defeated. Islam will be victorious in all the countries of the world, and Islam and the teachings of the Koran will prevail all over the world."[24]

Even though the Islamic "isms" had already started in the beginning of the last century by movements such as Tuheedis, the Oneness theology mainly known as *Wahhabbism* in Saudi Arabia, or the Muslim Brotherhood in Egypt, it was Khomeini who gave birth to an Islamic state. Khomeini also revived a fading religion that was overwhelmed by the Western culture of the twenty-first century. As Ayatollah Bager al-Sadr, a Shi'ite Muslim theologian, said, "The world as we know it today is how others shaped it. We have two choices: either to accept it with submission, which means letting Islam die, or to destroy it, so that we can construct a world as Islam requires."[25]

To the radical Muslims, Islam is on a decaying slope of the twenty-first century. They observe the corrosion of their society—the gradual invasion of the Western decadent and immoral subculture, which is in great contrast to that of Islam's value set forth by the lifestyle of their prophet Muhammad.

To them, Islam of the seventh century is on a rapid road to deterioration, and the one enemy that is speeding up this process is the West, with the United States as its head. "We the sons of the community of Hezbollah," a 1985 communique from Lebanon said, "consider ourselves a part of the world Islamic community, attacked at once by the tyrants and the arrogant of the East and the West.... Our way is one of radical combat against depravity, and America is the original root of depravity."[26]

September 11, 2001: A New Era

September 11, 2001, began a new era for America as well as for the world. Historically, the Western world faced an instant threat. The tide changed from a secular standoff with the Soviet bloc nations to a spiritual hold-up with religious zealots. America and the West were taken by surprise. The Muslim world was not. Millions of Muslims throughout the world were hoping and predicting such an event. These religious zealots considered America the enemy of their religion. America took a big hit, but its retribution was quick and swift. We have witnessed that for the past five years both in Afghanistan and Iraq. The question remains, though, have we won the war against radical Islam and these so-called "terrorist groups" after five years of war? Are we close to winning, and are we changing the hatred of the radical Muslims toward America and the American interests? The daily news should answer these questions. I believe that not only have we lost the war against the Islamic radicalism, but we have, through the past two wars, increased the potential and the progress of the radicalism!

The day following the U.S. attack on Afghanistan, bin Laden's message on a video was broadcast over *Al-Jazeera*, the Arabic satellite station. Bin Laden spokesman Suleiman Abu Ghaith made the opening statement, "What happened in the United States is a natural reaction to the ignorant policy of the United States. If it continues with this policy, the sons of Islam will not stop their struggle. The American people have to know that what is happening to them now is the result of their support of this policy."[27]

The words of Abu Ghaith may be irrelevant to most of us but not to the majority of Muslims. The common notion that is growing day by day in the Islamic world is that America is an enemy of Islam. Prior to Khomeini's revolution, every social and economical problem the people faced was believed to be stimulated by the CIA. When the shah's government started daylight-saving time in Iran, I was a young teenager. Most people believed that the change of an hour a day was the CIA plot to destroy the Islamic calendar. It was ridiculous. You would not believe how "popular" the CIA was in Iran! The point is that the United States was considered an enemy of Islam. This was in the seventies. That hatred toward the U.S. government has now broadened to a greater scale in the Muslim countries among millions and millions of Muslims. Can we afford this reputation?

The two wars in Iraq and Afghanistan, the standoff with Iran in their nuclear power plants, the civil war in Iraq, the election of Hamas in the Palestinian territories, the depicting of Muhammad's caricature in Western media, and other incidents that will take place in the near future have placed and will place America and Western Europe in a colossal collision with the Islamic world. The question is, what must we do?

Solution

I would suggest that we need to make the following responses if we desire to find a solution to the Islam crisis. First of all, we must understand that we are dealing with a religious ideology and not a political policy. Policies can be compromised, and an agreement can be reached—not so with religious mind-sets and statures. Therefore trying to establish political policies without considering the spiritual impact is a mistake and will have a counter effect. Promoting and enforcing democracy from outside an Islamic society, for instance, is promising but immature. Knowing the teaching of Islam, one will realize that such a concept is too farfetched. Even if it works, it will work *against* the purpose for which our Western politicians intend.

Examples of this fact are the election in Algeria and the landslide victory of Hamas in the Palestinian territory. In December of 1991, the Algerian government canceled elections after the first round of presidential elections showed that the Islamic Salvation Front (FIS) would win. These will also be the results in places like Saudi Arabia, Pakistan, Egypt, and other hotbeds of Islamic radicalism if democratic processes are placed without the neutralization of the Islamic beliefs first.

Islam is an enemy of the freedom of individualism and freedom as we know it in the context of Western civilization. The sooner we acknowledge this truth, the faster we will find the solution. The more our politicians flirt with the idea of a "peaceful Islam," the harder it will become for them to deal with the troubles that they are facing and will face with the Islamic world. Islam boldly declares:

> O you who believe! obey Allah, and obey the Messenger, and those charged with authority among you. If you differ in anything among yourselves, refer it to Allah and His Messenger, if you do believe in Allah and the Last Day: that is best, and most suitable for final determination.
>
> —SURAH 4:59

Many Muslim apologists are scrambling to prove that Islam holds a great deal of democracy within its constitutions. Studying the law, the tradition, the history, and the current places of Islam, one will soon realize that nothing could be further from the truth. The core foundation of democracy is the freedom of speech. Right? Absolutely wrong in Islam! We do not need to go any further than the recent reactions of the Islamic world toward Muhammad's caricatures in a Danish newspaper! According to an independent Web site tallying the total casualty count as a result of the controversy (based on verified news sources), as of March 16, there have been a total of 139 deaths and 823 injuries as a result of the violent protests by Muslims throughout the world.[28] If they react so incredibly violent toward the people who live outside of their covenant and their borders, what kind of reactions would one who comes from their own communities receive?

If democracy means free presidential or parliamentary elections, then the U.S. government has succeeded in establishing democracy in Afghanistan and Iraq, for the time being. The very fact that Afghanistan's constitution is based upon the Islamic law indicates that democracy, as we know it, would be impossible in Afghanistan. Its constitution describes Islam as its sacred and state religion. According to Article 3 of Afghanistan's constitution, no law may contradict the beliefs and provisions of Islam.

Article 3 [Law and Religion]
In Afghanistan, no law can be contrary to the beliefs and provisions of the sacred religion of Islam.[29]

The judicial branch and court system of Afghanistan are to use the Hanafi jurisprudence. Imam Abu Hanifa (A.D. 699–765), the founder of Hanafi school of *fiqh* (Islamic law), was a renowned Islamic scholar and jurist. The Afghanistan Islamic republic's top court is the *Stera Mahkama* (Supreme Court). Courts are allowed to use Hanafi jurisprudence in situations where the constitution lacks provisions. Even though the "*sharia* law" is not specifically mentioned, Hanafi jurisprudence is in fact one of the six branches of *sharia* law.[30]

The question remains, what does Islam say about other religions and freedom of individuals? The Quran states:

If anyone desires a religion other than Islam (submission to Allah), never will it be accepted of him; and in the Hereafter He will be in the ranks of those who have lost (All spiritual good).
—SURAH 3:85

Whatever it be wherein you differ, the decision thereof is with Allah: such is Allah my Lord: in Him I trust, and to Him I turn.
—SURAH 42:10

If not Him, you worship nothing but names which you have named,—you and your fathers,—for which Allah has sent down no authority: the Command is for none but Allah: He has commanded that you worship none but Him: that is the right religion, but most men do not understand.
—SURAH 12:40

Is that democracy?

A War of Ideology!

Islam cannot be reformed; it must be exposed for what it is. If you fight it physically, you will strengthen it, because Islam feeds on warfare and bloodshed. The Quran states:

> The punishment of those who wage war against Allah and His Messenger, and strive with might and main for mischief through the land is: execution, or crucifixion, or the cutting off of hands and feet from opposite sides, or exile from the land: that is their disgrace in this world, and a heavy punishment is theirs in the Hereafter.
>
> —SURAH 5:33

In order for us to win any ground against Islamic terrorism, Islam must be exposed for its violence, bloodshed, hatred, racism, degrading of women's position, adulterous affairs, spiritual darkness, and anti-West, anti-Christ, and anti-Christian stance.

The United States must strengthen the voices of those who have analyzed Islam and its history and who are not afraid to publish their research. The fear that Islam has produced against its opposers has left very little room for opposing opinions. The very fact that no news media in America printed the caricatures of Muhammad demonstrates that Islam has already established its footprints of fear in the hearts of Americans. It is shameful for a great nation like ours, which is a beacon for freedom, to fear the Islamic sharia. What shame on the American news media.

After twenty-seven years of the horror of the Islamic sharia practiced in Iran by the mullahs, Iran has now given birth to the first generation of men and women who are well versed in the laws of Islam and who are not afraid to oppose it. These voices need to be supported and strengthened. If the United States compromises with the spirit of Islam and protects the Islamic faith as some Western nations (like Australia) are in the process of doing, America will eventually fall. We will dig our own grave, and Islam will bury us. The Islamic faith and its teachings contradict every aspect of our freedom and the core belief of our system. Islam in its heart of faith is an enemy of America, whether we believe it or not. We are infidels through and through according to the teaching of Islam. The reason Islam is capable of standing and the Muslims are suffering to live in this land is because they want to change

America. By and by, they will convert the sons and daughters of this nation, and they will become a powerhouse.

In an open letter to the pope, the Archbishop of Izmir (Smyrna) in Turkey, Rev. Guiseppe Germano Barnardini, spoke of a recent gathering of Christians and Muslims for the purpose of interfaith dialogue. He said that a Muslim leader once told him: "Thanks to your democratic laws, we will invade you. Thanks to our religious laws, we will dominate you."[31]

In an article published in the *San Ramon Valley Herald* on July 4, 1998, Omar Ahmad, chairman of the board of Council on American Islamic Relations (CAIR), was quoted as saying that Muslims should not assimilate into American society. He said, "If you choose to live here (in America)... you have a responsibility to deliver the message of Islam. Islam isn't in America to be equal to any other faith, but to become dominant. The Koran... should be the highest authority in America, and Islam the only accepted religion on Earth."[32] Mr. Ahmad believes that "everything we need to know is in the Koran." CAIR is an Islamic civil liberties group based in Washington DC and is supported by many influential people. Since its founding in 1994, CAIR has been receiving sizable donations, invitations to the White House, and highly respected media attention toward its programs such as its full-page story in *USA Today* on its distribution of 25,000 free Qurans.[33]

Other powerful Islamic organizations such as the Middle East Policy Council (MEPC) have been promoting Islamic indoctrination in our schools throughout the country. MEPC has been sponsoring a social studies course known as the *Arab World Studies* (edited by Audrey Shabbas).[34]

These Islamic organizations are not just exposing Americans to their doctrines for the sake of *understanding*, but rather are exploiting and planning to convert Americans to the faith of Islam. For instance, all sixth- and seventh-graders in the state of California had to go through this course in their social studies classes.

An article on WorldNetDaily.com in 2002 reports that parents were outraged when they found out the children were being indoctrinated with the Islamic sharia. Elizabeth Christina Lemings, a teacher in the Byron, California, Union School District, was unaware of the course until her seventh-grade son brought home the handouts. The handouts included the history of Islam and the life of Muhammad. There were twenty-five Islamic terms that had to be memorized, six Arabic phrases, twenty Islamic phrases to be learned, five pillars of faith, and ten key Islamic prophets and disciples to be studied.

"We can't even mention the name of Jesus in the public schools," Mrs. Lemings declared, "but they teach Islam as the true religion, and the students are taught about Islam and how to pray to Allah. Can you imagine the barrage of lawsuits and problems we would have from the ACLU if Christianity was taught in the public schools, and if we try to teach about the contributions of Matthew, Mark, Luke, John, and the apostle Paul? But when it comes to furthering the Islamic religion in the public schools there is not one word from the ACLU, People for the American Way, or anybody else. This is hypocrisy."[35]

Assist News Service (ANS) reports that students are to pretend that they are Muslims, wear Muslim clothing to school, stage their own jihad via a dice game, and pick out a Muslim name for their own out of a list of thirty. When the students were asked what they thought about the course, some described it as "fun," and others thought it was a "pretty culture."[36]

According to Middle East Policy Council, the Shabbas Islamic workshop has been taught in 175 cities in 43 states to more than 16,000 educators since 1985. Millions of kids in America have been exposed to the 500 plus pages of teachings of the *Arab World Studies* curriculum. This is an amazing effort in our public schools, where the name of Jesus Christ is forbidden to be mentioned and proclaimed.[37]

The question is, how do we reconcile freedom of religion and freedom of Islam in America? Islam's appetite is the world, and America is on the top of the agenda. Can our politicians do anything about the spread of this deadly poison in our nation? I greatly doubt it. This is where the role of the church comes in.

Poverty and Oppression

You have already learned in earlier chapters of this book that there are conditions that breed radical Islam, including socioeconomic conditions such as poverty, oppression, animosity, and warfare. America must establish a policy of promoting economic empowerment in Islamic nations. Unemployment and hopelessness are breeding grounds for radical Islam. I believe that the landslide victory of Hamas in the Palestinian territory is a great example of this fact. Palestinians, in general, have never been Islamic zealots. The Palestinian uprising began in 1987 as a result of the social and economic conditions of the Palestinians in Gaza and the West Bank.

On December 10, 1987, three days after the start of the *Intifada*, in an interview broadcast on Israeli radio, the mayor of Gaza, Rashad al-Shawwa, summed up the condition of the Palestinians' morale by stating the following:

> One must expect these things after twenty years of debilitating occupation. People have lost hope. They are frustrated and don't know what to do. They have turned to religious fundamentalism as their last hope. They have given up hoping Israel will give them their rights. The Arab States are unable to do anything, and they feel that the PLO, which is their representative, also has failed.[38]

I believe that the struggle between Israel and the Palestinian people took off on the wrong foot just like radical Islam and the United States. I believe that the Israelis have never quite understood the vibes of an Islamic culture. Of course, the entire development of the statehood of Israel was built upon the wrong foundation. The land of Israel should have never been annexed and divided by the League of Nations. The Balfour Declaration was a corrupt foundation. It was in contradiction to God's Word and plan for Israel. The land of Israel has belonged to the Jewish people since 2000 B.C. God gave that land to Abraham and his descendants, the Jewish people, through Isaac. Israel doesn't belong to anybody else—Arabs or non-Arabs. Peace is impossible to achieve in Israel for many reasons, which could be the entire discussion of another writing. But peace cannot be achieved, mainly because the land cannot be divided. God will not allow it.

For our purposes here, we must discuss the political condition and a political solution. On that note I must declare that Hamas should never have won a landslide election this year in Palestine. They did win because of the unwise treatment of the Palestinians by the Israelis. The Palestinian uprising (*Intifada*) in 1987 was a boiling point of the frustration of the Palestinian society. Instead of dealing with the root of the problem, Israel dealt with the problem itself. And again, more violence, bloodshed, and isolation of the Palestinian people led to more strength for Hamas and growth of radical Islam among the Palestinian people. Thus Hamas has now become a powerhouse in Israel, and the Israeli government must deal with it. Can they? Not in their current political and spiritual conditions.

If America is to win the war against radical Islam, America must start at ground level—eliminate the oppressive (both social and economic) conditions of the countries with which the United States has major relations, countries like Pakistan, Saudi Arabia, Kuwait, Turkey, and Egypt. We must suffocate that which breeds radicalism—not dealing with the problem, but rather with the root and cause of it. It is like fighting a mole; the best way is to eliminate its food under the ground. Once its source of food is gone, the mole is gone as well.

Protectors of Faiths, or Exposers of the Truth?

Again we must recognize that we are engaged in a spiritual battle with radical Islam whether we would like to admit it or not. I like to put it this way: Islam is at war with the Western mind-set and Western lifestyle. Almost everything in America and the West is an abomination to the Islamic teaching. The teaching of Islam and the traditions of Muhammad contradict every aspect of the American philosophy, society, and history. Islam was on a direct collision path with the West from day one, when Muhammad began sending out messengers to tribes and kingdoms outside of the Arabian Peninsula, "enlightening" them. Islam demands conversion of the world's mind and subjugation of all authorities. The Quran commands:

> O you People of the Book! believe in what We have (now) revealed, confirming what was (already) with you, before We change the face and fame of some (of you) beyond all recognition, and turn them hindwards, or curse them as We cursed the Sabbath-breakers, for the decision of Allah must be carried out.
>
> —Surah 4:47

No choice or mercy is granted. No reasoning is permitted. It is a system of totalitarian subjection. What if one does not abide or obey? The Quran says:

> Fight those who do not believe in Allah nor the Last Day, nor hold that forbidden which has been forbidden by Allah and His Messenger, nor acknowledge the Religion of Truth, (even if they are) of the People of the Book, until they pay the Jizya with willing submission, and feel themselves subdued.
>
> —Surah 9:29

The word *fight* in the above verse is translated from the word *Qatiloo* in Arabic, which actually means "to kill." Thus the above verse should read:

> *Kill* [Slay] those who believe not in Allah nor the Last Day, nor hold that forbidden which has been forbidden by Allah and His Messenger, nor acknowledge the religion of Truth, (even if they are) of the People of the Book, until they pay the Jizya with willing submission, and feel themselves subdued.
> —SURAH 9:29, EMPHASIS ADDED

Yusuf Ali, the translator of the Quran from Arabic into English, was highly educated in England. He knew that Western people would not accept the violent language of the Quran, so he often toned down his translation to make it more adaptable to the Western culture and mind-set, which has been formed on the basis of a Christian conscience. Did you note what the commandment in the Quran says? "Kill those who believe not in Allah...even if they are of the People of the Book [Christians, Jews, and Sabians]."

I could quote many passages and verses in the Quran that command such violence against those who refuse the faith of Islam. The point I am trying to get across to you is the fact that Islam is in battle against all those who repudiate, reject, and refuse the Islamic faith. Islam and the Islamic adherents consider the Western societies evil and unclean. Homosexuality, pornography, Western music, Hollywood's pop culture, and Christianity are all points of abomination and desecration to the Islamic commandments and faith.

After four years of separation due to my conversion from Islam to Christianity, my family decided to visit me. First they thought that I had, literally, lost my mind. My mother tried to put me in a mental hospital through the Iranian Embassy in Stockholm. Finally after four years of cutting me off completely, my older sister and mother decided to come and see me and try to convert me back to Islam. At that time I lived in Spain and worked among the Iranian refugees. My sister, I noticed, had become more religious. She prayed more often and acted very religious and defiant of me. I also detected that she washed her hands and face more often than a religious person would usually do. When I inquired why she had become so concerned about cleanliness, she told me blatantly that I was unclean. "You have become a Christian, and you are unclean according to Islam, so every time I kiss you or touch you I have to wash myself." That is the mind-set of Islam.

To radical Muslim groups such as Al-Qaeda, Hezbollah, Muslim Brotherhood, Hamas, and many others, the West is the personification of evil and desecration of the faith of Allah. In Article 13 of the Hamas Communiqué, the organization bases its structure upon the "raised banner of Jihad in the face of the oppressors in order to free the country and the people from the [oppressors'] desecration, impurity, and evil."[39] To Hamas, Israel and America are the forces of evil, impurity, and desecration of their religion.

Article 7 of the Hamas Charter states:

> The Day of Judgement will not come until the Moslems fight the Jews (killing the Jews), when the Jew will hide behind stones and trees. The stones and trees will say O Moslems, O Abdulla, there is a Jew behind me, come and kill him. Only the Gharkad tree, [evidently a certain kind of tree] would not do that because it is one of the trees of the Jews.[40]

The above hadith is not a made-up philosophy of Hamas but rather Muhammad's teachings and the practices of Islam. The Quran commands:

> The Jews say: "Allah's hand is tied up." Be their hands tied up and be they accursed for the (blasphemy) they utter. Nay, both His hands are widely outstretched: He gives and spends (of His bounty) as He pleases. But the revelation that comes to you from Allah increases in most of them their obstinate rebellion and blasphemy. Amongst them we have placed enmity and hatred till the Day of Judgment. Every time they kindle the fire of war, Allah extinguishes it; but they (ever) strive to do mischief on earth. And Allah does not love those who do mischief.
>
> —SURAH 5:64

In verse 82 of the same surah we read:

> Strongest among men in enmity to the Believers will you find the Jews and Pagans; and nearest among them in love to the Believers will you find those who say, "We are Christians": because amongst these are men devoted to learning and men who have renounced the world, and they are not arrogant.

As you see, there is great animosity in the Quran against the Jews. In the above verse there is a softer tone toward the Christians, but that of course was changed later when Muhammad was also rejected by the Christian tribes.

> O you who believe! take not the *Jews and the Christians* for your friends and protectors: they are but friends and protectors to each other. And he amongst you that turns to them (for friendship) is of them. Verily Allah guides not a people unjust.
>
> —SURAH 5:51, EMPHASIS ADDED

How can there ever be peace between the Muslims, the Jews, and the Christians with these kinds of commandments in the Muslims' *holy* Quran?

Islam's teaching must be exposed if we are to win the battle against radical Islam or so-called *fundamentalists*. The more effort put forth by our government or any other organization in providing space and tolerance for the Islamic faith, the greater the risk in the expansion of the ideology of Islam. No one in his right mind should allow a rattlesnake for a pet for his children. McCarthyism showed us the danger of Communism, and America raised a standard against it and prevented it from dominating the world. Today we face a very similar danger, yet much deadlier, with Islam. The problem is that Islam under the banner of religion is protected by the constitution and feared by the violence that it bears in its bosom. Tolerance, understanding, political correctness, religious freedom, and claims of "peaceful Islam" are the neutralizing forces and pavers of the path for Islam.

Can we do anything about it? The *Jyllands-Posten* in Denmark has begun the process—not so much as in drawing a silly caricature but rather by bringing to the surface the hidden sentiments of the Islamic faith. Since those caricatures became public, the god of Islam has killed nearly 140 human beings (some were Christian believers who had no relation to the event) through the violence by Muslim demonstrators throughout the world. The depiction of Muhammad was more dishonorable than killing innocent people. *Wow!* What a *peaceful religion*!

I hope and pray that more voices like *Jyllands-Posten* may rise up and open the eyes of the world to what Islam is really all about. I wish the CIA, Mossad, and other *intelligent* organizations would plot such efforts. We must expose Islam worldwide before Islam dictates to the world what it should believe in.

Does America have enough guts, knowledge, and wisdom to do that?

7

The Palestinian Issue

It is evident that the Arab-Israeli conflicts are one of the main sources of the problems with Islamic fundamentalists. But why is it so difficult for these two Middle Eastern nations to get along with each other? In order to get to the root of the issue, we need a better understanding of the history between the Jewish and Muslim peoples.

Early Roots of Hatred

In the time of Muhammad, there were three main Jewish tribes who lived in Yathrib (later Medina). There were also other Jewish settlements further to the north, the most important of which were Khaybar and Fadak. Yathrib was predominantly a Jewish settlement. Muhammad hoped that the Jews of Yathrib would accept him and his new monotheistic religion, Islam. However, these tribes knew that Muhammad could not be a prophet of Jehovah God since he was not from the seed of David. They resisted Muhammad, therefore, and his message. This led to much hostility between the Jews and the Muslims.

Two Jewish tribes, Banu Qaynuqa and Banu al-Nadir, were besieged by the Muslim army and forced into exile. According to Ibn Ishaq in *Sira*, the biography of Muhammad, the third Jewish tribe, Banu Qurayza, sided with the Quraish, the tribe of Muhammad who opposed him violently. Together they attempted to attack Medina in an effort to overcome the Muslim army. This was a most serious challenge to the Islamic community and their faith. The military effort failed, and the Banu Qurayza was in turn besieged by Muhammad's army. Adult males were put to death, and the women and children were sold into slavery. The men were massacred by the Muslims digging trenches in the marketplace in Medina, and the men of Qurayza were brought out in groups into the trenches and their necks were struck.

129

Islamic tradition refers to the conversion of one of the Jewish leaders by the name of Ibn Salam to Islam. Muhammad hoped that Salam's conversion to Islam would be followed by other Jews and that Muhammad would be recognized as a prophet, but that did not happen. The Quran refers to this in Surah 26:197:

> Is it not a Sign to them that the Learned of the Children of Israel knew it (as true)?

During this period Muhammad changed the direction faced during prayer (*Qibla*), from the site of the former temple in Jerusalem to the Kaaba (cubic house) in Mecca. The change of *Qibla* was a command from Allah both reflecting the independence of the Muslims as well as a test to discern those who truly followed the revelation of Muhammad. The Quran refers to this in the following verses:

> Thus have We made of you an Ummat justly balanced, that you might be witnesses over the nation, and the Messenger a witness over yourselves; and We appointed the Qibla to which you used, only to test those who followed the Messenger from those who would turn on their heels (from the Faith). Indeed it was (a change) momentous, except to those guided by Allah. And never would Allah make your faith of no effect. For Allah is to all people most surely full of kindness, Most Merciful. We see the turning of your face (for guidance) to the heavens: now shall We turn to a Qibla that shall please you. Turn then your face in the direction of the sacred Mosque: wherever you are, turn your faces in that direction. The people of the Book know full well that that is the truth from their Lord. Nor is Allah unmindful of what they do.
> —SURAH 2:143–144

When Muhammad first began receiving his revelations from Allah, he tried to convince the Jews that his revelations were the continuation of Judaism (and Christianity), the religion of the People of the Book, or the Bible. Before he left Mecca, he still faced Jerusalem in prayer. However, after he received revelation from on high to change direction, he faced Mecca in prayer. When the Jews confronted him about this change, Muhammad had to fight back theologically, striking out on a new path in his new competitor religion to survive.[1]

Muhammad constantly received revelation against the Jews. There are numerous verses in the Quran against the Jewish people. Surah 2:88 says: "They [referring to the Jews] say, 'Our hearts are the wrappings (which preserve Allah's Word: we need no more).' Nay, Allah's curse is on them for their blasphemy."

The root word here in Arabic is the word *Kafara*, which means the act of denying or blaspheming or rejecting the teaching of Allah and his prophet Muhammad. Here Allah puts a curse on the Jewish people because they rejected Muhammad's revelation. In verse 90 of the same surah the Quran states:

> Miserable is the price for which they have sold their souls, in that they deny (the revelation) which Allah has sent down, in insolent envy that Allah of His Grace should send it to any of His servants He pleases: thus have they drawn on themselves Wrath upon Wrath. And humiliating is the punishment of those who reject Faith.
>
> —SURAH 2:90

Abdullah Yusuf Ali comments on this verse: "Racial arrogance made the Jews adverse to the reception of Truth when it came through a servant of Allah (Muhammad)."[2]

> The Jews say, "Allah's hand is tied up." Be their hands tied up and be they accursed for the (blasphemy) they utter....Amongst them [Jews] we have placed enmity and hatred till the Day of Judgment.
>
> —SURAH 5:64

Again, Allah puts a curse on the Jewish people. In the same surah, verse 82, it says, "Strongest among men in enmity to the Believers [Muslims] will you find the Jews and Pagans." And in Surah 2:65–66, Allah turned a whole village of Jewish people into apes because they broke the Sabbath!

From these verses and many others, and also through the many hadith, we understand that because Muhammad was renounced and resisted by the Jews; therefore, Muhammad's god, Allah, does not like the Jews.

Colonization and Oil

The Muslim Safavieh and Mughal Empires fell in the eighteenth and nineteenth centuries, respectively. The Muslim Ottoman Empire remained strong for another century and a half. Its siege of Vienna in 1683 failed, as it had in 1529. By 1699, the Ottomans had suffered several defeats by the Holy Alliance of Austria, Poland, Venice, and the Russians. Greece became independent in 1829, and in 1830, Algeria was occupied by the French. In 1922, the Ottoman Empire was abolished and replaced by the Turkish republic.

The eighteenth and nineteenth centuries became an era of European colonization of the Muslim states. In 1869, the French opened the Suez Canal from the Mediterranean to the Red Sea—the most impressive engineering feat of the nineteenth century. By the beginning of 1900 there were few Islamic states that were not dominated by the West. The British and French took control of most of the Islamic world.

However, the days of colonialism were short-lived, and before World War II, most of the former colonies gained formal independence. Nearly all the remainder became independent after the war and joined the United Nations—Iraq in 1932, Syria in 1947, Indonesia in 1950, Egypt in 1952, Morocco, Tunisia and Sudan in 1956, Malaysia in 1957, Nigeria in 1960, and Algeria in 1962.

In 1864, oil was discovered as a major source of energy. In 1908, the British army established its importance by their use of it for military machinery. Oil was essential for victory on the battlefields of World War II. Whatever was happening with oil in the Middle East affected countries everywhere.

Over half of the world's oil reserves are in the Middle East. The major exporters are Saudi Arabia, Iraq, Kuwait, United Arab Emirates, and Iran. In 1960, Iran, Kuwait, Saudi Arabia, Iraq, and Venezuela formed the Organization of Petroleum Exporting Countries, or OPEC, to fight for direct access in exporting oil. OPEC later grew to thirteen member states.

The Zionist Movement

The nineteenth century had seen a growing persecution of the Jews in Russia and Eastern Europe, and in 1882 a new wave of immigrants began to arrive in Israel. Many were members of the Hovevei Zion movement who were interested in settling the land and working in agriculture. Most of these immigrants came from Russia and Romania.

Israel had been without any political state for a thousand years. So Theodor Herzl, an Austrian-Hungarian writer, founded the international

Zionist movement with the primary goal of establishing a Jewish state. This movement later gave birth to the Balfour Declaration, a document issued by British foreign minister Arthur James Balfour, which endorsed the creation of the first national Jewish homeland in two thousand years in Palestine. It also guaranteed civil and religious rights of Arabs living there.

The mandate system was established by Article 22, Paper of the Covenant of the League of Nations, as formulated at the Paris Peace Conference in 1919. Under this article it was stated that the territories inhabited by peoples unable to stand by themselves would be entrusted to advanced nations until such time as the local population could handle their own affairs.[3]

In this context, Israel was to be granted a British mandate with its administration implementing the terms of the Balfour Declaration. The text of the mandate specifies the historical connection of the Jewish people to Israel and the commitment of the British government to facilitate, by means of immigration and settlement on the land, the establishment of a Jewish national home. Moreover, a Jewish agency was to be established as a recognized body with whom the administration would negotiate and cooperate. Two years later after World War I, the League of Nations mandated Palestine to Great Britain.[4]

By 1936, two hundred eighty thousand Jews had arrived in Palestine from Europe, escaping the brutality of Nazi Germany. The Holocaust, which resulted in the deaths of six million Jews at the hands of the Nazis, incited worldwide sympathy for the persecuted Jews, which gave the Zionist movement the attainment of a Jewish homeland.

Arab-Israeli Conflict Begins

With the increase of Jewish immigration to Israel, hostility of the Arabs toward the Jewish immigrants grew stronger. A rash of Palestinian-Arab riots broke out, to which the outside world paid little attention.

In the summer of 1946, Jewish guerillas under the leadership of Menachem Begin blew up British government offices in the King David Hotel. Ninety-one Jewish, British, and Arab civil servicemen were killed.

Within a year, Britain requested a special session of the United Nations' General Assembly. In 1947, the General Assembly proposed the partition of Palestine into two separate states—Arab and Jewish—both west of the Jordan River. Thirty-three UN members voted for the resolution; thirteen, including the eleven Muslim states, voted against it.

On May 14, 1948, Israel declared its independence. The British high commissioner sailed for home marking the mandate end, and David Ben-Gurion became the first prime minister of the state of Israel. Within hours, Israel's survival was in question. Five Arab states attacked Israel, but their lack of unity made them no match for the better trained Israeli Army, many of whom were World War II combat veterans.

The war ended in October of 1949; however, it was just the beginning of the Arab-Israeli conflicts of the twentieth century. Some seven hundred thousand Palestinians fled or were driven from what had been British-mandated Palestine. Israel annexed large tracts of land. Jordan and Egypt held onto the West Bank and Gaza Strip, respectively. Control of Jerusalem was split between Israel in the west and Jordan in the east.

In the 1950s, Arab unity became the focus of the Arab nations. Any show of defiance against foreign influence won admiration among the Arabs, such as that of Gamal Nasser of Egypt, who was a hero to the Arabs. In July of 1956, Egypt, under Nasser's leadership, nationalized the French-run Suez Canal and brought back a sense of pride among the Arabs. However, that pride did not last long. Britain and France conspired to recapture the canal with Israeli help. Israel invaded Sinai in October, and Britain and France occupied the canal zone; but in November of that year they had to withdraw under U.S. pressure.

In June of 1967, Egypt together with Syria and Jordan attacked Israel, initiating the Six-Day War. Israel simultaneously attacked Egypt, Syria, and Jordan after destroying the Egyptian air force in a surprise attack. The Israeli Air Force inflicted a devastating defeat upon the Arab armies.

During the Six-Day War, Israel not only defeated the Arab armies but also captured the Sinai Peninsula and Gaza Strip from Egypt, the Golan Heights from Syria, and the West Bank and East Jerusalem from Jordan. Israel celebrated this dramatic victory, which had more than doubled the size of its territory. For the Arabs it was *al-Naqsa*, the setback.

Palestinians were scattered all over the Middle East, with their main concentration in Jordan. Yasser Arafat took control of the Palestine Liberation Organization (PLO) and moved to Jordan, where he created a threat of civil war. King Hussein's army forced Arafat to leave Jordan, so he and the PLO moved their activity to Lebanon.

In 1972, PLO guerillas invaded the Israeli dorm at the Olympics in Munich, killing eleven Israeli athletes. On October 6, 1973, Egypt and Syria attacked Israeli forces in Sinai and the Golan Heights during the Jewish fast of Yom Kippur. They made initial gains but had to retreat after Israeli counterattacks.

In 1974, the Arab league recognized Yasser Arafat as the only legitimate leader of the PLO. In July of 1976, Israeli commandos rescued ninety-eight Israeli hostages in Entebbe, Uganda, held by Palestinians who hijacked an Air France Airbus. In the summer of 1985, the PLO struck again, hijacking TWA flight 847 in Beirut, Lebanon. One hundred fifty passengers were held hostage for seventeen days.

Attempts at Peace and Further Clashes

Anwar Sadat became the new leader of Egypt in 1970. He realized that the Arabs did not have a chance of winning against the Israelis, so why not make peace with them? This great leader visited Jerusalem in November of 1977, offering peace to the Jewish state, an unprecedented move by an Arab leader. This historical visit was greatly welcomed by the Jewish people and Prime Minister Menachem Begin.

In the fall of 1978, an incredible move was taken by Israel and Egypt at Camp David. The two rival countries negotiated peace, with the United States as their mediator. In September, Egypt, Israel, and the United States signed Camp David accords at the White House. Israel agreed to hand back Sinai to Egypt in return for peace and normalization. Anwar Sadat stunned the Arab world by signing a peace treaty with the state of Israel, and Egypt was immediately suspended from membership in the Arab league. Sadat was a secular Muslim strongly opposed to the radical Islamic movement in his country. He was also open to the beliefs of other religions. Harald Bredesen, one of the founders of the Charismatic movement in America, had an audience with Sadat and witnessed to him of the gospel of our Lord Jesus Christ.

In 1979, a new crazed dictator seized power in the Middle East. This time it was in Iraq by a man named Saddam Hussein, who showed his true colors of violence from the first day he took over parliament by executing many of Iraq's ministers. In 1981, Saudi Arabia, fearing an invasion by Iraq's or Iran's fundamentalists, formed an alliance with Kuwait, Bahrain, Qatar, United Arab Emirates, and Oman.

On September 16, 1982, Israel-allied Christian militias entered the Sabra and Shatila refugee camps in Beirut and massacred about two thousand unarmed Palestinians after PLO fighters had been forced out of Lebanon by Israel.

In December of 1987, the Palestinian *Intifada* (uprising) against Israeli rule started in the West Bank and Gaza. Young Palestinian demonstrators hurled stones at Israeli troops in the occupied territories, and the military responded with curfews, arrests, and deportations. More than twenty thousand people were killed or injured. As violence grew, life became harder for the Palestinians living in Israel. Many immigrated to other parts of the world.

On August 2, 1990, Iraqi troops invaded Kuwait, and within hours Saddam Hussein set up a puppet government. The Iraqi soldiers looted Kuwait and destroyed everything they could. Saudi Arabia, fearing that Iraq would invade their country, appealed to the United States for help. President Bush responded by deploying more than five hundred forty thousand troops onto the most sacred of Muslim ground.

The United Nations Security Council took a strong stand against Saddam Hussein. The United Nations demanded immediate withdrawal of Iraqi troops from Kuwait and imposed economic sanctions against Hussein's government. They also authorized the United States, with its allies, to use force in liberating Kuwait.

In January of 1991, the U.S. military commenced relentless bomb attacks against Iraq's military machine, destroying Hussein's military infrastructure. In a desperate act, Hussein began bombing Israel with Scud missiles, hoping to get Israel involved and arouse sympathy from the Arab nations who supported military action against Iraq. Even though the war was justified, once again the West had to mediate in the Middle East.

In September 1993, Yasser Arafat and Israeli Prime Minister Yitzhak Rabin signed the Declaration of Principles in Washington on the basis of the Oslo Accord. Israel recognized the PLO and gave them limited autonomy in return for peace and an end to Palestinian claims on Israeli territory.

On February 25, 1994, a militant Jewish settler massacred twenty-nine Palestinians who were praying at the main mosque in Hebron. In July of the same year, Arafat made a triumphal return to Gaza to take up his new position as head of the new Palestinian Self-rule Authority, after nearly twelve years of running the PLO from Tunis.

On October 26, 1994, another historic event took place in the United States. Israel and Jordan signed a peace treaty with the mediation of the United States.

In September of 1995, Arafat and Rabin signed the Taba agreement, known as Oslo II, in Washington to expand Palestinian self-rule in the West Bank and Gaza and allow Palestinian elections, which were held on January 20, 1996.

On October 23, 1998, Israeli President Benjamin Netanyahu signed the Wye River Memorandum outlining further Israeli withdrawal from the West Bank after U.S. pressure to end eighteen months of stagnation on the Israeli-Palestinian peace track. Upon completion of each phase of Palestinian commitments, Israel agreed to transfer a specified percentage of land to the Palestinians within the context of "further redeployments" as stated in previous agreements.

Final negotiations between Israel and the Palestinians were deadlocked as the deadline for a framework agreement was missed. As these peace talks stop and resume, violence and bloodshed continues. The Hamas Islamic Militia persists in its strategy of suicide bombings, killing innocent civilians, and Israel continues to strike back.

Israel Divided

There are four major elements within Israel's political system. Each represents a nucleus of power that cannot be disregarded. The peace of Israel rests upon the unity, if possible, of these four groups. These four elements are:

1. Political Israel
2. Spiritual Israel
3. Political Palestinians
4. Radical Palestinians

Group one, *political Israel*, is formed, for the most part, by a group of secular Jews whose stance is not based upon the Torah and biblical values, but rather on the identity of a race of people, the Jewish people. On the other hand, the second group, named *spiritual Israel*, represents the group of Jews whose position is founded on more than just a race issue; their identity is based upon strong religious conviction, history, and tradition.

On the opposite pole from these groups, there are groups three and four.

Group three, *political Palestinians*, is made up of the Palestinians whose goal is to create an independent Palestinian state within the land of Israel, a state within a state. The fourth group, *the radical Palestinians*, is the toughest of the four, representing the group of Palestinians whose purpose is the eradication of the state of Israel.

Often in our reasoning we want to eliminate what we consider to be the source of the problem in order to reach a solution. When it comes to Israel, that kind of reasoning will not work. All of the mentioned groups have a part in the conflict, and it is impossible to eradicate or ignore any of them in order to achieve a peaceful solution for the conflict in the Middle East. Each of these groups has deep roots in the land of Israel, and one cannot attempt to uproot them without disastrous consequences.

Again, we must study the nature of a problem before we can come to a resolution. Therefore let us carefully look at these four groups and consider their goals and their efforts.

Group four: radical Palestinians

One of the major difficulties in reaching a peaceful solution for Israel is the Islamic Palestinian militia known as *Hamas*, the fourth element fueling Israel's political system. We can take a look at the philosophy of this group by reading the following passage, which is found on the Hamas Web site:

> **To confront Sharon's massacres: Escalating resistance, serious Arab action and reprisal and not returning to humiliating negotiations**
>
> Zionist aggression against our people witnessed a new escalation in the past few days represented in intensifying storming operations of Palestinian cities and targeting liquidation of more intifada activists. The step follows the moral and security defeat that befell the Zionist occupation at the hands of martyr heroes who blew up the Zionist security theory and proved failure of terrorist Sharon's government in achieving security for Zionist occupiers. Following the Quds and Haifa operations that terrorized the Zionists, Sharon resorted to political steps such as occupying the "Orient House" then followed it with escalation in military aggression that led to the martyrdom of numerous Palestinians. In a single day, yesterday Sunday, six Palestinians were martyred in Rafah, Gaza and Nablus

including two small children in a fresh cold-blooded massacre by the occupation army. Such escalation aims at increasing pressures on our people and pushing them to despair of continuation of resistance against occupation in addition to pressuring the Palestinian Authority to return to effective security coordination and resume policy of detention of Palestinian freedom fighters. The PA actually responded by arresting a number of Hamas cadres at the pretext of having links to the martyrdom operation in Al-Quds. In the light of such Zionist escalation and aggression, the Zionist enemy circulated possibility of resuming political talks with the PA. A number of Arab parties also exerted efforts in a bid to revive the negotiations' dead body. Faced by such developments we would like to affirm the following:

1. The escalation of Zionist terrorism and aggression against our people reflects the Zionist occupation and the Sharon government's misery and moral defeat. They are trying to score illusionary victories over the Palestinian people to preserve their existence and cohesion.

2. The Zionist enemy's signs about political negotiations with the PA and readiness to accept a political settlement in addition to activating role of terrorist Peres in the light of continuation and escalation of repression, terrorism and aggression target distracting the attentions and ensuring international support to criminal Sharon's policy and terrorism.

3. We affirm the importance of unity of our people on the option of intifada, resistance and steadfastness in its capacity as the sole option capable of ejecting occupation and putting an end to Zionist aggression and terrorism God willing.

4. Returning to discussions on reviving negotiations with the Zionist enemy and resuming the so-called peace process is a stab in the back of the blessed intifada and lets down our people's Jihad, brave resistance and martyrs' blood. Our people did not indulge in this intifada and resistance and did not offer martyrs and sacrifices only to submit to the criminal enemy's demands and return to humiliating negotiation with it. Any step in this direction on the part of any Palestinian or Arab party would be met with anger on the part of our people along with the Arab and Islamic peoples.

5. We affirm that resistance would persist and escalate and that the criminal Zionist enemy would never know sleep or security as long

as occupation continued. Our stationed Palestinian people will not take heed of suspicious calls voiced by defeatists to halt resistance or martyrdom operations at weak pretexts. Persistence of occupation and its daily bloodbaths against our people boost the necessity for escalation of resistance and continuation of martyrdom operations.

6. We denounce the state of Arab and Islamic impotency in face of the Zionist aggression. We invite the Arab and Islamic peoples to restore their role in support of their Palestinian brothers. We also urge the Arab and Islamic governments to shoulder their responsibility in resisting aggression and adopt serious practical steps in confrontation of Sharon and his terrorist gang and not to remain captive to losing bets on the American role. It is high time for the Arab and Islamic countries to sever all kinds of relations and contacts with the Zionist enemy and to pressure the American administration through its interests in the region.[5]

Note that point four of the Hamas declaration says that any attempt to resume "the so-called peace process" would be considered "a stab in the back of the blessed intifada" and would let down "our people's Jihad." Hamas continues by stating that such an attempt "would be met with anger on the part of our people along with the Arab and Islamic peoples."

As long as Hamas continues its hateful stand against Israel, there will be no peace in Israel. Hamas is a terrorist organization hated by the Israelis, despised and feared by westerners, yet admired by the majority of the Palestinians.

I saw a report done by a major news network in the West Bank after the bombing of a pizza restaurant in Jerusalem by the Hamas. "Which one of you wants to be a suicide bomber for Hamas?" the American reporter asked the crowd of young Palestinian boys swarming about him. To his surprise, every boy in that crowd raised his hand with a huge smile and excitement on their faces. Recently, a Palestinian TV children's show called *The Children's Club*, which is modeled on the American program *Sesame Street*, aired an episode in which young boys with raised arms chanted, "We are ready with our guns; revolution until victory; victory."[6]

Hamas is not only a terrorist organization, but also an ideology in the hearts of many young Palestinians. Their ideology is based upon the teaching and the traditions of Muhammad and the Islamic hateful stance against the Jewish people.

What about the other groups' ideology and goals?

Group one: political Israel

Group one, political Israel, simply desires peace without any bloodshed. Even though it represents varying opinions, it is the easiest to deal with of the four. For example, Ariel Sharon is a right-wing hardliner. He was the leader of the right-wing Likud Party until November 2005, when he left that party to form a new party, Kadima (Forward).[7] His policies indicate that his goal is to ensure total security for Israel on his terms, which means keeping the maximum of land for the Jewish state and giving the very minimum to the Palestinians. Ehud Barak, on the other hand, would probably do anything for peace, including giving up Jerusalem for it. At a session in the Israeli parliament Sharon said, "Barak does not have the right to give up Jerusalem, which the people received as a legacy."

Group two: spiritual Israel

The second group, the ultraorthodox Jews, were not quite in the game until the assassination of Yitzhak Rabin by a Jewish right-wing extremist in 1995. The Jewish extremists regarded Rabin as a traitor for agreeing to trade Israel's land for peace. Religious parties and ultraconservative secular groups together are a powerful force against giving up any part of the occupied territories.

Group three: political Palestinians

The third group, political Palestinians, desire to take the West Bank, including Jerusalem and Gaza, and create a Palestinian state independent from Israel.

Political Israel and political Palestinians have been negotiating for peace since 1974, when the PLO was officially recognized by the Arab League. They have not yet reached an agreement, and I believe they will never reach an agreement and achieve a peaceful solution. Why? Because they have ignored the two other major players in the game—the ultraorthodox Jews (spiritual Israel) and the Hamas (radical Palestinians).

Political Israel hopes that the PLO will eventually subjugate Hamas and other radical Islamic groups. They only want to deal with the PLO. *The PLO should be the party controlling Hamas,* they think, not knowing the true nature of Hamas. The PLO has no concern, at this time, with Hamas, because Hamas is helping its cause. *Let them do our dirty work,* the PLO thinks.

Hamas's goal—the eradication of the Jewish race—is evident by the warfare they have waged on the Jewish people. Killing thousands of innocent people who have no animosity against them is their solution for achieving their goal. If it were a political goal, they would have a different strategy. They have shown their cards from the beginning of play.

The Way to True Peace

With the death of Yasser Arafat on November 11, 2004, the incapacitating stroke of Ariel Sharon in January 2006, and the election victory of Hamas in January 2006, the possibility of a peaceful end to the centuries-old hatred and violence between the Jews and the Muslims is more uncertain than ever. The dynamics of these four major political elements has changed, the leadership is evolving, and the violence continues on its upward climb.

Recognizing these four different groups and understanding their goals, one is led to think—*These guys are playing Russian roulette; how can they achieve peace? How can four ideologies that are in absolute contradiction to one another reach an agreement?* These are very good questions.

Sometimes politicians play a game that has no end and no solution. It is like the blacksmith who thought that he could fix a shoe for any four-legged animal until he was presented an elephant. Sure, he could bend and stretch the horseshoe to fit the elephant, but who in the world could lift the elephant's leg up and nail the shoe into it? Not a blacksmith!

In this way, the politicians around the world have been racking their brains and draining their resources to bring about a peaceful solution to the Arab-Israeli conflict. Possible? Not until they get help from the elephant trainer.

Peace in Israel is unrealistic because the pieces that need to come together do not fit the peace puzzle. No human government or social or political genius can make these four pieces of the puzzle fit together. This is because they are not considering a fifth element—God.

If we do not consider God in this equation, we are missing the vital piece, because it is for God's sake that groups two and four exist. If God wasn't in the equation, as some politicians believe, there wouldn't be any conflict between the Arabs and the Jews. If there was no God, Israel would not be Israel. Hamas would not exist, nor would the ultraorthodox Jews. There wouldn't be any radical Islamic militant groups, and there wouldn't be any peace negotiations.

So if God is the main part of this equation, why are we trying to solve the problem of Israel, as well as radical Islam, without Him?

Israel Inherits a Promise

Nearly four thousand years ago, a man named Abram from Ur of the Chaldeans, which is known today as the country of Iraq, was chosen by God to become the father of the nation of Israel. We read about this promise in the first book of Moses, the Book of Genesis:

> Now the LORD had said to Abram:
>
> "Get out of your country,
> From your family
> And from your father's house,
> To a land that I will show you.
> I will make you a great nation;
> I will bless you and make your name great;
> And you shall be a blessing.
> I will bless those who bless you,
> And I will curse him who curses you;
> And in you all the families of the earth shall be blessed."
> —GENESIS 12:1–3

This passage of Scripture is known as the *Abrahamic covenant*, a treaty, if you would, between God and Abram, whose name was later changed to *Abraham*. The purpose of this covenant with Abraham was to create a nation that would be consecrated unto God.

After the fall of Adam, there was a separation between God and man. Man sought his own gods and walked his own ways apart from the purpose that God had for His creation. As a result, different societies lived in anarchy, and people did what was right in their own eyes. People worshiped all kinds of things. There was no law, order, or peace.

But God had a plan—to redeem mankind from the chaos. To do that,

He had to send a deliverer, one who was the Way—one who was not part of the chaos Himself, but an outsider; someone who would understand our condition, yet be separate from it. Who could that person be? It couldn't be a human, for all have sinned. How could a blind person lead another blind person?

God decided to make His own Son, Jesus, the deliverer. He had to become one of us for us to behold Him. If He appeared as glorious as He is, no human being would dare to approach Him. In order for Him to become one of us, He had to become flesh and come through a group of people who were separate from all idol worshipers of that time. He had to be born among a group of people who knew the one true God. So God had to cleanse a group of people. He had to consecrate them, separate them from the rest, so that the Messiah could come forth from them to the world.

God chose Abram, a Hebrew from Iraq, to be the father of this people. When Abram received God's call, he was seventy-five years old and had no children. Recognizing the dimension of this call, Abram cries to God, "Lord God, what will You give me, seeing I go childless, and the heir of my house is Eliezer of Damascus?" (Gen. 15:2).

Then the Lord answered Abram:

> And behold, the word of the LORD came to him, saying, "This one shall not be your heir, but one who will come from your own body shall be your heir." Then He brought him outside and said, "Look now toward heaven, and count the stars if you are able to number them." And He said to him, "So shall your descendants be."
> —GENESIS 15:4–5

With the naked human eye, one can count six thousand stars. The descendants would be beyond what Abram could imagine.

So God decided that out of this faithful man He would create a nation through which the Messiah could come to the world. In order for a people to exist, they must have a place of dwelling, where they exercise sovereignty and institute laws and regulations by which their identity is recognized.

Not only did God give Abram a promise for a group of people, but He also gave him a promise of a land—the land of Canaan, known today as Palestine.

And the LORD said to Abram, after Lot had separated from him: "Lift your eyes now and look from the place where you are—northward, southward, eastward, and westward; for all the land which you see I give to you and your descendants forever."

—GENESIS 13:14–15

Note that the promise of the land was not only for Abram, but also for his descendants forever.

The unfolding of these promises had to be all God's plan so that no man could mess it up. The promise of a child was fulfilled when Abram was one hundred years old, twenty-five years later. There was no way Abram could get the glory for that. Although, as we will see in the next chapter, he did interfere.

When ten years went by after the promise of a child, Abram and his wife, Sarai (later *Sarah*), tried to help God out. Sarai gave Abram her maidservant, Hagar, so that they might bear a child through her. The result of that plan was a boy named *Ishmael*, not the promised child of God's plan, but a child resulting from man's plan. Ishmael is known to be the father of the Arabs. Fifteen years after the birth of Ishmael, Isaac, the promised child and the progenitor of the Jewish people, was born.

This event is important in understanding the present-day Israeli-Arab conflict. From the very beginning there was a fight between the two brothers. Isaac was born out of God's promise, whereas Ishmael was born out of human effort. Recognizing the position that the two boys held, Abraham prayed to God for Ishmael, "Oh, that Ishmael might live before You!" (Gen. 17:18). Abraham was not praying for the survival of Ishmael, but for God's blessings upon him.

The Lord said to Abraham:

And as for Ishmael, I have heard you. Behold, I have blessed him, and will make him fruitful, and will multiply him exceedingly. He shall beget twelve princes, and I will make him a great nation.

—GENESIS 17:20

God is not a respecter of persons. He did not choose Isaac above Ishmael. But Isaac was born as a result of a promise. God had to bring forth someone from a promise or else man would have a part in His redemptive plan. And that would not be possible; it had to be God all by Himself.

In the above verse, God also shows His love for Ishmael and how He blessed Ishmael. We can see that promise fulfilled by looking at the Arab nations. There are more Arabs today than there are Jews. Arabs have never gone through persecutions as the Jews have. There have never been any attempts in history by the various kingdoms to annihilate the Arabs. Arab lands are full of black gold—oil; they are rich beyond description. So God has indeed blessed them. Arabs have more lands and more people and more wealth.

But the promise, the Messiah, had to come through Isaac, the Jewish people. That is why the Jewish people have gone through so much opposition in their four thousand years of history.

Out of one man, advanced in years, Abram, God brought forth a people, a nation. A people must have their own identity, an expression of ideas, thoughts, and character. Without a land that would be impossible. So God gave the land of Canaan, known today as *Erets-Israel*, to Abraham and his descendants for an everlasting possession.

> Also I give to you and your descendants after you the land in which you are a stranger, all the land of Canaan, as an everlasting possession; and I will be their God.
>
> —GENESIS 17:8

Note the words *an everlasting possession*. This promise was repeated over and over again to the patriarchs. This leads us to a very legitimate question: Would God change His promise to Abraham? If He did, then that would make God a liar.

So now, we have two possible views to take on the current struggle in Israel:

1. There is no God, and this religious stuff is not for today.

2. There is a God who is the absolute truth and in Him there is no darkness, therefore He cannot lie. The Bible says, "Let God be true but every man a liar" (Rom. 3:4). God cannot lie, for whatever He says comes to be. (See Hebrews 11:3.)

Most of our politicians have chosen the first view. What has been the result? How many years have they tried to negotiate peace for Israel? There is more bloodshed among the Israelis and the Arabs than ever before. How long will they continue before they realize that the peace of Israel is beyond their grasp?

A Return to God's Word

In 1947, the General Assembly of the United Nations proposed the partition of Palestine into two separate states, Arab and Jewish, both west of the Jordan River, which resulted in the beginning of today's problem. How could man dictate what God had already established as an everlasting covenant? Can one succeed in opposing God? God is a merciful God, but mercy does not mean compromise. Truth cannot be altered in order to be politically correct.

"What about the Palestinians?" one may ask. Historically, they have no claim upon the land of Israel. It is as if I were to vacate my property for a long period of time, and a passerby takes possession of it for the time I am gone. Would he have the right to any claim on my property?

The Jews took possession of Erets-Israel more than thirty-five hundred years ago, long before the Palestinians were in existence. The Palestinian people only occupied the land while the Jews were dispersed. This may not be politically correct, but it is true.

This leads to the question, what should be the proper treatment of the Palestinians living in Israel?

Israel has to abide by the laws of the God, who gave them the land, if they want to abide in it in peace. The commandment was:

> For the LORD your God is God of gods and Lord of lords, the great God, mighty and awesome, who shows no partiality nor takes a bribe. He administers justice for the fatherless and the widow, and loves the stranger, giving him food and clothing. Therefore love the stranger, for you were strangers in the land of Egypt.
> —DEUTERONOMY 10:17–19

If Israel were to treat Palestinians according to the above verse, *Intifada* would have never begun, and Hamas would not be in existence today.

I remember the day my good friend Pastor Yusuf from Haifa drove me to Jerusalem. He is a Palestinian Christian who was born and raised in Israel, but he is from Arab descent.

He was so kind when he found out that I wanted to go to Jerusalem. He offered to take off from his work and drive me there. The trip takes three hours from Haifa to Jerusalem, and even though he is not familiar with the streets of Jerusalem, he was still willing to take me. I took him up on his offer, and we headed out to Jerusalem.

As we entered the city, he got onto a street that only buses were allowed on. As soon as he realized it, he decided to turn around and find the way out. Of course it was too late; the police saw us and stopped us.

While the policeman was writing him a ticket, another car drove by. The policeman waved her off the road, and she stopped. She was an Israeli Jewish woman. The policeman let her go without giving her any ticket. We were right behind that vehicle and saw the entire process. After he let her go, he came back to us and gave Pastor Yusuf a ticket. Pastor Yusuf asked the policeman why he didn't give the woman a ticket. The policeman refused to answer him. Pastor Yusuf told the policeman it was because he was an Arab, and she was a Jew.

Both were Israelis, both born in Israel, but one Arab and the other a Jew. Pastor Yusuf was mad and hurt, as was I, but then he smiled and said, "I forgive him with the love of Christ." He is a Christian, and a good one, and he must forgive.

That would not be the case with a radical Muslim. This kind of humiliation, which is the mildest example, may be tolerated by some, but not by the Islam of the seventh century.

Can Israel Make Peace With Islam?

In an interview with Fox News on Monday, September 24, 2001, former Israeli President Benjamin Netanyahu said:

> Militant Islam, a virulent strain of Islam, wants to reverse a thousand years of history, and they want to destroy the main engine of the West which is the United States.... So they will attack you again and again and again. And unless you dismantle this network and the regimes that support it are neutralized, the consequences will be tremendous.[8]

What Netanyahu did not understand was the fact that there are millions and millions of these fanatical Muslims. You can't kill them all! The more you dismantle, the more of them you have to deal with. They increase when they die in a martyr's death for their god.

On the other side, we see President Bush declaring, "The idea of a Palestinian state has always been part of the vision, so long as the right to Israel to exist is also respected."[9] This declaration is of course welcomed with huge open arms by the Arab nations.

President Mubarak of Egypt is one of the strongest allies of the United States in the Arab world. He has had his share of having to crack down on radical Islamic organizations like Al Jihad in Egypt. In a conference with the twenty-two ministers of the Arab League countries in October 2001, Mubarak said: "We support all measures taken by the United States to resist terrorism."[10] He explained his support with these words: "We are against terrorism because we have been burned by it."[11] To Mubarak, like many other Arab leaders, the problem begins with the Palestinian issue, which he said "has great importance in the efforts to eradicate the roots of terrorism."[12]

One worrisome idea that has come about in the current situation is "peace for land." Because of the fear created by the Islamic fundamentalists throughout the world, Western allies, especially the United States, may play with the idea that the establishment of a Palestinian state will rid the world of Islamic terrorism. President Bush spoke about this recently in a press conference.

The goal of radical Islam is not a Palestinian state. *It is the eradication of the state of Israel.* The day the Israelis signed the Oslo Peace Accord was the day Israel asked for more trouble. The underlying goal of the Oslo Accord was the establishment of two states: Palestine and Israel, living together in peace and security within the territory of the Palestine Mandate. Arafat's goal was to establish an independent Palestinian state with east Jerusalem as its capital. Is that possible?

I was so troubled the day I sat in the Palestinian police station in Bethlehem, trying to convince the chief of police to allow me to continue our Christian meeting at the Hotel Bethlehem. The night before, we had organized a citywide meeting inviting the people of Bethlehem, the majority of whom were Muslims, to hear the gospel of Jesus Christ. Five minutes into our service, a group of radical Muslims rose in protest yelling and cursing us for proclaiming Jesus as the Son of God. The irony was that Jesus was born in that city. The following day we were taken to the police station and told that our meeting was canceled. We were threatened by the Hamas and had no choice but to leave the city.

If the United States or any other European government thinks that by establishment of a Palestinian state they will solve the world's terror problem, they are gravely mistaken. The United States may think that it is not giving in to the terrorists' demands, but the fact remains that President Bush's statement about a Palestinian state is exactly that.

In a *BBC News Talking Point*, one of the comments reads, "Ultimately Israel would have to give the Arab land back as per the requirements of UN resolutions. History shows when twelve-year-old boys start dying for a right cause, they can never be defeated. Israel must understand this."[13]

As long as the Jews remain Jews and the Arabs remain Muslims, there will be no peace between these two sons of Abraham. This is a very hard statement, but it is absolutely the truth.

So what is the solution?

The solution is simply to eliminate the idea of two separate states—Israel and Palestine. Israel must have complete domain and sovereignty over the entire land, including the West Bank and Gaza. The Palestinians born in Israel must have the same rights as the Jewish people—and be treated as the citizens of Israel. Those who do not desire such citizenship must be deported to the land of their forefathers—Jordan, Syria, or elsewhere.

This concept may seem too simple, and even foolish in the eyes of complicated philosophers and politicians, yet it is the only solution for any peace in Israel.

8

God's Plan for Iran

Iran straddles the crossroads of our world, bridging the continents of Europe and Asia. Geographically, it is placed in a very key position.

The second largest country in the Middle East, Iran's land area of 636,000 square miles is about one-sixth of the size of the United States. It is surrounded, on the north, by former republics of the Soviet Union. On the northwest corner are Armenia and Azerbaijan, and on the northeastern side is Turkmenistan. The great Caspian Sea lies in the northern Midwest. With 144,000 square miles, it is the world's largest inland sea and home to the renown sturgeon whose eggs are the famous Persian caviar. To the east, Iran borders Afghanistan and Pakistan, and on the west, Turkey and Iraq. The southern border is mainly the gulf (the Gulf of Oman and the Persian Gulf). At the southern tips of these two gulfs are the Arab nations of Kuwait, Bahrain, Qatar, Oman, United Arab Emirates, and, of course, the largest of them all, Saudi Arabia.

Iran's landscape is dominated by deserts and mountains. Iran is one of the most mountainous countries in the world with mountain ranges such as the Alburz (560 miles long) and the Zagrus, which is about 200 miles in width. Mount Damavand, the tallest peak, towers high (18,934 feet) above the Alburz range. The two largest deserts, Dasht-e-Kavir and Dasht-e-Lut, cover an area of 500 by 200 miles and 300 by 200 miles, respectively.

The Persian Empire

Iranian (Persian) history is as old as the known history of the first human civilizations. The Iranian Plateau and the plains of Mesopotamia were the dwelling places of the first families of the human race.

Two of the first known people groups were the Sumerians and the Elamites. The Sumerians lived in the region of Ur, where Abraham lived, in Mesopotamia.

They established the first large-city civilization. The Elamites lived in southwestern Iran. The cultural development of Sumer and Elam ran parallel.

Iran, which means "the land of the Aryans," is a combination of three empires: Pars (Persians), Medes, and Elamites. Around 1000 B.C., groups of herding nomads known as the Aryans (Persians and Medes) migrated to the provinces of Fars (Pars). As the numbers of these Aryan tribes grew stronger in the Iranian Plateau, so did opposition from neighboring kingdoms, mainly the Assyrians. The constant incursions from the Assyrians brought unity among the tribes of Persians, Medes, and also Elamites, which eventually led to the establishment of one of the greatest kingdoms of that era, the Achaemanid Empire.

The Achaemanid (Hakhamaneshian) Empire (559–330 B.C.) was led by a great military leader known as Cyrus the Great. He was the son of Cambyses, the prince of Persia, and was born about 599 B.C. In 559 he became king of Persia (including Media and Elam). In 538, Cyrus conquered Babylon on the night of Belshazzar's feast, and then the ancient dominion of Assyria was also added to his empire. (See Daniel 5:30.) Cyrus was anointed by Jehovah God. As a matter of fact, Cyrus's name was prophesied two hundred years prior to his birth by the prophet Isaiah. In Isaiah 45 we read:

> Thus says the LORD to His anointed,
> To Cyrus, whose right hand I have held—
> To subdue nations before him
> And loose the armor of kings,
> To open before him the double doors,
> So that the gates will not be shut:
> "I will go before you
> And make the crooked places straight;
> I will break in pieces the gates of bronze
> And cut the bars of iron.
> I will give you the treasures of darkness
> And hidden riches of secret places,
> That you may know that I, the LORD,
> Who call you by your name,
> Am the God of Israel.
> For Jacob My servant's sake,
> And Israel My elect,

I have even called you by your name;
I have named you, though you have not known Me."

—Isaiah 45:1–4

Many great kingdoms had been oppressors of the Jews. Cyrus, on the contrary, became known to them as a "shepherd" (Isa. 44:28; 45:1). God had raised him to help His people. God anointed and called Cyrus for His plan for the Jewish people.

Soon after the conquest of Babylon by the Persians, Cyrus issued the decree that had been prophesied by the prophet Jeremiah, setting the Jews free after seventy years of captivity in Babylon. (See Ezra 1.) Not only did Cyrus liberate God's people from captivity, but he also guaranteed their safe return to their homeland and the rebuilding of the city of Jerusalem. The edict of Cyrus for the rebuilding of Jerusalem marked a great epoch in the history of the Jewish people. (See 2 Chronicles 36:22–23; Ezra 1:1–4; 4:3; 5:13–17; 6:3–5.)

It has been said that the Persian Empire was the world's first empire in which one ruler governed many different peoples. Under Cyrus's reign, the Persian Empire extended from India to Ethiopia, comprising one hundred twenty-seven provinces. (See Esther 1:1; Daniel 6:1.) These provinces were governed by provincial governors known as *satraps*.

The Persian Empire is remembered for many of its accomplishments. They were the first people to create a visual telegraph system. Semaphore beacons were erected on mountaintops allowing messages to be rapidly passed from one town to the other. Persians also worked out a monetary system.[1]

Cyrus was known to be a tolerant and just ruler. He was a great defender of human rights and was respectful of customs and religions. Conquered nations under him kept their rights and customs. Cyrus pardoned his valiant enemies and granted high positions of importance to them in the provinces. This was further practiced by other Persian monarchs. For example, King Artaxerexes commanded Ezra when he returned to Jerusalem:

> And you, Ezra, according to your God-given wisdom, set magistrates and judges who may judge all the people who are in the region beyond the River [Euphrates], all such as know the laws of your God; and teach those who do not know them.
>
> —Ezra 7:25

Due to the fair principles of the Persian kingdom, Persia became known as a territory where many persecuted took asylum.[2]

The following are some governing principles practiced by the Persians:

- *Government*: constrained by constitutional limitations (Esther 8:8; Dan. 6:8–12)

- *Municipal governments*: provided with dual governors (Neh. 3:9, 12, 16–18)

- *The princes*: were advisors in matters of administration (Dan. 6:1–7)

- *Status of women*: queen sat on the throne with the king (Neh. 2:6)

The Achaemanid Empire declined after Cyrus and was finally defeated by Alexandra of Macedon (356–323 B.C.).

Iran Today

Iran is a bridge between the West and the East. Because of its strategic importance, Iran has endured many afflictions by invading armies, such as the Greeks, Romans, Arabs, Mongols, and the British and Russian forces.

Under Cyrus the Great, from the Achaemanid dynasty, the empire was united and known as the Persian Empire, which, at the time, covered much of the known world. As we said, Cyrus was known to be a generous ruler. The nations he conquered were allowed to keep their traditions, religions, and language. Because of the expansions of the Persian Empire into the neighboring territories, there are now over seventy ethnic groups (people groups) that consider Iran their homeland. These people groups include Jews, Armenians, Assyrians, Kurds, Turks, Baluchi, Azeri, Turkemen, Ghashghai, Arabs, Mongols, and Afghanis. The majority of these ethnic minorities have been loyal in keeping their customs, languages, and religions. Of course, since the Islamic Revolution in 1979 with its strict ordinance and the cruel rules of the mullahs, life has been very difficult for those who are not practicing Shi'ite Muslims. The Islamic government of Khomeini purged Iran of almost all Jews and followers of the Islamic Baha'i sect, which is considered an abomination faith. Before the 1979 Islamic Revolution, there were eighty-five thousand Iranian Jews living in Iran. Today, according to Operation World, they number about twenty-five thousand.[3] Constitutionally the rights of Jews, Zoroastrians, and Christians are guaranteed, but in practice they are greatly persecuted.

The Times of the Nations

In the Book of Acts we read:

> And He has made from one blood every nation of men to dwell on all the face of the earth, and has determined their preappointed times and the boundaries of their dwellings.
>
> —ACTS 17:26

Here we see that every nation has boundaries and preappointed times. I believe that the "preappointed times" are the times of God's visitation upon the nations. The Bible also calls it a "time of life" (Gen. 18:10).

When Jesus approached Jerusalem He cried out:

> For days will come upon you when your enemies will build an embankment around you, surround you and close you in on every side, and level you, and your children within you, to the ground; and they will not leave in you one stone upon another, because you did not know the time of your visitation.
>
> —LUKE 19:43–44

Here Jesus declares the judgment upon the city of Jerusalem, which took place in A.D. 70 because they did not recognize their appointed time, the day of their visitation.

I have noticed that one of the most difficult things for the people of God to recognize is God's timing—God's timing for them, God's timing for their call, and God's timing for their nation. Most Christians operate outside of God's timing for their lives. They start their ministries out of time, they start their businesses out of time, they publish a book out of time, they marry out of time, and so forth. And as a result of miscalculating the times of God for their lives, they either give birth to a wrong thing or abort a right thing.

Understanding God's Timing

The Bible says, "To everything there is a season, a time for every purpose under heaven" (Eccles. 3:1).

God does everything according to His purpose and His timing. Often we are willing to obey God, but we miss the timing of our obedience. For those of us who are *runners*, or, better said, *energized by God's Spirit*, we have a tendency to allow our zeal to decide the timing of the things of God, and we run ahead of God's time. It is like a baby born out of due time. It will be an underdeveloped child with underdeveloped organs. Such is the case with those of us who run ahead of God's timing. Our impatience can cause great harm and heartache to our natural and spiritual life.

Ishmael was a good example. He was born as a result of an ambitious soul that did not wait upon God. We read in Genesis 16:1–3:

> Now Sarai, Abram's wife, had borne him no children. And she had an Egyptian maidservant whose name was Hagar. So Sarai said to Abram, "See now, the LORD has restrained me from bearing children. Please, go in to my maid; perhaps I shall obtain children by her." And Abram heeded the voice of Sarai. Then Sarai, Abram's wife, took Hagar her maid, the Egyptian, and gave her to her husband Abram to be his wife, after Abram had dwelt ten years in the land of Canaan.

This happened ten years after God had promised Abraham a child. Sarah had waited these ten years and had become impatient. She was losing face in her culture by being barren, so she thought she would help God out. What bold thinking! So she suggests an outlandish solution: "Please, go in to my maid; perhaps I shall obtain children by her." Abraham acquiesced, and the result was devastating. Their impatience and lack of knowledge of God's way and timing gave birth to one of the most troublesome conditions on this planet. The Bible says:

> For it is written that Abraham had two sons: the one by a bond-woman, the other by a freewoman. But he who was of the bond-woman was born according to the flesh, and he of the freewoman through promise, which things are symbolic. For these are the two covenants: the one from Mount Sinai which gives birth to bond-

age, which is Hagar—for this Hagar is Mount Sinai in Arabia, and corresponds to Jerusalem which now is, and is in bondage with her children—but the Jerusalem above is free, which is the mother of us all. For it is written:

"Rejoice, O barren,
You who do not bear!
Break forth and shout,
You who are not in labor!
For the desolate has many more children
Than she who has a husband."

Now we, brethren, as Isaac was, are children of promise. But, as he who was born according to the flesh then persecuted him who was born according to the Spirit, even so it is now. Nevertheless what does the Scripture say? "Cast out the bondwoman and her son, for the son of the bondwoman shall not be heir with the son of the freewoman."
—GALATIANS 4:22–30

Four thousand years have passed since Ishmael was born, and yet his descendants are still persecuting the sons of the child born by God's will. What a tremendous price we pay when we miss God's timing. The Lord spoke to Abraham:

And He said, "I will certainly return to you according to the time of life, and behold, Sarah your wife shall have a son." (Sarah was listening in the tent door which was behind him.)... "Is anything too hard for the LORD? At the appointed time I will return to you, according to the time of life, and Sarah shall have a son."
—GENESIS 18:10, 14

Note what the Lord said to Abraham about the timing of this miracle— "according to the time of life." In verse 14 we read, "at the appointed time." According to the above passages of Scripture, God had a specific time in mind for the fulfillment of His promise.

Some people believe and teach that if one has faith, the answer to one's petition will come instantly. But according to Genesis 15:6, that is not so. Abraham believed God and His promise twenty-five years before it took place. Faith doesn't speed up God's plan and its timing. It just brings it to pass. If Sarah had a revelation of this, we would not have all the conflict that we have today between the Arabs and the Jews.

Time, for us, is the process of maturing into the things of God. If God brings us to maturity before He calls us, then we will not walk in faith. From the time we hear the call of God to the time we fulfill that call, God takes us through a process of faith and maturity in the Spirit.

David was anointed as a king when he was only fifteen years old, but he did not take the seat of a king until he was thirty years old. For fifteen years he was a fugitive, running for his life from Saul. This period of fifteen years was actually a very short period in comparison to what other Bible characters went through to mature to the calling of God. David sought God constantly, and that made him mature faster in the things of God than others like Moses, who did not start his ministry until he was eighty years old.

We need time not only to be conformed to the will of God, but also for the process of God's will to unfold. Four hundred years went by between the Old and New Testaments. God was quiet for four hundred years before He spoke through John the Baptist. Why did God have to wait for four hundred years? The Israelites had to become exhausted in their own efforts at achieving righteousness; otherwise they would not be ready for the righteousness of God through Jesus Christ. The Bible says:

> But when the fullness of the time had come, God sent forth His Son, born of a woman, born under the law, to redeem those who were under the law, that we might receive the adoption as sons.
> —GALATIANS 4:4–5

The law was a tutor, or a nanny, to lead men to Christ. If Jesus had come right after Malachi, people would not have received Him at all. So we see that there is a specific and perfect timing for all the purposes of God on this planet.

In the Book of 1 Chronicles, we read about the army of David, men of different tribes of Israel with different talents and giftings of God.

> Of the sons of Issachar who had understanding of the times, to know what Israel ought to do, their chiefs were two hundred; and

all their brethren were at their command.

—1 Chronicles 12:32–33

Because the children of Issachar had an understanding of the times, they were empowered with the ability to take right action.

Here in America we have an understanding of natural time, but many Christians lack knowledge of the spiritual time. What takes place in the spiritual realm determines what will take place in the natural. If we recognize the timing of God, we will then understand the physical timing of things—when, where, and how.

The many questions raised as a result of September 11, for example, show how we, the church, lack an understanding of the hour in which we live. Of what was September 11 a result? Our disobedience? God's judgment on America? Why did it happen to the United States? Did it have any spiritual significance? Was it a prophetic sign? Was it the beginning of a new era? If it was, did we see it coming? And if not, why?

I believe that 9/11 was a "thorn in the flesh" of the church in America. God commanded Israel to deal with the Philistines. If Israel disobeyed God, the Philistines would become a thorn in their side. Let me explain what I mean. Today the church in America carries the responsibility of 50 percent of all the gospel introduced to the world. There is not a nation on this planet that produces more witness for the gospel of God than the United States of America. I believe this is why America is the most blessed nation on this earth.

> But he who did not know, yet committed things deserving of strips, shall be beaten with few. For everyone to whom much is given, from him much will be required; and to whom much has been committed, of him they will ask the more.
>
> —Luke 12:48

And yet with all the mission efforts of the church in America toward other nations, the Islamic world has been, except for a few organizations, neglected almost completely. Churches simply didn't care and didn't want to obey the Great Commission for the Islamic world. God has a claim on harvest in the Muslim world. But how could they believe without someone proclaiming the good news to them? The efforts of a few small organizations were not sufficient to meet the 1.3 billion souls! Something drastic had to take place to wake up the church to the demand of God for harvest in the Muslim world! What could that be?

September 11 and other violent incidents by the radical Muslims have changed that. Now God's people are concerned about the Muslim world, and many efforts are being put forth to reach them, including TV broadcasts. And I firmly believe that if these efforts are not sufficient, we will see more violence from the radical Muslims.

The church needs the functioning of the children of Issachar, men and women who are aware of God's purpose and plan for these last days and who know what God's people ought to do. There are those who are always ready to warn us with End-Time prophecies, and we thank God for them. However, we also need concrete and clear knowledge of the time in which we live. We need a better understanding of the action called for in this hour so that we can walk not in fear, but in absolute certainty of and obedience to God's will; that is, so we can walk a sure walk of faith.

Fear is due to lack of knowledge of God's plan, purposes, and timing. For instance, the new threats by Ahmadinejad, the president of Iran, and Iran's development of nuclear energy have scared many people here in the West, including many Christians. I understand when the world is afraid, but the church must know and understand the plan, purposes, and timing of God.

Faith comes from having revelation knowledge of God's will. It is an assurance, confidence, and certainty. Fear, the opposite of faith, is the result of a lack of knowledge of and belief in God's will.

When the disciples, together with Jesus, were caught in the midst of the storm on the Lake of Galilee, Jesus was sound asleep. The disciples, on the other hand, were trying to save themselves and Jesus. After they had frustrated themselves with their efforts at saving the whole company, they came to Jesus complaining. "But He was in the stern, asleep on a pillow. And they awoke Him and said to Him, 'Teacher, do You not care that we are perishing?'" (Mark 4:38).

Jesus woke up and rebuked the storm:

> Then He arose and rebuked the wind, and said to the sea, "Peace, be still!" And the wind ceased and there was a great calm. But He said to them, "Why are you so fearful? How is it that you have no faith?"
>
> —MARK 4:39–40

Why were the disciples so afraid, even though Jesus was with them in the boat? First, because they didn't know who Jesus was. And second, because they weren't aware of God's purpose and plan. If they had known and trusted God's plan—that Jesus was supposed to die for the sins of humanity on a cross outside of the city of Jerusalem and not in the middle of a lake due to a raging storm—they too would have fallen asleep in peace, allowing Jesus to deal with the wind and the waves. Their lack of knowledge of God's will gave birth to fear in their lives.

Fear can only abide where there is no knowledge of God's will. Why were most people in America and the Western world scared to death after September 11? Simply because they had no knowledge of the will of a loving God. They walk in ignorance, disobedience, and fear. It is the same for God's people. If we lack knowledge of the time and of His will, we will also walk in darkness and fear.

God's Timing for Iran

Do we recognize the time of God's visitation for our nation as well as other nations? Do we know when God is planning to visit people with His grace, mercy, and power? And do we realize that God is now visiting the nation of Iran, the beginning of His dealings with the Islamic world?

If we had recognized God's timing, we, the church of Jesus Christ, would have been ready for this awesome move of God that is now taking place in Iran. Jeremiah prophesied this move of God in Iran twenty-seven hundred years ago. In Jeremiah 49:34–39 we read:

> The word of the LORD that came to Jeremiah the prophet against Elam, in the beginning of the reign of Zedekiah king of Judah, saying, "Thus says the LORD of hosts:
>
> 'Behold, I will break the bow of Elam,
> The foremost of their might.
> Against Elam I will bring the four winds
> From the four quarters of heaven,
> And scatter them toward all those winds;
> There shall be no nations where the outcasts of Elam will not go.
> For I will cause Elam to be dismayed before their enemies

And before those who seek their life.
I will bring disaster upon them,
My fierce anger,' says the LORD;
'And I will send the sword after them
Until I have consumed them.
I will set My throne in Elam,
And will destroy from there the king and the princes,' says the
    LORD.
'But it shall come to pass in the latter days:
I will bring back the captives of Elam,' says the LORD."

Note verse 38: "'I will set My throne in Elam, and will destroy from there the king and the princes,' says the LORD." Isn't this what is happening in Iran right now? Did we see it? And do we see it now? God is working one of the most awesome moves that has ever taken place on this planet, and yet most of the church world doesn't even know. For the first time in the history of an Islamic nation, thousands upon thousands of Muslims are converting to Christ. This is a phenomenal miracle. God is pouring out His Spirit in Iran, and the faith of the gospel is being established in the hearts of the Iranian populace for the first time in their history. God is establishing His throne in a radical Islamic nation. Iran is becoming a prototype of the fall of Islam in the hearts of millions of ex-Muslims. This is amazing and glorious! I believe that within the next few years millions of Iranians will become strong Christians and great witnesses for Jesus in the Muslim world.

Thank God for those few who have heard the cry of this servant of God, and thank God for the rest of you who will hear it through this book. Hallelujah!

The Time of Visitation

Often God visits a people right after a breakdown in their national pride. Pockets of revival can be seen at different times in the history of a country, through various individuals and events. However, a nationwide revival often occurs after the entire nation is broken in its pride.

The Soviet Union is a great example of this fact. For seventy years the Russian people experienced the brutality of an iron-fisted system. Communism broke their national pride and opened the hearts of the Russian people. From 1978 to the year 2000 I crisscrossed the former Soviet bloc nations, and also the Soviet Union. We could not find a large enough arena for all the people that rushed to our meetings to hear the gospel of Jesus Christ. The hunger in the hearts of people was so amazing. They were broken, and they needed comfort, hope, peace, and blessings.

Within a few years after the fall of the Soviet iron-fisted regime, churches grew at a phenomenal rate. Pastor Ulf Ekman's ministry in Sweden began a mission venture to the Soviet bloc countries. Within four years they established four hundred churches in the Soviet Union alone. Other ministries also claim great successes in these nations, all as a result of a hunger produced in the hearts of millions of people who experienced oppression and a breakdown in their national pride. The Bible says, "When He slew them, then they sought Him; and they returned and sought earnestly for God" (Ps. 78:34).

People always cry after God when they are in a desperate condition. And when the people's cry increases before God, then an answer comes from on high, and God visits the people with His mercy.

Before the birth of Christ, Israel was broken down by the hard rule of the Roman Empire. The Bible tells us that there were souls in Israel hungry for a change. In the Book of Luke we read:

> And behold, there was a man in Jerusalem whose name was Simeon, and this man was just and devout, waiting for the Consolation of Israel, and the Holy Spirit was upon him. And it had been revealed to him by the Holy Spirit that he would not see death before he had seen the Lord's Christ. So he came by the Spirit into the temple. And when the parents brought in the Child Jesus, to do for Him according to the custom of the law, he took Him up in his arms and blessed God and said:
>
> "Lord, now You are letting Your servant depart in peace,
> According to Your word;
> For my eyes have seen Your salvation
> Which You have prepared before the face of all peoples,
> A light to bring revelation to the Gentiles,
> And the glory of Your people Israel."
>
> And Joseph and His mother marveled at those things which were spoken of Him. Then Simeon blessed them, and said to Mary His

mother, "Behold, this Child is destined for the fall and rising of many in Israel, and for a sign which will be spoken against (yes, a sword will pierce through your own soul also), that the thoughts of many hearts may be revealed."

Now there was one, Anna, a prophetess, the daughter of Phanuel, of the tribe of Asher. She was of a great age, and had lived with a husband seven years from her virginity; and this woman was a widow of about eighty-four years, who did not depart from the temple, but served God with fastings and prayers night and day. And coming in that instant she gave thanks to the Lord, and spoke of Him to all those who looked for redemption in Jerusalem.

—LUKE 2:25–38

Simeon and Anna were two of God's consecrated people who sought God for the deliverance of Israel. Anna prayed and fasted for some sixty years. Jesus came as a result of a great hunger for His salvation.

In order for God to move in a nation and among a people, there must always be a group of people who hunger after God. "Blessed are those who hunger and thirst for righteousness, for they shall be filled" (Matt. 5:6).

The Islamic government of the Ayatollah Khomeini broke down the national pride of the Iranian people through much hardship, death, and sorrow. Iran is now broken by the forces of radical Islam. The Iranian people were one of the proudest groups of people that I have ever seen. But they are now broken. And this brokenness has produced a great hunger in their souls for the truth. That hunger is the igniter of one of the greatest moves of God in human history. God is doing something in Iran beyond anyone's imagination.

Iran, the Beginning of the Fall of Islam!

Iran has been a key nation in God's plan in times past, and I believe that God will use Iran today, again for His plan of salvation for the Muslim world. I believe that Iran is the axe that God will put to the tree of Islam to break the strength of Islam in the Muslim world.

In order for Islam to be exposed for what it is, its nature and philosophy must be put into practice. This is why I believe that radical Islam must arise. Muslims must see the reality of what they believe. They must taste the truth of Islam. Once they taste the hatred, division, bloodshed, and fear that Islam advocates, then they will know that Islam is a religion of death and destruction.

Islam has enough venom within its ideology to poison itself, if we leave it alone. Once doubt begins inside a Muslim community about the truth of Muhammad and his religion, there is no redemption for the Islamic faith. And this is when the church needs to proclaim the gospel of love and power.

Iran is the first example of the fall of Islam. After the Islamic Revolution of Ayatollah Khomeini in 1979, the Iranian society became the training ground for a return to seventh-century Arabian culture and Muhammad's cruel and demonic traditions. War broke out with Iraq, their neighboring country, and these two Muslim nations killed more than two million of their own people over eight long years. Death and sorrow were a daily part of life in Iran. Joy was un-Islamic, according to Khomeini.

Khomeini brought the reality of seventh-century Arabian culture into the twentieth-century life of Persian people. He broke the national pride and trust that the majority of the Iranian people had in Islam as he practiced the grim reality of this religion. He brought death, sorrow, and destruction to millions of lives in that land, exposing the nature of true Islam and of Allah, a god who is hateful, vengeful, and incredibly merciless. By word of mouth, I heard from a credible source that one official from the Iranian government said, "Islam was a sick cow which Khomeini shot and put an end to."

Before the Islamic Revolution, the Iranian society was closed and religious. The shah tried hard to secularize the nation and bring the people to a place where they would not be blindfolded in their religious ideologies. What the shah of Iran and his father tried to do for more than fifty years, Khomeini accomplished in just a few.

Once people had a taste of the true Islam, they were no longer respectful and fearful of it. In a recent uprising of university students against the Islamic regime, the demonstrators chanted, "Death to Ayatollah Khamenei."[4] Ayatollahs are the highest rank of clerics in the Shi'ite Islamic faith; therefore, defaming them is defaming Islam and its laws.

Muslims cannot defy their spiritual leader unless they are hateful toward that system of belief. For the first time in the history of Iran and any Islamic nation, we are seeing a bold defiance of Islam by Muslims. This is a miracle. And this is the beginning of the fall of Islam in many Islamic nations.

We, the body of Christ here in America and the West, need to prepare for this massive harvest that is ahead of us in Iran and the Muslim nations. We need to raise national leaders who are on fire for God and will lead further the move of God in their nations, such as Iran, Afghanistan, Pakistan, Egypt, and other Islamic nations. God has already opened the airwaves into these countries. There are no longer any Islamic forces that can hinder the preaching of God's Word in their nations. So this is just the beginning of a glorious ride. We will be witnesses of God's mighty hand of salvation in these nations.

So get ready, buckle up, because I am declaring a prophetic word, just as Elijah declared to Ahab: Gird up, because I hear the sound of the rain. Hallelujah!

9

Iran's Christian Soldiers

Persecution strengthens the church. That is a proven fact. The blood of those martyred for Christ has always paved the way for a great move of God. Satan does not understand that the more people of God he kills, the more of them he must deal with. As these persecuted leaders boldly declare their unshakable faith in Christ—even as some of them lose their lives—great spiritual strength arises in the hearts of their followers. As the martyrs shed their blood, the believers who witness their great faith in God develop an uncompromising resolve to be true to Christ.

Persecution has affected the church since its beginning soon after the Day of Pentecost. Herod the king stretched out his hand to harass some from the church in Acts chapter 12. He first killed James the brother of John, and then he took a bold step and put Peter, one of the main apostles of the church, in prison. What did the church do? In Acts 12:5 we read, "Peter was therefore kept in prison, but constant prayer was offered to God for him by the church."

The church went into a "constant prayer" mode. You know what that is? It is raw power. Prayer produces the purest form of power—God's power. In Acts 8:1 we read a similar story: "Now Saul was consenting to his death. At that time a great persecution arose against the church which was at Jerusalem; and they were all scattered throughout the regions of Judea and Samaria, except the apostles."

It looked as though the devil had won the battle against the church, but a gasoline fire cannot be put out with water. The more water you throw at it, the more you will spread the fire. The persecution in Jerusalem was a blessing. It spread the gospel to other regions. We read in Acts chapter 8:

> As for Saul, he made havoc of the church, entering every house, and dragging off men and women, committing them to prison.

Therefore those who were scattered went everywhere preaching the word. Then Philip went down to the city of Samaria and preached Christ to them. And the multitudes with one accord heeded the things spoken by Philip, hearing and seeing the miracles which he did. For unclean spirits, crying with a loud voice, came out of many who were possessed; and many who were paralyzed and lame were healed. And there was great joy in that city.

—ACTS 8:3–8

Philip was chosen by the apostles to serve the tables in the church in Jerusalem. Man chose him to serve tables, but God ordained him to win souls and bring healing to the sick. Now they had revival not only in Jerusalem but also in Samaria!

The sequence of events that occurred in Acts mirrors almost what has taken place in Iran. Many Christian leaders left the country as a result of the 1994 persecutions against the church by the Iranian government. As a result, Iranian ministries are scattered over every continent. In nearly every major city around the world there is at least one Iranian church.

Yet even though the government pushed many Christian leaders out of the country, they have been unable to stop a tremendous, sovereign move of God in Iran, evidenced by the conversion of thousands upon thousands of Iranian Muslims. Open Doors Ministry recently reported: "One Shi'ite cleric in the Ministry of Education declared publicly that an average of fifty Iranian young people were known to 'convert secretly to Christian denominations' every day."[1]

Actually, fifty people a day is a very low estimate. The rate of conversion is so drastic that during the past twelve months top government officials have publicly warned the Iranian populace against a number of "foreign religions" targeting the country with illegal propaganda.[2]

God's Special Forces

In this chapter we are going to introduce you to some of Iran's Christian soldiers. Some of them have fled their country to live in Christian freedom and liberty around the world. Others are God's Special Forces, living lives in service to Jesus Christ in the midst of great persecution and danger in the country of Iran. Like the U.S. Army's Special Forces, these Christian soldiers are determined to complete their mission for God regardless of the cost.

Sara: A Brand-new Believer

It was the morning of January 17, 2005, when Zohreh, the Iranian woman who answers the calls from Iran at our office, told me that Sara had left four messages on our answering machine. She said it was very urgent and asked that I please call her back. I made the long-distance call to Sara, who lives in a well-known city located in the central part of Iran.

As soon as Sara answered, I noticed the stress in her voice. "What is the matter?" I asked her.

"My husband called the police on me this morning and told them that I have rejected Islam and have become a Christian," she said with a cracking voice. "Two policemen came to our house, and they started making a report. I was very afraid, and my children were crying. I told the policemen, 'The children are afraid. I need to take them outside to calm them down.' When we got outside, I took a cab, and we all went to my friend's house. What do I do now? Please help me!" I heard the intense fear in her voice, so I tried to calm her with encouraging words from the Scriptures.

What do I do now, Lord? I thought to myself. After a long conversation with Sara, I convinced her to stay where she was until I could find a place to put her—possibly in Tehran, the capital.

That morning I sent an e-mail to all of our partners and asked them for prayer for Sara. Here is the text of that message:

> I just had a very distressing call from one of our new believers in Iran. Sara is the mother of five teenage children. She and her children have recently accepted the Lord. She came to our conference in Turkey, and the Lord healed her and filled her with the Holy Spirit. Today her husband called the police and registered her as a *mortad*, one who has converted to Christianity, the penalty for which is imprisonment or even death. She fled with her children when the police came, and all six of them are on the run tonight. At this time she is staying with a friend. They were very scared. Please pray for protection and peace for Sara and her children tonight. Also pray for her husband, that God may visit this man and that the fear of God may come upon him.

Sara's husband was a religious Muslim man and had recently married another woman. According to Islamic law, a Muslim man is permitted to have four wives plus many concubines. Even though this is an Islamic law, in reality all the families in Iran, especially the women who are victimized by their husbands, despise it.

Sara and her children reacted harshly to his decision to marry another woman. To justify his sinful act, her husband called the police and reported her as an *apostate* (one who has left Islam and converted to another religion). It is a very serious crime in Islam and carries the death penalty.

We found a place for Sara and her children in Tehran, but Sara decided to stay in her home town and face her punishment. But she said that she could not stay at her friend's home with five kids, so she had gone back to her house. When I talked with her again a few days later, Sara was much calmer.

She was scheduled for a trial in a religious court. Because the city where she lived was one of the Muslim hardliners' seats of politics, I advised her that she would be better off leaving that city. I was afraid for her life. However, she was convinced otherwise. She didn't want to run. She kept saying that Jesus would deliver her out of this trial. Then I tried to instruct her how to behave in the court and what to say before the judge. She said that she had read somewhere in the Bible that when they bring you before the judge in defense of your faith, the Word said not to worry about what to say or not to say, because at that moment the Holy Spirit will teach you what to say. I thought to myself, *Here is a brand-new believer, and she has more faith in the Scriptures than I do at the moment.* I tried to encourage her and assured her that many of us were praying for her.

At her first trial, Sara's husband did not show up. Then Sara was scheduled for a second trial, and again, her husband did not appear. Finally the judge dismissed the case. However, her husband divorced Sara and took custody of her children.

Sara's case is a mild case of persecution when compared with so many other believers in Iran who have been imprisoned, tortured, and who lost all their belongings, families, jobs, educational opportunities, and even their lives. According to VOA (Voice of America), the United States has designated Iran as a "country of particular concern" because of its denial of religious freedom.[3] The list also includes China, Burma, North Korea, and Sudan.

The United Nations Universal Declaration of Human Rights declares,

"Everyone has the right...in public or private, to manifest his religion in teaching, practice, worship, and observance."⁴ People in Iran—like people everywhere else—should be allowed to practice their religion freely.

Yet Christians in Iran have been warned by the government to follow many regulations. Church members are required to carry membership cards, and copies of these cards must be submitted to the government. No one is to be admitted to a Christian service without a membership card and an identity check. Meetings are to be held only on Sundays, and church officials may not admit new members without informing the Ministry of Information and Islamic Guidance. Evangelical churches are especially pressured not to evangelize among Muslims.⁵

Bishop Haik Hovsepian-Mehr

Under traditional sharia (Islamic law), conversion by any Muslim to a non-Muslim religion is apostasy and is punishable by death. A Christian responsible for the conversion of a Muslim (i.e., evangelizing) also risks his own life.

The martyrdom of several key evangelical pastors in Iran underscores the severity of these regulations that the government has placed on the church.

Bishop Haik Hovsepian-Mehr, an Armenian, was superintendent of the Assemblies of God in Iran and pastor of Tehran's Assembly of God congregation, known as *Jamiat-e Rabbani*. He was greatly loved by Christians from many denominations, and he was a key person in drawing the attention of the world to the persecution of the Christians by the Islamic government of Khomeini.

I met Bishop Haik in 1984 in a Christian conference organized by the Iranian Christian Fellowship of London, held at a Christian retreat center outside of London called Ashburnham. He told me that before the revolution, he could get hardly any Muslims to visit their church service. But a few years after the revolution, hundreds of Muslims would come to the church, staying during the service and for hours afterward. "I couldn't get rid of them; they had all kinds of questions for which they wanted an answer. They were hungry for the truth," he told me. Because he was from an Armenian (Christian) background, Bishop Haik had a great love of preaching the gospel to Muslims.

Haik was a man of God who believed in the God-given right of a person to believe according to his conscience. He loved the people of Iran, whether

Christian or Muslim, and he did not care for the authorities' warnings. He would rather obey his Master and lose his life than obey a demonic law enforced by a group of hateful radicals.

Bishop Haik disappeared on January 19, 1994, and his body was found on January 20. His family, however, was not notified of his death for another eleven days. He had been tortured and stabbed. Authorities stated that he had been murdered by unknown assailants, but it is generally recognized that he was a victim of a government death squad. Two days before his death, Bishop Haik wrote, "I am ready to die for the cause of the church so that others will be able to worship their Lord peacefully and without so much fear."[6]

Mehdi Dibaj

Bishop Haik was also a key figure in bringing the world's attention to the abuses against Christians in Iran. He had appealed to the United Nations for an investigation. He was especially visible in working for the release of Mehdi Dibaj.

Rev. Mehdi Dibaj was born into a Muslim family and converted to Christ after reading a Christian tract as a teenager. He was first arrested in 1979 and spent sixty-eight days in jail. In 1984 he was arrested again on apostasy charges for converting from Islam to Christianity decades earlier. In jail he experienced mock executions and regular beatings.

In 1988 his wife divorced him and was converted back to Islam after being threatened with death by stoning. Church and family members took Dibaj's children into their own homes. While still in prison, Rev. Dibaj wrote these powerful words to his son: "What a privilege to live for our Lord and to die for Him as well."

On December 21, 1993, after being in prison for nine years, an Islamic court in the city of Sari sentenced Rev. Dibaj to death. His crime, according to the *sharia*, was based on the charge of apostasy. He had abandoned Islam and become a Christian. Once the news of Rev. Dibaj's death sentence reached the rest of the world, many Iranian believers throughout the world prayed for him. Many, like Bishop Haik, worked toward his release.

On January 16, 1994, Rev. Dibaj was released from prison after much pressure was put on the Iranian government from the world communities.

Following his release, Rev. Dibaj traveled around Iran for several months encouraging believers.

Six months after his release from prison, Rev. Dibaj was mysteriously abducted while on the way to his daughter's birthday party, and he paid the ultimate price for his faith in Christ Jesus. He was martyred on June 24, 1994.

The following is the celebrated written defense that Rev. Dibaj delivered to the Court of Justice in the city of Sari in Iran on December 3, 1993:

> *In the Holy Name of God who is our life and existence:* With all humility I express my gratitude to the Judge of all heaven and earth for this precious opportunity, and with brokenness I wait upon the Lord to deliver me from this court trial according to His promises. I also beg the honored members of the court who are present to listen with patience to my defense and with respect for the Name of the Lord.
>
> I am a Christian. As a sinner I believe Jesus has died for my sins on the cross and by His resurrection and victory over death, has made me righteous in the presence of the Holy God. The true God speaks about this fact in His Holy Word, the Gospel (*Injil*). *Jesus* means Savior, "because He will save His people from their sins." Jesus paid the penalty of our sins by His own blood and gave us a new life so that we can live for the glory of God by the help of the Holy Spirit and be like a dam against corruption, be a channel of blessing and healing, and be protected by the love of God.
>
> In response to this kindness, He has asked me to deny myself and be His fully surrendered follower, and not to fear people even if they kill my body, but rather rely on the creator of life who has crowned me with the crown of mercy and compassion. He is the great protector of His beloved ones as well as their great reward.
>
> I have been charged with "apostasy!" The invisible God who knows our hearts has given assurance to us, as Christians, that we are not among the apostates who will perish but among the believers who will have eternal life. In Islamic Law (Sharia'), an *apostate* is one who does not believe in God, the prophets or the resurrection of the dead. We Christians believe in all three!
>
> They say, "You were a Muslim and you have become a Christian." This is not so. For many years I had no religion. After searching and studying I accepted God's call and believed in the Lord Jesus Christ in order to receive eternal life. People choose their religion, but a

Christian is chosen by Christ. He says, "You have not chosen me but I have chosen you." Since when did He choose me? He chose me before the foundation of the world. People say, "You were a Muslim from your birth." God says, "You were a Christian from the beginning." He states that He chose us thousands of years ago, even before the creation of the universe, so that through the sacrifice of Jesus Christ we may be His. A *Christian* means one who belongs to Jesus Christ.

The eternal God who sees the end from the beginning and who has chosen me to belong to Him, knew from the beginning those whose hearts would be drawn to Him and also those who would be willing to sell their faith and eternity for a pot of porridge. I would rather have the whole world against me, but know that the Almighty God is with me. I would rather be called an *apostate*, but know that I have the approval of the God of glory, because man looks at the outward appearance but God looks at the heart. For Him who is God for all eternity, nothing is impossible. All power in heaven and on earth is in His hands.

The Almighty God will raise up anyone He chooses and brings down others, accepts some and rejects others, sends some to heaven and others to hell. Now because God does whatever He desires, "Who can separate us from the love of God?" Or who can destroy the relationship between the creator and the creature or defeat a life that is faithful to his Lord? The faithful will be safe and secure under the shadow of the Almighty! Our refuge is the mercy seat of God who is exalted from the beginning. I know in whom I have believed, and He is able to guard what I have entrusted to Him to the end until I reach the kingdom of God, the place where the righteous shine like the sun, but where the evil doers will receive their punishment in the fire of hell.

They tell me, "Return!" but to whom can I return from the arms of my God? Is it right to accept what people are saying instead of obeying the Word of God? It is now forty-five years that I am walking with the God of miracles, and His kindness upon me is like a shadow. I owe Him much for His fatherly love and concern.

The love of Jesus has filled all my being, and I feel the warmth of His love in every part of my body. God, who is my glory and honor and protector, has put His seal of approval upon me through His unsparing blessings and miracles.

This test of faith is a clear example. The good and kind God reproves and punishes all those whom He loves. He tests them in preparation for heaven. The God of Daniel, who protected his friends in the fiery furnace, has protected me for nine years in prison. And all the bad happenings have turned out for our good and gain, so much so that I am filled to overflowing with joy and thankfulness.

The God of Job has tested my faith and commitment in order to increase my patience and faithfulness. During these nine years He has freed me from all my responsibilities so that under the protection of His blessed Name, I would spend my time in prayer and study of His Word, with a searching heart and with brokenness, and grow in the knowledge of my Lord. I praise the Lord for this unique opportunity. God gave me space in my confinement, brought healing in my difficult hardships, and His kindness revived me. Oh what great blessings God has in store for those who fear Him!

They object to my evangelizing. But if one finds a blind person who is about to fall in a well and keeps silent, then one has sinned. It is our religious duty, as long as the door of God's mercy is open, to convince evil doers to turn from their sinful ways and find refuge in Him in order to be saved from the wrath of the Righteous God and from the coming dreadful punishment.

Jesus Christ says, "I am the door. Whoever enters through me will be saved." "I am the way, the truth and the life. No-one comes to the father except through me." "Salvation is found in no-one else, for there is no other name under heaven given to men by which we must be saved." Among the prophets of God, only Jesus Christ rose from the dead, and He is our living intercessor forever.

He is our Savior and He is the (spiritual) Son of God. To know Him means to know eternal life. I, a useless sinner, have believed in this beloved person and all His words and miracles recorded in the Gospel, and I have committed my life into His hands. Life for me is an opportunity to serve Him, and death is a better opportunity to be with Christ. Therefore I am not only satisfied to be in prison for the honor of His Holy Name, but am ready to give my life for the sake of Jesus, my Lord, and enter His kingdom sooner, the place where the elect of God enter everlasting life. But the wicked enter into eternal damnation.

May the shadow of God's kindness and His hand of blessing and healing be and remain upon you forever. Amen. With Respect,

YOUR CHRISTIAN PRISONER,

MEHDI DIBAJ[7]

If you go to Farsinet.com, you can find the following quote by Mehdi Dibaj at the bottom of his written defense:

> I have always envied those Christians who were martyred for Christ Jesus our Lord. What a privilege to live for our Lord and to die for Him as well. I am filled to overflowing with joy; I am not only satisfied to be in prison...but am ready to give my life for the sake of Jesus Christ.[8]

Tateos Michaelian

Just days after Dibaj disappeared, Bishop Haik's successor as chairman of the Council of Protestant Ministries and pastor of St. John's Armenian Evangelical (Presbyterian) Church disappeared. Tateos Michaelian's family was called to identify his body on July 2, 1994.

A young woman was arrested for his shooting death. Authorities originally stated that she was part of the Mujahedin Khalq organization (an opposition group), but in 1995 a report by Middle East Concern (MEC) gave new evidence, obtained from a high-level Iranian government contact, that he was murdered by a death squad acting on the instructions of "the highest authority" within the Iranian political leadership.[9]

In addition to pastoring, Michaelian had translated many Christian books into Persian. Before his death, he had agreed to help with a new translation of the Persian Bible, now called the "Michaelian Project" and being translated by Elam Ministries in partnership with Wycliffe Bible Translators.[10]

Other Christian Martyrs

Since the persecution of Christians in Iran escalated after the beginning of the Khomeini revolution, several other Christians have been martyred. In chronological order, these include: Rev. Arastoo Sayah, Muslim convert (1979); Brother Bahram Dehqani-Tafti, Muslim convert (1980); Brother Manuchehr Afghani, Muslim convert (1988; ICI only learned of this martyrdom in 1995); Rev. Hossein Soodmand, Muslim convert (1990); and Muhammad Bagher Yusefi, a Muslim convert, who was an Assemblies of God pastor and cared for Mehdi Dibaj's children. He was found hanging from a tree near his home on September 28, 1995.[11]

The list goes on of men and women who have suffered greatly at the hand of the Iranian Islamic government. Some were shot, some stabbed to death, some tortured, and others hanged. Many were imprisoned and lost their dignity. Some have even lost their faith, not able to handle the torture and humiliation they experienced in prison. These are the men and women who have joined the martyrs of the Book of Hebrews:

> And what more shall I say? For the time would fail me to tell of Gideon and Barak and Samson and Jephthah, also of David and Samuel and the prophets: who through faith subdued kingdoms, worked righteousness, obtained promises, stopped the mouths of lions, quenched the violence of fire, escaped the edge of the sword, out of weakness were made strong, became valiant in battle, turned to flight the armies of the aliens. Women received their dead raised to life again. Others were tortured, not accepting deliverance, that they might obtain a better resurrection. Still others had trial of mockings and scourgings, yes, and of chains and imprisonment. *They were stoned, they were sawn in two, were tempted, were slain with the sword. They wandered about in sheepskins and goatskins, being destitute, afflicted, tormented*—of whom the world was not worthy. They wandered in deserts and mountains, in dens and caves of the earth. And all these, having obtained a good testimony through faith, did not receive the promise, God having provided something better for us, that they should not be made perfect apart from us.
>
> —HEBREWS 11:32–40, EMPHASIS ADDED

The Gospel Through Christian Broadcasts

In spite of the persecution and tragedy faced by non-Muslims in Iran, the Christian church is growing in Iran—spurred by a fresh, sweeping move of the Holy Spirit and strengthened through the fellowship of suffering believers. Missions experts estimate twenty to thirty thousand indigenous evangelical and Pentecostal believers today, most of them from Muslim backgrounds.[12]

This growing number of believers is disturbing to the radical Islamic government. Authorities have become particularly vigilant in recent years in curbing what is perceived as increasing proselytizing activities by evangelical Christians.[13] One of the government's greatest concerns is the newly developing Christian TV broadcasts that are being aired daily over Iran by several ministries based in America, including Nejat TV. According to Yahya R. Kamalipour, professor and head of the Department of Communication and Creative Arts at Purdue University Calumet in Hammond, Indiana, and author of *Global Communication*, Iranian air space today is electronically penetrated by more satellite TV signals and radio stations from around the world than any other nation, many of these from Christian broadcasters.[14]

Although satellite dishes are illegal in Iran, Kamalipour states that U.S. satellite channels can be picked up in Iran by households equipped with illegal satellite dishes, disguised on the rooftops in defiance of the government's anti-dish stance. Although there are no accurate viewer estimates, reportedly anywhere from three million to five million Iranian households are equipped with receiving dishes.[15]

Satellite TV is the greatest tool of evangelism for the Muslim countries. I am so privileged to be a part of this groundbreaking work, which has resulted in thousands of Iranians coming to Christ—many of whom become such fervent believers that they risk their lives to share the gospel in their Islamic countries.

Those who are familiar with Muslim outreach know how hard it can be. Muslims love to argue about their faith with Christians. Sometimes it can take several years of constant witnessing to Muslims before they are even willing to read the Bible, because they believe that the Bible has been "altered" by Christians and is no longer the book that Jesus "wrote." In addition, Muslims are convinced that their religion is the final and the best of all other religions. Thus, Muslim evangelism can be very frustrating with endless talks, arguments, and even violent reactions.

On the other side, in this age of technology, God has provided tools of evangelism that are extremely efficient, such as radio and satellite TV. This is not to undermine the importance of personal evangelism. However, when it comes to reaching the masses, no other tool is as effective as radio and especially satellite TV.

There are many advantages with TV programs that are aired via a satellite station, often based in another country. First of all, the censorship by the local government is completely eliminated. Secondly, the people are reached where they are, right in their homes. They can't argue with someone who is talking to them through their TV set! They listen to the message even if they dislike the person. They may change the channel if one offends them. But for the most part, the message of the gospel is intriguing to them, especially when the program is a healing service. Muslims love miracles. Through a TV or radio program the Word of God can be sown into their hearts. Moreover, a satellite program goes where the majority of missionaries cannot go—to the unreached villages and towns and communities.

Nejat TV—the beginning of revival

About the same time the persecution arose against the church in Iran, the Lord was preparing me for TV broadcasts into the Middle East.

In 1997 I began Fishermen's House Church in Tulsa, Oklahoma, with two families. Shortly thereafter we rented an empty space for our office and church services. The space was an empty shell. We made a deal with the landlord to lease us the space for five years at a price of three dollars per square foot. In return, we would finish the space with our own money, building our offices and a sanctuary. He agreed, and we began the process.

As we were building our rented facility, I saw in my spirit that I would one day tape TV programs out of my office. So when we built the space, I had my office built to be twice the necessary size, thinking of the vision for the TV broadcasts. Today, half of my office is used for our Nejat TV set.

In 2001, I had a call from one of my good friends and a board member of our ministry who asked me if I was willing to go to Philadelphia to pray for two Christian women who had cancer. I told him that I was willing to go, and then I added, "Why don't you also organize a healing service in your church?"

On the day of the healing service, I was in prayer for many hours, praying especially for the healing of these two ladies with cancer. Around four o'clock, the Lord spoke to me. He said, "Tonight there will be one of My servants in the service. He will give you $90,000. Use $50,000 for your two upcoming crusades in India, and use the remaining $40,000 to buy equipment for television broadcasting. You will soon be on TV in Iran."

I thought to myself, *Ninety thousand dollars? That is not possible. If I get $1,500 out of the offering tonight, I will be tap dancing after the service.*

So I started bargaining with the Lord. I brought it down to $35,000, which is what I had faith for. It wasn't long before I recognized my foolishness. *Why am I bargaining with the Lord?* I reasoned. *If it is me thinking this up, it will not happen, but if it is God, why am I arguing with Him?*

That night it happened exactly as the Lord had told me. There was a man in the service who gave me $90,000. And I did exactly what the Lord had told me. I paid for the two crusades, through which more than three hundred thousand Hindus were saved, and with the remaining $40,000 I bought the equipment for the TV broadcasting.

On May 18, 2003, our ministry aired its first Christian satellite program into Iran via a secular Iranian satellite station based in California. That day our two phone lines were jammed with calls from Iran. Calls and e-mails came in all that week from Iranians who were more than ready to accept Jesus as their Lord and Savior, and each week the number increased to the point that we had to hire more people and add four more lines to our phone system. Iranians and Afghans were calling from the Middle East and all over the world, waiting on the line for ten to twenty minutes before they had a chance to be prayed for.

Ever since that first broadcast, the calls and e-mails have not stopped coming. Multitudes of Iranian Muslims are turning to Christ everywhere. It is a mass revival. Many of them see a dream or a vision of Jesus. Ninety-nine percent of all the people who contact us accept Jesus almost instantly—something that was unimaginable even a few years ago.

This is the result of Iranians tasting the reality of Islam and becoming desperate for a change. Iran is on the brink of another revolution, this time orchestrated by the Spirit of God. This will be a revolution that will bring millions of Iranians into God's righteous kingdom. Hallelujah!

From May 10, 2003, through mid-April of 2006, we broadcast three hours of programming over the Jamm-e-Jam satellite station, based in California, into Iran. In April 2006, Trinity Broadcasting Network (TBN) became a partner with our Nejat TV network, and our three hours weekly became an hour of broadcast every day. And now with an increase of broadcasters, a twenty-four-hour station (TBN Nejat TV) will start September 1, 2006, broadcasting Christian programming in the Farsi language over two satellite stations (Hot Bird 6 and Tellstar 5), covering almost all this planet. To God be the glory!

The following are just a few of the thousands of responses we have had to the Nejat TV broadcasts. These precious Iranian converts have become a part of God's Special Forces in that land of darkness:

A call from Zabul (near Afghanistan border)

A few moments ago, I saw your program from India on TV. I was very touched by your program. If the religion of Jesus has this kind of power and signs, I will give all that I have. I am a Shi'ite Muslim, but I want to ask Jesus Christ, the prophet of God, the Spirit of God, or the Son of God, or whoever you say He is...I beg of Him to solve my problems from my soul, and heart, because I believe in His religion.

A young Iranian girl calls.

Hello, my name is H— (She sounds very nervous and excited on the phone.) I am calling from Iran, the Fars province. When I saw your program, my heart...don't know, I don't know, how I am feeling. Would you please, for God's sake, pray for me also? (She is crying.) I need help. I plead with the Prophet Jesus to help me also.

An Iranian man is saved.

This man called and spoke to us on the phone for a long time. Ever since he was ten years old, he had questions about the integrity of Islam and its relationship to women. When he saw our program for the first time, he said that he felt as though someone from heaven came down and spoke to his heart. He felt that this message was the truth that he needed to hear and for which he had been longing all his life. He accepted the Lord right after our program.

"There is no way I can describe to you the lightness that I felt in my heart after the prayer," he said. He wrote down the prayer of salvation that I said at the end of the Nejat program and prayed that same prayer all day long in his store (a flower shop) for many days.

Muslims are used to praying the same prayer over and over again. He kept calling us but couldn't get through. He wanted to know what he needed to do now that he is a Christian. "Is it OK for my body to be buried in a Muslim graveyard if I am killed by the Iranian government because of my faith?" he asked.

He lives in northern Iran, and there are no churches there. He was so hungry to know the truth and to do God's will.

A couple from Mashhad, Iran, are saved.

This couple called our office right after watching our program and were ready to receive Jesus as their Lord and Savior. Partway through the middle of the salvation prayer ("Jesus, I repent from all my sins . . ."), the man interrupted and said, "Ma'am, how holy His words are!"

After they finished praying, the phone counselor told him that now angels are rejoicing, and that all his sins were forgiven and forgotten. Again he interrupted and said, "You couldn't be serious! Are you? Is this that simple? You mean simply, just like that, our sins are wiped away by His blood?" The phone counselor assured him that this is what the Word of God says in the Bible.

The simplicity of the message brought great conviction upon his heart. "Islam is just a dictatorial belief," he said. "When we are born, they recite verses from the Quran in one ear, and when we die they do the same in another ear. In between birth and death they fill us with all lies. Oh, God, this Christianity is so simple!" he said with a sigh of relief.

A *basiji* in Tehran, Iran, is saved.

Muhammad Reza called our office with this question: "Is drinking a sin in Christianity?" The phone counselor asked him how old he was. "Twenty years old," he replied. "I am a *basiji* (special military force of the Iranian government), and we are forced to do *namaz* (Muslim prayer, five times daily)," he continued. "It seems there is a fight going on inside of me." He had so many questions. "I read somewhere that Jesus said people are His sheep. Why does He compare people to sheep?" After hearing the message of the gospel about Jesus, "the Great Shepherd," he gave his heart to the Lord. Then there was silence, and the phone counselor could hear the sound of *Azan* (the call to prayer) from a mosque nearby. Then Muhammad Reza said, "Thank You, Jesus, for this new birth." After the prayer there was a rest in his voice.

A woman in Switzerland is visited by Jesus and saved.

This woman kept praying to the prophet Jesus and calling His name. One night she had a dream. She saw Jesus with Moses and saw that Jesus was exalted above Moses. Jesus said to her, "Woman, why do you keep calling Me?"

"Prophet Jesus, I love You, and I need Your help," she responded.

Jesus told her that she could not come to Him unless she was dressed like the rest of the people. Fatemeh looked around and saw that everyone was dressed in white linen. She asked the Lord, "How can I get such a dress?" Jesus told her to read one of the books of the Old Testament (Exodus 40).

She had never heard about such a book (Exodus) in the Farsi language before. When she woke up, she called her nominal Christian friend and asked her if there was such a book in the Bible. Her friend told her that there was a book in the Old Testament by that name. She was able to get a Bible and anxiously looked for the book that Jesus had told her to read.

To her amazement, she found the book of the Bible and the chapter where it was written about the holy garment of Aaron. She asked her friend how she could find such a garment. "It is impossible!" her friend told her. She kept asking around with no avail. Then one day she came across our program. It was Monday morning when she called, and that day I answered the phone. She asked me if I knew how to find such a robe.

"Yes, I do," I answered her assuredly. I told her where that dress was. I opened my Bible and read Revelation 19:7–8 for her. As I shared with her, she wept and finally accepted Jesus as her Lord and Savior. Praise God!

A woman's daughter is healed, and she is saved in Shiraz, Iran.

A woman called and asked for prayer for healing of her daughter in Tehran. "Sir, please help; my daughter's kidneys have shut down!" I told her that she needed to believe. "I believe!" she said firmly. I said to her that her Muslim kind of faith in Jesus is not enough, she must believe in Jesus as Lord and Savior. She kept insisting that she had a great love for Jesus, but that she couldn't deny Islam yet. "Let me see His power first," she said and continued begging me to pray. Finally I gave in and prayed.

The woman called me a couple of days later and told me that her daughter was miraculously healed that same night. Her doctor had a nightmare that night about not knowing what to do to help this woman.

The following day the woman was completely healed, and the doctor said that it was only by a miracle. She and her other daughter both accepted Jesus as their Lord and Savior.

God's Light in the Darkness of Islam

Numerous people who call us come to the Lord together with their entire immediate family. We have prayed over the phone with as many as twenty-two family members all gathered together in one room praying the prayer of salvation on their knees.

One such family who accepted the Lord soon after we began broadcasting now has forty family members who have come to the Lord! To God be all the glory.

Together with the other evangelical Christian ministries that are reaching into Iran through satellite TV and radio broadcasting, the light of the gospel of freedom through Jesus Christ our Lord is reaping a harvest. The religion of Islam has held a grip on Iran for more than fifteen hundred years. But today thousands of Iranian and Afghan people have come to Christ as a result of these broadcasts.

Yet violent persecution continues, and conversion to Christianity during the last decade has resulted in beating, imprisonment, torture, and even execution. It is possible that some of these Muslim converts will pay the ultimate price of martyrdom for their beliefs, as we read earlier in this chapter. But despite the risks, Iran's Christian soldiers are rising up in strength and are hungry to learn more about Jesus. They have learned the truth, and the truth has set them free and created a vibrant, underground movement that is spreading the light of God in this land once dominated by the darkness of Islam.

10

Dreams and Visions in Iran

O ne of the ways that God has chosen to communicate the message of the gospel to the Iranian people is through dreams and visions. This is the fulfillment of Isaiah's declaration:

> So shall He sprinkle many nations.
> Kings shall shut their mouths at Him;
> For what had not been told them they shall see,
> And what they had not heard they shall consider.
>
> —ISAIAH 52:15

A great majority of the thousands of converts who are coming to Christ in Iran have had a dream or vision from the Lord. At times the Lord Jesus Himself has appeared to them and spoken with them. Antioch Ministries in San Jose, California, which reports fifty thousand Iranian Muslim conversions through its satellite TV ministry begun in 2002, reports: "Almost 50 percent of those who call the office have had a dream about Jesus."[1]

Pastor Matt Beemer of World Harvest Bible Church in Manchester, England, in an e-mail to our office, explains two of the reasons Iranians are so open to hearing from God through dreams and visions. "Many Iranians have visions and dreams. It seems much more so than what I see among other people groups. I believe one reason is because their culture is very story based, and this is one of the best ways for God to communicate with them. Another reason is that it seems right now is a very special season of God's grace among the Iranian people throughout the world."

The Islamic faith is so engraved in the hearts and souls of the Muslim people that it often takes a supernatural manifestation of God to convince them about the Lordship of Jesus Christ. To Muslims, Islam is a complete system that encompasses every aspect of their lives, particularly the way they think. Islam is absolute in its teaching about Jesus Christ. Over and over again, the Quran states that Jesus was no more than a prophet.

> *Christ the son of Mary was no more than a Messenger*; many were the Messengers that passed away before him. His mother was a woman of truth. They had both to eat their (daily) food. See how Allah makes His Signs clear to them; yet see in what ways they are deluded away from the truth!
>
> —SURAH 5:75, EMPHASIS ADDED

Islam not only teaches that Jesus was only a prophet, but also that to believe otherwise is blasphemy and an unpardonable sin. It is so dogmatic in its theology that it goes a step further and puts a curse on all those who believe that Jesus was the Son of God.

> The Jews call 'Uzair a son of Allah, and the Christians call Christ the Son of Allah [God]. That is a saying from their mouth; (in this) they but imitate what the Unbelievers of old used to say. *Allah's curse be on them*: how they are deluded away from the Truth!
>
> —SURAH 9:30, EMPHASIS ADDED

With this falsehood engraved in the souls of Muslims, how can one convince them that Jesus was the Son of God? This is why miracles and the manifestation of the Spirit of God are absolute necessities for a successful ministry among Muslims. It is interesting to me that every single Iranian convert who sees Jesus in a dream or a vision knows without a shadow of a doubt that the One in the dream or vision was actually Jesus. In other words, they do not confuse Him with Muhammad or one of their Imams.

Dreams and Visions in the Old Testament

The Bible tells us about dreams and visions. The Book of Job has a wonderful passage of explanation about the way God uses visions and dreams:

> For God may speak in one way, or in another,
> Yet man does not perceive it.
> In a dream, in a vision of the night,

When deep sleep falls upon men,
While slumbering on their beds,
Then He opens the ears of men,
And seals their instruction.
In order to turn man from his deed,
And conceal pride from man,
He keeps back his soul from the Pit,
And his life from perishing by the sword.

—JOB 33:14–18

We have many examples in Scripture of dreams and visions that God used to reveal Himself to His people. Paul (Saul) had a vision of Jesus near the city of Damascus, which resulted in his conversion. (See Acts 9:1–5.) Cornelius, a Gentile centurion, had a vision of an angel who told him to send for Peter and listen to Peter's message. This resulted in the conversion of Cornelius and his entire family. (See Acts 10.)

In the Old Testament, from time to time God protected His people from harm and communicated His message to them, and also to the Gentiles, through visions and dreams.

God showed Jacob in a dream that He was blessing him by supernaturally changing the genetic makeup of his herd. (See Genesis 31.) God warned Laban, Jacob's father-in-law, not to treat Jacob unjustly because God's hand was upon him to carry the seed of the Messiah.

Dreams and Visions in Iran

Through one of our weekly Nejat broadcasts, a young girl by the name of Leila, from a religious family in the city of Shiraz, accepted Jesus as her Lord and Savior. She began witnessing to her family immediately after her conversion, which is often the case with new converts.

Her sister, Nasrin, who lives in Tehran, resisted her greatly. So also did her father. Her mother, after watching our program, was the only other family member who accepted Jesus.

Her father entered into a temporary marriage, which is a practice permitted by Islamic *sharia* law in Iran. His action brought great doubt and confusion to the entire family. Leila telephoned me to ask me to pray for her dad and her entire family. I assured her that God would touch her entire family if she continued to believe God for them.

A few weeks later, Leila's sister, Nasrin, saw our program from Tehran. God touched her during the program. When we talked by phone, she told me, "I was so shaken by the content of your program and wept through almost the entire half-hour show." That day Nasrin accepted Jesus, and she became on fire for Jesus. Before her conversion she could not stand her sister talking about Jesus, but now she herself cannot stop talking about Jesus all the time to her friends and colleagues.

As Leila and Nasrin continued to witness to their family members, more and more family members came to Christ—except Leila's dad. One day as they were all watching our program, *Roz-e-Nejat* (*Day of Salvation*), Leila's father challenged my offer at the end of our program. At the end of each program I ask people to touch their TV sets for a point of contact so that as I am praying God may touch their bodies for healing. Leila's father laid his hand on the TV set and began mocking my words: "See, nothing is happening; this man is a charlatan...." He continued on that line of thought.

That night Leila's father had a dream. In the dream, Jesus appeared to him and began speaking with him. But he couldn't understand a word of what Jesus was saying. Then he saw me standing by the side of Jesus and interpreting the words of Jesus into the Farsi language for him. He woke up from the dream very afraid. When he went back to sleep, the exact same dream was repeated three times. When he woke up the third time, he got out of his bed, got down on his knees, repented and accepted Jesus as his Lord and Savior. There was a great joy in that family for his salvation.

I once witnessed to a Muslim from Morocco. He was not convinced that Jesus could wash his sins away. However, he was very interested in seeing me again and talking some more about Jesus.

The next day I met with him again. He told me, "Last night I had a dream! I saw myself drowning in the sea. I cried out to God, and a man came down from heaven who was dressed in white, shining clothes. I could not see the man's face, but he stretched out his hands to save me and pulled me out of the water."

"My friend," I said, "Jesus is the One who pulled you up out of the water. He is showing you that He will pull you out of your sin and save your life." Because of his dream and my explanation, this man from Morocco was finally able to understand the gospel, and he accepted the Lord into his heart.

Sometimes through a dream God shows the promotion that awaits His people. Joseph, Jacob's son, had several dreams in which he saw that his father and mother and his brothers would bow before him. (See Genesis 37.) It was not proper for Joseph to share that dream with his family, since he was the youngest brother. Yet his dream revealed God's plan for Jacob and his household of seventy-two people to be delivered from the famine that would strike the land of Israel. Joseph's dreams and his ability to interpret dreams brought him before Pharaoh and secured the highest position in Pharaoh's kingdom. (See Genesis 37; 40.) In a dream God showed Pharaoh about the seven years of prosperity and famine in his land, which led to the migration of Israel to Egypt. (See Genesis 41.)

One of the Persian workers at Pastor Matthew Beemer's church in Manchester, England, passed along the following testimony about a significant dream of a man in Iran:

> A middle-aged couple who had fled to Manchester, England, from northwest Iran became believers in Jesus Christ and were baptized in water. Their asylum case was closed, and the judge said they were not refugees but illegal immigrants. After about four months of faithful attendance at the church, we prayed and believed God for intervention for their visa. Suddenly a four-year visa was issued. This was not the first miracle that God performed.
>
> I used to go to fellowship with them once or twice a week and prayed with them. We read the Bible and shared the Word of God. They told me about their son in Turkey, who they needed to join them. They had not seen this son for more than two years.
>
> While in prayer, Jesus told me that the son would return in seven days' time, and I declared this to them. That same night the father had a dream in which Jesus told him that his son would be in the UK in seven days. Exactly seven days later the only son of this family, aged nineteen, arrived in the UK.
>
> We rejoiced in the Lord and thanked Him for His faithfulness.

Dreams and Visions to Gentiles

In the Bible, God sometimes had to speak His Word to His people through their enemies because His people had more faith in the words of their enemies than in the words of God. That was certainly the case with Abraham and Gideon. In both cases God spoke in a dream to the Gentile nations and warned them about His people.

After Abraham lied about his relationship with Sarah, telling the Gentile king Abimelech that she was his sister and not his wife, God warned Abimelech in a dream about Sarah. (See Genesis 20.) Why did Abraham lie? He was afraid that Abimelech would kill him because he had a beautiful wife. What happened to God's promise to him for his protection?

In the case of Gideon, God had to give a dream to a Midianite, Israel's enemy, to motivate Gideon to action. (See Judges 7.) Gideon was too weak in his faith to believe the Word of God by himself. He had to go to the enemy camp and hear the dream and its interpretation out of the mouth of his enemy to believe that he would win the battle against them.

God often works the same way with His people today. How often do we Christians wait to fully trust God until after we have heard through the mouth of a non-Christian doctor, business associate, or lawyer what He has already told us?

In the Book of Daniel we see several dreams through which God exalted His people and revealed His plan for the future of Israel and the Gentile nations.

A few weeks prior to our crusade in 1991 in Karakul, a city located in eastern Kyrgyzstan near the border of China, God revealed Himself through dreams to two Kyrgiz men, both Muslims. In the dream, an angel of the Lord told each man that in the month of May a man would conduct some meetings in the football stadium. "Go and listen to the message he brings," the angel said.

One of them, a young man, found out about the crusade through our coordinator. This young man was hungry for God, and he accepted Jesus during our crusade. He is now one of the key helpers in the church in that city. His family also accepted Jesus eventually.

The other young man also accepted Christ and joined the church that was started after our crusade.

The Bible also tells us about visions. While *dreams* are the revealed will of God in our unconscious state, *visions* take place when we are awake. A vision can be an *open vision*, which is what you would see with your naked eyes—as real as watching something on TV or in a movie. A vision can also take place in a state of being that is known as a *trance*.

In Acts 9, Paul had an open vision on the road to Damascus.

> And Saul, yet breathing out threatenings and slaughter against the disciples of the Lord, went unto the high priest, and desired of him letters to Damascus to the synagogues, that if he found any of this way, whether they were men or women, he might bring them bound unto Jerusalem. And as he journeyed, he came near Damascus: and suddenly there shined round about him a light from heaven: And he fell to the earth, and heard a voice saying unto him, Saul, Saul, why persecutest thou me? And he said, Who art thou, Lord? And the Lord said, I am Jesus whom thou persecutest: it is hard for thee to kick against the pricks. And he trembling and astonished said, Lord, what wilt thou have me to do? And the Lord said unto him, Arise, and go into the city, and it shall be told thee what thou must do. And the men which journeyed with him stood speechless, hearing a voice, but seeing no man. And Saul arose from the earth; and when his eyes were opened, he saw no man: but they led him by the hand, and brought him into Damascus. And he was three days without sight, and neither did eat nor drink.
>
> —ACTS 9:1–9, KJV

So you see, here Paul heard the voice of Jesus and saw a bright light. Paul was wide awake when this took place. He was very conscious of his surroundings.

I know of an Iranian man who was arrested by the Iraqis and put in jail. After three years of torture, he decided to commit suicide and obtained some pills in prison. Just as he was preparing to take the pills and end his life, he heard an audible voice from heaven tell him, "Call upon the name of Jesus." The voice repeated this message three times.

Finally, in desperation, the man said, "Jesus." Later, that man told me, "When I said, 'Jesus,' something lifted from my heart. I felt lighter."

He threw the pills away and later was released from prison. He traveled to Sweden and lived in a refugee camp. One of the people from our ministry team found him there and told him about the gospel. When he heard the name *Jesus*, he exclaimed, "I know Him! I accepted Him." We discipled him, and he continues to serve the Lord.

In Acts chapter 10 we see a different type of vision, one in which the body becomes senseless to its natural surroundings, almost like an ecstasy.

On the morrow, as they went on their journey, and drew nigh unto the city, Peter went up upon the housetop to pray about the sixth hour: And he became very hungry, and would have eaten: but while they made ready, he fell into a trance, and saw heaven opened, and a certain vessel descending unto him, as it had been a great sheet knit at the four corners, and let down to the earth: Wherein were all manner of fourfooted beasts of the earth, and wild beasts, and creeping things, and fowls of the air. And there came a voice to him, Rise, Peter; kill, and eat. But Peter said, Not so, Lord; for I have never eaten any thing that is common or unclean. And the voice spake unto him again the second time, What God hath cleansed, that call not thou common. This was done thrice: and the vessel was received up again into heaven.

—ACTS 10:9–16, KJV

John Gill's *Exposition of the Bible* describes the trance of Peter with these words:

He fell into a trance; or an ecstasy, or an ecstasy fell upon him; it was what was supernatural, and came from above, and did not arise from any natural cause in him; he was as it were out of the body, and entirely in the spirit; all the bodily organs and senses were shut up, and all sensible objects removed from him; and he was wholly intent on what was proposed to him in the vision, which filled him with wonder and astonishment.[2]

Several former Muslims have seen visions as I baptized them. I baptized one Muslim convert, a young woman, in a retreat camp outside the city of Stockholm, Sweden. When she came up out of the water she just stared into the air as if she were in a trance. I couldn't see what she was focusing on, so I asked her, "What is happening?"

She said, "I see the Lord in the water with us, and He is talking to me."

It is important to understand that when a Muslim experiences a dream or vision, he takes it very seriously. Muslims do not believe that Allah gives dreams or communicates with people, so when something like that happens to one of them, it is really out of the ordinary. They talk about it all the time.

J. Christy Wilson Jr., a veteran missionary to the Muslim world, related the following story:

In July of 1991, John Wimber [of Vineyard Ministries] ministered at Gordon-Conwell Theological Seminary. In the last service he asked all to pray silently and to ask the Lord to glorify Himself through us. I prayed that God would use my wife and me to reach Muslims with signs and wonders. As the meeting ended, I thanked John for coming. He told me the Holy Spirit had shown him my request. "You were asking God to use you with signs and wonders to reach Muslims, weren't you?" "Yes, exactly," I replied. "The Lord had heard," he said, "and is going to answer your prayer."

Though Dr. Wilson has gone home to the Lord, the Lord is definitely using signs and wonders, dreams and visions to reach the Muslim world.

Since Bible days, God has used people's dreams and visions to lead, guide, and warn His people about their lives. The Bible contains nearly two hundred references to dreams and visions.

A report by the Southern Baptist International Mission Board, titled "Bleeding Edge," indicates that a common feature among former Muslims who converted to Christianity is the fact that God moves into their lives through signs, miracles, dreams, visions, and wonders. It is not surprising, then, that God would use dreams and visions, such as were used to bring individuals to Himself in the Bible, to bring Muslims to Himself today. In lands where people have never seen the words of God in written form, God is still speaking to them and revealing Himself to them through dreams and visions. It is not the only way for Him to reach them, but case after case shows that it is one way. Missionaries have a choice to either ignore the reality or dare to believe and ask that God would invade their friends' dreams, too, and reveal the truth of Jesus Christ to them as He has done in the lives of countless individuals.

11

The Challenge to the Church

The church of Jesus Christ is, I believe, one of the greatest revelations of God to mankind. The church is today what Jesus was when He walked in His physical body on the earth. God manifested His will and plan through what Jesus said and did while He walked on the earth. When Jesus ascended on high, the Holy Spirit descended, and on the Day of Pentecost, the church of Jesus Christ was born. Through the church God can manifest Himself to the world. Aside from the church, there are no institutions or organizations on this planet that have the ability and the knowledge to manifest the will and the plan of God for mankind. The church is it. The Bible declares a very strong statement about the mission of the church:

> But if I am delayed, I write so that you may know how you ought to conduct yourself in the house of God, which is the church of the living God, the pillar and ground of the truth.
>
> —1 TIMOTHY 3:15

The church is "the pillar and ground of the truth." In other words, the church is the foundation, keeper, and supporter of the truth. Without the church, the knowledge of men is hollow ground—it is sinking sand. God has ordained that His manifold wisdom may be manifested through His church (Eph. 3:10). Jesus said, "You [the believers—the church] are the salt of the earth." He also said that the church is the light of the world (Matt. 5:13–14). Salt preserves, and light illuminates. We are to declare and manifest the truth and preserve it, keep it from contamination of the world. If the church fails to do so, then consequently it is not operating for what it was birthed. Jesus said, "You are the salt of the earth; but if the salt loses its flavor, how shall it be seasoned? It is then good for nothing but to be thrown out and trampled underfoot by men" (Matt. 5:13).

Notice what Jesus says happens when we lose our ability to operate for what we were born: "It is then good for nothing." This kind of church is nothing but piles of dirt and human traditions, good only to be mocked by the world.

When it comes to the Muslim world, what is the church's responsibility? Well, according to the words of Jesus, we must first proclaim the truth to them (*illumination*). We must also keep the gospel truths among them (*preservation*). Fifteen hundred years have passed since Muhammad declared that he was the last prophet of God. There are 1.3 billion Muslims on this planet. Looking at the demographics of church missions, one will soon notice that the Islamic world has been definitely neglected. It is no surprise that the Islamic world mocks Christianity in the West. It is no wonder that people in Islamic nations believe that all the people in the Western Hemisphere are followers of Jesus Christ. What a misconception! I wonder where they collected such a wrong impression!

If you go to Iran today, tens of thousands of Muslims will tell you what Christianity is all about—salvation, healing, manifestation of God's power. Why is their perception of Christianity completely different than that of the rest of the Muslim world? One reason is because they have seen and heard the true gospel of Jesus Christ from our TV broadcasts for the past three years. Nejat TV continuously receives calls from sick people in Iran who have not yet seen our TV programs but have been told by their Muslim family members that if they call our office in America they can be healed from their sicknesses.

Why weren't they referred to the orthodox churches in Iran? It is simply because those churches do not preach Jesus Christ as healer and savior of the Muslim people. Almost all the people who are being converted to Christianity because of TV programs that are broadcasting the gospel have wanted to know more about Christianity and have visited orthodox churches in Iran as a result. Because they have no knowledge of the church situation, these Muslims think that all Christians are the same. Thus after watching our programs for a few times, they make a church visit to get more information about the Christian faith.

However, nearly every single one of these orthodox churches in Iran has refused to receive these Muslims. The priests tell them that their church is for *Christians* and that *Muslims* are not allowed to come in. The Muslims then call us and ask us why they aren't allowed in the church. Well, it is because those are not real churches. They have a form of Christianity but not the Christ! The truth is very clear, like the light of the day. The Bible says, "For God so *loved* the *world*" (John 3:16, emphasis added). That world includes Muslims. Consequently, if you refuse the gospel to Muslims, then you are not preaching the God of the Bible! The orthodox church in Iran is merely busying itself keeping the customs and traditions of their forefathers.

Jesus said that if we follow Him, He will make us fishers of men (Matt. 4:19). If a believer—or a church—is really alive in Christ, that person or church will be responding to the harvest of God by fishing for men. Following Jesus and having a desire for the souls of men *go hand in hand.* They are knit together—one follows the other. Therefore we can ask the question: if a person has no desire for souls, is he or she truly following Jesus?

We are the salt of the earth and the light of the world, yet the Islamic world has been neglected. I believe that the recent uprising of radical Islam throughout the world is a cry within the souls of the Islamic world for the salvation of God. The level of hunger that we have been hearing and seeing coming out of Iran for the truth of the gospel of Jesus Christ is absolutely astonishing. An example of this is what I experienced recently in a leadership training conference for Iranian believers held in Turkey. We had six teaching sessions per day, and each lasted up to an hour and a half. In addition to this, we had two prayer meetings each day. From 7:30 in the morning to 9:30 at night, I was literally swamped by these new believers. They did not give me a moment's peace to myself! They were like sponges soaking up every moment and every word, hungering for the truth of God's Word. This hunger must be fed—but by whom? If not the church of the living God, who then is able to feed them the bread of life?

God has laid a massive responsibility on the church. Paul says it in 2 Corinthians 5:

> Now all things are of God, who has reconciled us to Himself through Jesus Christ, and has given us the ministry of reconciliation, that is, that God was in Christ reconciling the world to Himself, not imputing their trespasses to them, and has committed to us the word of reconciliation.
>
> Now then, we are ambassadors for Christ, as though God were pleading through us: we implore you on Christ's behalf, be reconciled to God. For He made Him who knew no sin to be sin for us,

that we might become the righteousness of God in Him.
                                              —2 CORINTHIANS 5:18–21

God reconciled the world to Himself and has given us "the word of reconciliation" and also "the ministry of reconciliation." In other words, God has done His part; now we must do ours. Our part is almost as important as His, because if people never have a chance to hear that God has made the provision of salvation through Christ Jesus, it is as though it has never happened for them. The word or the ministry of reconciliation is as important as the work of reconciliation itself. Paul stresses this fact by saying, "We are ambassadors for Christ, as though God were pleading through us." Listen to what he says: God is pleading through us. Isn't that amazing? God has made us copartners with His Son in this great plan of salvation for mankind. Glory be to God.

God is not slack in His doings. If we do not respond to His calling, He will lay it on others who are able to carry such a great responsibility. We are privileged to be partakers of the gospel. This is not a matter of choice. It has been given to us by the Most High. Will we carry it?

In 1990, the Lord spoke to me about the former Soviet republics in Central Asia, such as Azerbaijan, Kyrgyzstan, and Kazakhstan. The Lord told me that I had four years before the doors to these states would be closed for mass crusades. Communist Russia had oppressed Islam for the past seventy years in these states, but now we had an open window before these states became independent and returned to their roots. That four-year period was the window. I was able to do four crusades in Kyrgyzstan and Kazakhstan before the doors were completely closed on public meetings. In one of our crusades in Kyrgyzstan, thousands of Muslims were saved and several churches were founded as a result of that crusade in the city of Karakul. How I wish I had been able to do more, but unfortunately, I couldn't raise enough support. Today Kyrgyzstan is an Islamic state and prohibits evangelism.

An Awakening Time

The church as a whole has denied the Islamic world. Because of persecution, hardship, or whatever our reason may be, we have neglected the proclamation of the truth of the gospel to one-fifth of the world's population. The gospel must be preached into all the world as a witness to all groups of people before the end can come (Matt. 24:14). All nations (people groups) have not heard the gospel; therefore, Jesus cannot come for His church. What does God do then?

Among all the forces that Satan has raised against the church and God's people throughout history, Islam, it seems, has been the most successful of them all. Islam feeds upon violence, bloodshed, and fear. And since it has a strong religious covering, it has penetrated the hearts of millions of people—1.3 billion people to be exact.

The gospel has been proclaimed to almost all groups of people, except the Muslim world. It is safe to assume that Islam is the last frontier before the return of Jesus. I believe that September 11 marked the beginning of the last chapter of human history before the return of God's Holy Son. Two questions remain: What is ahead for the history of the church? And how is the church going to break through the Islamic walls raised before us?

In my spirit, I foresee the fall of several nations into the hands of radical Islam. These nations are Saudi Arabia, Pakistan, Egypt, and Algeria. I wish that I knew the timing of it, but I do not. I just know that the earth is about to be shaken with these powers, which are becoming more and more visible. Are we ready for what is ahead?

The United States knew the threat of radical Islam, but it was not ready for the September 11 tragedy. What would happen if a radical Muslim group could explode an atomic bomb on a key city in the Western Hemisphere? What would be the outcome of such an incident? What would happen if that ever took place on our soil? Can we recover from such a disaster?

September 11 was a wake-up call for the church and for the people outside of the church. The people outside of God's covenant always live in reaction to things. We, the church, must live by faith and the foreknowledge of the truth. After September 11, most people were afraid of traveling. But I knew it was the safest time for traveling because I knew how radical Muslims think. I knew they would not strike again so soon.

Knowledge produces safety and soundness. A thief comes at night, when everyone is asleep. The Bible says:

> But know this, that if the master of the house had known what hour the thief would come, he would have watched and not allowed his house to be broken into.
>
> —LUKE 12:39

The enemy strikes when we are not watching. We do not live by senses but by faith. The way of faith says that now is an acceptable time, and today is the day of salvation.

Seize the Time

The time for the Muslim world is here. The harvest in these nations is ripening and in some, like Iran, is already starting to be gathered. What do we do?

The start of our Nejat TV broadcasts in Iran and the efforts of a handful of other ministries reaching in Iran have signaled the first time in the history of the church that we are seeing a breakthrough in an Islamic nation. Not just any nation—rather one of the most forceful radical Islamic nations on the earth.

But the fields are white unto harvest in these Islamic nations. Where are the workers? What must take place before we recognize that God is demanding a harvest from the Islamic nations? The Iraq war is an indication that politics alone cannot deal with the Islamic world. The daily news of Islamic suicide bombers is awakening us to the challenge that lies before us. The time to take action in the Islamic world is here.

I have a constant burden for the church in Iran. God is moving gloriously in Iran, and tens of thousands of Muslims are converting to the faith of the gospel of God. But there are no churches or pastors to take care of them. Like the apostle Paul, who told the Corinthian church that a "great and effective door has opened" (1 Cor. 16:9) for him in Macedonia, I see the great and effective door opening in Iran.

The church—you and I—must become workers in this great harvest. We must find the resources to train and disciple these Muslim converts and send them back into the harvest to bring more into the kingdom of God. It doesn't take much to do a great work for God, just a few willing and submitted vessels. This great open window in Iran, one of the strongest Muslim nations in the world, is the first example of the fall of Islam.

Let me give a couple of suggestions that will help you to see this great opportunity and to seize it.

1. Form a prayer meeting in your church or home group and begin to pray for the following:

- Pray for laborers for this massive harvest in Iran, and other Arab nations, especially for more pastors.

- Pray for an outpouring of God's Spirit in the Muslim nations with signs and wonders.

- Pray for the underground church in Muslim countries.

- Pray for the establishment of more Christian satellite TV stations in the native languages of the Muslim nations, such as Turkish, Azeri, and Arabic, and for newly established TV broadcasts like Nejat TV.

- Pray for the development of leaders in the church, especially those from a Muslim background, and for leadership training materials, Bibles, and teaching materials. (Bibles are scarce in Iran since the Iranian government shut down the Bible society's office.)

- Pray for the home groups forming all around the country of Iran as a result of TV broadcasts.

- Pray for wisdom for our political leaders in dealing with radical Muslims.

- Pray that God would expose the darkness of the Islamic faith and that the spirit of blindness over the Muslim nations would be broken.

2. Take the following steps to getting involved:

- Support outreaches among the Muslims, such as Nejat TV, that are fruitful and that establish the church.

- As led by God, respond to opportunities to go or send others into Muslim nations as they open to foreign assistance.

We live in an incredible time, a time when we will see the glorious manifestation of sons of God. Paul, by the Spirit of God, writes to the church in Rome:

> For I consider that the sufferings of this present time are not worthy to be compared with the glory which shall be revealed in us. For the earnest expectation of the creation eagerly waits for the revealing of the sons of God.
>
> —Romans 8:18–19

There are millions of people who would do anything to hear the good news of Jesus Christ. We, the body of Christ, have a great responsibility before our God. One day at the judgment seat of Christ we have to give Him a record of what we have done in the flesh during our earthly life. What are we doing with the gospel of God's Son? I challenge you today to take a bold step and fulfill God's plan. There are multitudes in the valley of decision waiting for your response. Do something for the Muslim world and for His glory.

> Ask of Me, and I will give You
> The nations for Your inheritance,
> And the ends of the earth for Your possession.
>
> —Psalm 2:8

Notes

Introduction

1. "Senate Ready to Up War Aid," October 7, 2005, CBS News, accessed at http://www.cbsnews.com/stories/2005/10/06/iraq/main917420.shtml on March 1, 2006.

2. Ibid.

3. "President Bush Hosts Iftaar [sic] Dinner at White House," Office of the Press Secretary, October 17, 2005, accessed at http://www.whitehouse.gov/news/releases/2005/10/20051017-5.html on March 1, 2006.

4. Joseph Farah, "Healthy Islam-skepticism," Between the Lines, *WorldNet-Daily*, accessed at http://www.worldnetdaily.com/news/article.asp?ARTICLE_ID=35347 on March 1, 2006.

5. Reuters, "Tehran Pulls Its Assets Out of Europe," GulfNews.com, accessed at http://www.gulfnews.com/indepth/irancrisis/more_stories/10013175.html on March 1, 2006.

6. Associated Press, "Iranian President Meets Palestinian Leaders in Syria," FoxNews.com, accessed at http://www.foxnews.com/story/0,2933,182388,00.html on March 1, 2006.

7. "Palestine Liberation Organization," from Wikipedia, the Free Encyclopedia, accessed at http://en.wikipedia.org/wiki/PLO on March 1, 2006.

8. Mitchell Bard, "The Intifada," Jewish Virtual Library, accessed at http://www.jewishvirtuallibrary.org/jsource/History/intifada.html on March 1, 2006.

9. Ibid.

10. Khaled Hroub, *Hamas: Political Thought and Practice* (Washington DC: Institute for Palestine Studies, 2000), 329.

11. "Hamas Sweeps to Election Victory," *BBC News*, January 26, 2006, accessed at http://news.bbc.co.uk/2/hi/middle_east/4650788.stm on March 1, 2006.

12. William Shakespeare, *Julius Caesar*, Act III, Scene ii.

1—God at Work in Iran

1. Arianne Ishaya, PhD, "From Contributions to Diaspora: Assyrians in the History of Urmia, Iran," as viewed at http://www.nineveh.com/Assyrians%20in%20the%20History%20of%20Urmia,%20Iran.html on January 27, 2006. For more about the life of Justin Perkins, see http://famousamericans.net/justinperkins/.

2. Iranian Christians International, Inc., cited in "Keys to the Iranian Heart," InterVarsity International Student Ministries, InterVarsity.org, accessed at http://www.intervarsity.org/ism/article_item.php?article_id=397 on May 5, 2006.

3. William McElwee Miller, *Ten Muslims Meet Christ* (Grand Rapids, MI: Wm. B. Eerdmans Publishing Company, 1984).

4. Julian Lukins, "Behind the Black Veil," *Charisma*, June 2004.

5. "Persecution against Christian Converts in Iran Escalating," posted December 2, 2005, by *Christian Today*, and accessed at http://www.christiantoday.com/news/middle-east/persecution.against.christian.converts.in.iran.escalating/367.htm on December 6, 2005.

6. Ibid.

7. Ibid.

8. Ibid.

9. "ICI Ministry Report: 25 Years," Iranian Christians International (ICI), as viewed at http://www.farsinet.com/ici/ on January 27, 2006.

10. "Church Growth—Islamic Government Has Strengthened Churches," DAWN Friday Fax 1999 #43, accessed at http://www.jesus.org.uk/dawn/1999/dawn9943.html on May 5, 2006.

11. "Iranian Muslims Embracing Christianity in Record Numbers," Press Release from IAM, June 14, 2004, as viewed at http://www.iam-online.net/Press_release_PDFs/IAMTVrelease_FINAL.doc%20(Read-Only).pdf on January 27, 2006.

12. Ibid.

13. Testimony received by IAM and forwarded to Reza Safa for this book. For more information about IAM, go to http://www.iam-online.net/index.html.

14. For more information about Bridging the Gap Ministries and Donald Fareed, go to http://www.persianministries.org.

15. "Iran's Underground Church Grows Amid Persecution," *Maranatha Christian Journal*, as viewed at http://www.mcjonline.com/news/04a/20040811b.shtml on January 27, 2006.

16. Ibid.

17. "ICI Ministry Report: 25 Years."

18. For more information about Pastor Kourosh Barani or the Toronto Iranian Christian Church please go to http://www.farsinet.com/iactoronto.

19. The testimony of Amir was adapted from information Amir sent to our ministry at Harvester's World Outreach.

20. Homa's testimony was given in a phone conversation with a *Roz-e-Nejat* phone counselor.

21. The story of Mostafa's healing came to us as a result of their first phone message on October 30, 2003, and subsequent telephone conversations.

22. For more information about Pastor Matt Beemer or World Harvest Bible

Church in Manchester, England, go to http://www.goyewhbc.com.

2—The Spirit of Islam

1. Abdullah Yusuf Ali, *The Meaning of the Holy Qur'an* (Bartesville, MD: Amana Corporation, 2001), 208.

2. "Demographics of Islam," from Wikipedia, the Free Encyclopedia, as viewed at http://en.wikipedia.org/wiki/Demographics_of_Islam on February 1, 2006.

3. "Shi'ism," Ask the Jamiat, Jamiat.org, as viewed at http://www.jamiat.org .za/isinfo/shi.html on June 9, 2006.

4. For a brief, concise history of Islam that expands upon the history in this book, see "Islam," *CQ Press in Context,* as viewed at http://www.cqpress.com/ context/articles/epr_islam.html on February 2, 2006, and excerpted from the *Encyclopedia of Politics and Religion,* ed. Robert Wuthnow, 2 vols. (Washington DC: Congressional Quarterly, Inc., 1998), 383–393.

5. Much of this history is adapted from Reza Safa, *Inside Islam* (Lake Mary, FL: Charisma House, 1996), 29–32.

6. Robin Wright, *Sacred Rage: The Wrath of Militant Islam* (New York: Simon and Schuster, 1985), 99.

7. Ibid., 83–84.

8. Mark A. Gabriel, PhD, *Journey Into the Mind of an Islamic Terrorist* (Lake Mary, FL: FrontLine, 2006), 97.

9. "Sahih Bukhari," from Wikipedia, the Free Encyclopedia, as viewed at http://en.wikipedia.org/wiki/Sahih_Bukhari on June 8, 2006. *Sahih al-Bukhari* [The Correct Books of Bukhari], English translation by Dr. Muhammad Muhasin Khan, USC-MSA Compendium of Muslim Texts, University of Southern California, can be accessed at http://www.usc.edu/dept/MSA/fundamentals/ hadithsunnah/bukhari/.

10. Hadith No. 1095, accessed at Al Islam, http://hadith.al-islam.com/bayan/ Display.asp?Lang=eng&ID=1095 on June 9, 2006.

11. Hadith No. 1099, accessed at Al Islam, http://hadith.al-islam.com/bayan/ Display.asp?Lang=eng&ID=1099 on June 9, 2006.

12. Hadith No. 1104, accessed at Al Islam, http://hadith.al-islam.com/bayan/ Display.asp?Lang=eng&ID=1104 on June 9, 2006.

13. Hadith No. 11, accessed at Al Islam, http://hadith.al-islam.com/bayan/ Display.asp?Lang=eng&ID=11 on June 9, 2006.

14. Hadith No. 12, accessed at Al Islam, http://hadith.al-islam.com/bayan/ Display.asp?Lang=eng&ID=12 on June 9, 2006.

15. Hadith No. 57, accessed at Al Islam, http://hadith.al-islam.com/bayan/ Display.asp?Lang=eng&ID=57 on May 10, 2006.

16. Nikki R. Keddie, ed., *Religion and Politics in Iran* (New Haven, CN: Yale University Press, 1983), 180–181.

17. Dilip Hiro, *Holy Wars: The Rise of Islamic Fundamentalism* (New York: Routledge, 1989), 63.

18. Wright, *Sacred Rage*, 179.

19. Ibid., 180.

20. Jill Smolowe, "A Voice of Holy War," *TIME*, March 15, 1993, 31–34.

21. Ibid., 33.

22. Wright, *Sacred Rage*, 35.

23. John Cloud, "Atta's Odyssey," *TIME*, October 8, 2001, 67.

24. Wright, *Sacred Rage*, 36.

25. Ibid., 37.

26. Robin Wright, *In the Name of God: The Khomeini Decade* (New York: Simon and Schuster, 1989), 87.

3—America and Iran at Odds

1. Gary Sick, *All Fall Down: America's Tragic Encounter With Iran* (New York: Random House, Inc., 1985), viii.

2. John Hagee, *Jerusalem Countdown* (Lake Mary, FL: FrontLine, 2006), vii.

3. Ibid.

4. Muhammad Mehdi Khorrami, "Iranians in the U.S.," *PBS Online: Beyond the Veil*, as viewed at http://www.internews.org/visavis/BTVPagesTXT/Iranians_in_US.html on February 22, 2006.

5. These statistics were taken from the 2000 census and were published in *Namak*, an English-language magazine covering entertainment, culture, and lifestyle topics for the Persian community. Viewed at http://www.namakmag .com/demographics.html on February 22, 2006.

6. Nicholas Schmidle, "The Paradox of Anti-Americanism in Iran," *The Daily Star* (Lebanon) and viewed at http://www.challenging-islam.org/articles/schmidle .htm on February 22, 2006.

7. Michael A. Palmer, *Guardians of the Gulf: A History of America's Expanding Role in the Persian Gulf, 1833–1992* (New York: Free Press, 1992), 6–7.

8. James A. Bill, *The Eagle and the Lion* (New Haven and London: Yale University Press, 1988), 4, 58; Elton L. Daniel, *The History of Iran* (Westport, CN: Greenwood Press, 2001), 127–129; Nikki R. Keddie, *Modern Iran* (New Haven,

CT and London: Yale University Press, 2003), 23, 73–76.

9. Kenneth M. Pollack, *The Persian Puzzle* (New York: Random House, 2002), 51.

10. Behzad Farsian, "Blame the British for the Problems of Iran," Gulfnews .com, as viewed at http://archive.gulfnews.com/articles/03/12/01/104246.html on February 22, 2006.

11. Muhammad Reza Pahlavi, *Answer to History* (New York: Stein and Day, 1980), 59.

12. Daniel, *The History of Iran*, 131.

13. Ibid., 133.

14. Ibid., 137.

15. Ibid.

16. "Bridge to Victory," *The Iranian*, November 3, 1997, excerpted with permission from "On Borrowed Wings," by Robert D. Burgener, as viewed at http://www.iranian.com/History/Nov97/WWII/index.html on February 23, 2006.

17. Daniel, *The History of Iran*, 143–144.

18. "Declaration of the Three Powers Regarding Iran: December 1, 1943," from Wikipedia, the Free Encyclopedia, as viewed at http://en.wikipedia.org/wiki/Tehran_Conference on February 23, 2006.

19. Daniel, *The History of Iran*, 147–148.

20. Pollack, *The Persian Puzzle*, 52; Stephen Kinzer, *All the Shah's Men* (Hoboken, NJ: John Wiley & Sons, Inc., 2003), 96.

21. Kinzer, *All the Shah's Men*, 134–141.

22. Ibid., 142–149.

23. Ibid., 160.

24. Daniel, *The History of Iran*, 153.

25. Pollack, *The Persian Puzzle*, 65.

26. Ibid.

27. Ibid., 66.

28. Pahlavi, *Answer to History*, 83.

29. Kinzer, *All the Shah's Men*, 167–171.

30. Pollack, *The Persian Puzzle*, 67.

31. Kinzer, *All the Shah's Men*, 204.

32. Pollack, *The Persian Puzzle*, xxv.

33. Ibid., 424.

34. Daniel, *The History of Iran*, 156.

35. Ibid., 146.

36. For a more thorough account of the inequitable conditions in the oil refineries, see Kinzer, *All the Shah's Men,* pages 62–70.

37. Greg Myre, "Hamas and Fatah Try to Reduce Tension After Shoot-out," *International Herald Tribune,* May 8, 2006, 3.

4—The Formation of the Islamic Revolution

1. Daniel, *The History of Iran,* 160.

2. Ibid., see also Pollack, *The Persian Puzzle,* 109.

3. Pollack, *The Persian Puzzle,* 74.

4. Ibid., 119.

5. Nafeez Ahmed, *Behind the War on Terror* (Gabriola Island, BC: New Society Publishers, 2003), 39.

6. Pollack, *The Persian Puzzle,* 124.

7. Kinzer, *All the Shah's Men,* 197.

8. Daniel, *The History of Iran,* 190–191.

9. Ibid.

10. Pollack, *The Persian Puzzle,* 134.

11. Ibid., 154–155.

12. Ibid.

13. Joseph Farah, "Iran President: Terrorist, Murderer," *WorldNetDaily,* Wednesday, August 31, 2005, as viewed at http://www.worldnetdaily.com/news/article.asp?ARTICLE_ID=46060 on February 24, 2006.

14. Daniel, *The History of Iran,* 189.

15. Ibid., 194.

16. "Sadegh Ghotbzadeh," from Wikipedia, the Free Encyclopedia, as viewed at http://en.wikipedia.org/wiki/Sadegh_Ghotbzadeh on February 24, 2006.

17. Sick, *All Fall Down,* viii.

18. Ibid., 293.

19. Ibid., 296–297.

20. Ruhollah Khomeini, *Islam and Revolution I: Writings and Declaration of Imam Khomeini (1941–1980),* Hamid Alqar, translator (Berkeley, CA: Mizan Press, 1981), 55.

21. Ibid., 40.

22. Pollack, *The Persian Puzzle,* 150–151.

23. Daniel, *The History of Iran,* 188.

24. Ibid.

25. Ibid., 208.

26. Pollack, *The Persian Puzzle*, 190.

27. Ervand Abrahamian, *The Iranian Mojahedin* (New Haven, CT: Yale University Press, 1989), 220.

28. Wright, *In the Name of God*, 99.

29. Abrahamian, *The Iranian Mojahedin*, 221.

30. Ibid., 223.

31. Wright, *In the Name of God*, 100.

32. Ibid., 105.

33. Pollack, *The Persian Puzzle*, 185–186.

34. Ibid., 193.

35. Ibid.

36. Bill, *The Eagle and the Lion*, 305.

37. Pollack, *The Persian Puzzle*, 235.

38. Ibid., 241.

5—Muhammad and God at War

1. Iranian Government Constitution, English Text, General Principles, Article 1, accessed at http://www.iranonline.com/iran/iran-info/Government/constitution-1.html on March 2, 2006.

2. Ibid., Article 2.

3. Khomeini, *Islam and Revolution I*, 265–266.

4. Iranian Government Constitution, English Text, General Principles, Articles 13 and 14.

5. International Religious Freedom Report 2004, released by the Bureau of Democracy, Human Rights, and Labor, accessed at http://www.state.gov/g/drl/rls/irf/2004/35497.htm on March 2, 2006.

6. Ibid.

7. Daniel, *The History of Iran*, 185–186.

8. Iran, "Current Church Growth Status," accessed at http://www.acts.edu/oldmissions/Iranhist1.html on March 2, 2006.

9. International Religious Freedom Report 2004.

10. "Haik Hovsepian Mehr," from Wikipedia, the Free Encyclopedia, accessed at http://en.wikipedia.org/wiki/Haik_Hovsepian_Mehr on March 2, 2006.

11. Iran, "Current Church Growth Status."

12. Thomas Sancton, "The Tehran Connection," *TIME*, March 21, 1994, quoted in "The Persecution of Christians in Iran," Jubilee Campaign, accessed at http://www.jubileecampaign.co.uk/world/ira1.htm on March 2, 2006.

13. Reported by Compass Direct, "Iranian Police Arrest Christian Pastor Khosroo Yusefi and His Family," Farsinet.com, accessed at http://www.farsinet .com/dibaj/khosroo_yusefi.html in January 2006.

14. "Islamic Republic of Iran," Operation World, accessed at http://www.gmi .org/ow/country/iran/owtext.html on March 2, 2006.

15. International Religious Freedom Report 2004.

16. "Report 2005: Iran," Amnesty International, accessed at http://web .amnesty.org/report2005/irn-summary-eng on March 2, 2006.

17. Ibid.

18. "Iran—Constitution," International Constitutional Law, accessed at http:// www.oefre.unibe.ch/law/icl/ir00000_.html#I000 on March 2, 2006.

6—America and Islam

1. John H. Haaren, "Charles Martel, A.D. 714–741 and Pepin, A.D. 741–768," *Famous Men of the Middle Ages,* accessed at http://www.authorama.com/famous -men-of-the-middle-ages-11.html on March 15, 2006.

2. Robert Morey, *The Islamic Invasion* (Eugene, OR: Harvest House Publishers, 1992), 36.

3. "Karl Marx," from Wikipedia, the Free Encyclopedia, accessed at http:// en.wikipedia.org/wiki/Karl_Marx on March 15, 2006.

4. Ibid.

5. Sayyid Qutb, *Social Justice in Islam,* translated by Hamid Alqar (Islamic Publications International, 2000), 132.

6. "Imperialism," from Wikipedia, the Free Encyclopedia, accessed at http:// en.wikipedia.org/wiki/Imperialism on March 15, 2006.

7. Qutb, *Social Justice in Islam,* 33.

8. Ibid.

9. Ibid., 131.

10. Jörg Lau, "Who's Afraid of Muhammad," *Sign and Sight,* accessed at http:// www.signandsight.com/features/588.html on March 15, 2006.

11. Ibid.

12. "Gunmen Shut EU Gaza Office Over Cartoons," CNN.com, February 2, 2006, accessed at http://www.cnn.com/2006/WORLD/meast/02/02/gaza

.cartoon/index.html?section=cnn_topstories on February 2, 2006.

13. Qutb, *Social Justice in Islam*.

14. Specific Surah reference unavailable; quoted in Qutb, *Social Justice in Islam*, 71.

15. Qutb, *Social Justice in Islam*.

16. Ibid., 68.

17. Khomeini, *Islam and Revolution I*, 205, 207.

18. Daniel, *The History of Iran*, 190–192.

19. Qutb, *Social Injustice in Islam*, n.p.

20. Stephen Zunes, "Military Response Would Feel Good but Nay [*sic*] Not Work," *USA Today*, September 17, 2001, accessed at http://www.usatoday.com/news/opinion/2001-09-18-ncguest2.htm on March 15, 2006.

21. Ibid.

22. Stephen Zunes, "Should U.S. Forces Strike Back Hard?" *USA Today*, September 18, 2001, 25A.

23. Mark Galli, "Now What?" *Christianity Today*, October 22, 2001, accessed at http://www.christianitytoday.com/ct/2001/138/51.0.html on March 16, 2006.

24. Wright, *Sacred Rage*, 21.

25. Galli, "Now What?"

26. Ibid.

27. Omar Shama, "Bin Laden Praises Terror Strikes; Vows No Security for U.S.," *Tulsa World*, October 8, 2001, A4.

28. Cartoon Body Count, Death by Drawing, accessed at http://www.cartoonbodycount.com/ on March 16, 2006.

29. The Afghanistan Constitution, accessed at http://www.oefre.unibe.ch/law/icl/af00000_.html on March 16, 2006.

30. Ibid.

31. John L. Allen Jr., "Europe's Muslims Worry Bishops," *National Catholic Reporter*, accessed at http://ncronline.org/NCR_Online/archives/102299/102299a.htm on March 16, 2006.

32. Lisa Gardiner, "American Muslim Leader Urges Faithful to Spread Word," *San Ramon Valley Herald*, July 4, 1998, referenced in Douglas J. Hagmann, "Sensitivity Training or Insanity?" from a Homeland Security report dated December 4, 2004, accessed at http://www.co-jet.org/cjet/4files/didyouknow1.htm on March 16, 2006.

33. Jeffrey MacDonald, "Getting the Holy Word Out," *USA Today*, June 2, 2005, D8.

34. "The Arab World Studies Notebook," Audrey Shabbas, editor, *Arab World and Islamic Resources*, accessed at http://www.makanalislam.com/Merchant2/merchant.mv?Screen=PROD&Store_Code=AWAIR&Product_Code=ARAB-WORLD on March 16, 2006.

35. "Islam Studies Required in California District," *WorldNetDaily*, January 11, 2002, accessed at http://www.worldnetdaily.com/news/article.asp?ARTICLE_ID=25997 on March 16, 2006.

36. Ibid.

37. Arab World Studies Notebook, *Middle East Policy Council*, accessed at http://www.mepc.org/workshops/awsn.asp on March 16, 2006.

38. Aryeh Shalev, *The Intifada; Causes and Effects* (Tel Aviv and London: Westview Press, 1991), 13.

39. Khaled Hroub, *Hamas: Political Thought and Practice* (N.p.: Institute for Palestine Studies, 2000), 269.

40. "The Covenant of the Islamic Resistance Movement," August 18, 1988, *MidEast Web*, accessed at http://www.mideastweb.org/hamas.htm on March 16, 2006.

7—The Palestinian Issue

1. James M. Arlandson, "Muhammad and the Jews," accessed at http://answering-islam.org.uk/Authors/Arlandson/jews.htm on March 17, 2006.

2. Ali, *The Meaning of The Holy Qur'an*, 41.

3. Article 22, Paper of the Covenant of the League of Nations, may be accessed at http://www.wzo.org.il/home/politic/mandate2.htm, as viewed on March 17, 2006.

4. The complete text for "The Palestine Mandate of the League of Nations, 1922," may be accessed at http://www.mideastweb.org/mandate.htm, as viewed March 17, 2006.

5. "From the Islamic Resistance Movement, Hamas, Palestine, August 20, 2001," accessed at http://www.jamiat.org.za/palestine/hamas.html on March 17, 2006.

6. Matthew Dorf, "Palestinian Children's Show Sparks Anger in Washington," *Jewish Telegraph Agency*, New York, August 17, 1998, accessed at http://www.satp.org/satporgtp/publication/faultlines/volume16/Article3.htm#26 on March 17, 2006.

7. "Profile: Ariel Sharon," *BBC News*, accessed at http://news.bbc.co.uk/1/hi/

in_depth/middle_east/2001/israel_and_the_palestinians/profiles/1154622.stm on March 17, 2006.

8. "Benjamin Netanyahu's Important Message," September 25, 2001, from a partial transcript from *Hannity & Colmes*, September 24, 2001, accessed at http://www.netanyahu.org/bennetimmes.html on March 17, 2006.

9. "Bush: Palestine State Was Always Part of Mideast Vision," *Jordan Times*, October 3, 2001, accessed at http://www.jordanembassyus.org/10032001004.htm on March 17, 2006.

10. "Arabs Warn Against Wider Attacks," *BBC News*, October 10, 2001, accessed at http://news.bbc.do.uk/1/hi/world/middle_east/1589750.stm on March 17, 2006.

11. Donna Bryson, "Arabs Afraid War Will Expand," *Tulsa World*, October 10, 2001, accessed at http://www.tulsaworld.com/assault/A_4_10_10.pdf on March 17, 2006.

12. Ibid.

13. "Sharon's Victory: What Next?" *BBC News Talking Point*, February 19, 2001, accessed at http://news.bbc.co.uk/1/hi/talking_point/1155983.stm on March 17, 2006.

8—God's Plan for Iran

1. Pahlavi, *Answer to History*, 36.

2. Ibid., 37.

3. Islamic Republic of Iran, *Operation World*, accessed at http://www.gmi.org/ow/country/iran/owtext.html on April 12, 2006.

4. Ali Reza, "Iranians Chant: 'Death to Khamenei,'" *Shia.com News*, accessed at http://www.shianews.com/hi/asia/news_id/0001722.php on April 12, 2006.

9—Iran's Christian Soldiers

1. "Iranian Pastor Moved to Military Prison," Compass Direct, *Open Doors*, accessed at http://odusa.com/ArchiveDisplay.asp?ID=F29A422A-6328-4B44-A305-A466F8745FF3&Category=News on February 21, 2006.

2. "Iran: Concern Mounts for Jailed Iranian Christian; Government Admits Christianity 'Out of Control,'" JihadWatch.org, as viewed at http://www.jihadwatch.org/dhimmiwatch/archives/003488.php on June 9, 2006.

3. David Gollust, "US Cites Eight Countries for Poor Record on Religious Freedom," *News Voice of America* (VOA.com), viewed at http://www.voanews.com/english/2005-11-09-voa2.cfm on February 21, 2006.

4. "Universal Declaration of Human Rights," adopted and proclaimed by

General Assembly resolution 217A (III) of December 10, 1948, as viewed at http://www.un.org/Overview/rights.html on February 21, 2006.

5. "Iran: Country Reports on Human Rights Practices—2001" released by the Bureau of Democracy, Human Rights, and Labor, March 4, 2002, as viewed at http://www.state.gove/g/drl/rls/hrrpt/2001/nea/825l.htm on February 21, 2006.

6. "Haik Martyred," *IISIC Bulletin*, as viewed on February 21, 2006, at http://www.isic-centre.org/Bulletins/94_Apr_May.pdf.

7. The Written Defense of the Rev. Mehdi Dibaj Delivered to the Sari Court of Justice—Sari, Iran, December 3, 1993, as viewed at http://www.farsinet.com/dibaj/ on February 21, 2006.

8. Ibid.

9. "New Evidence of Iranian Government Complicity in Killings," *Jubilee Campaign*, as viewed on February 21, 2006, at http://www.jubileecampaign.co.uk/world/ira7.htm.

10. "Bibles for the Iran Region," *Elam Ministries*, as viewed on February 21, 2006, at http://www.elam.com/articles/Translation/.

11. "Iranian Christians, Who Are They?" Iranian Christians International, as viewed at http://www.farsinet.com/ici/who.html on February 21, 2006. See also http://www.farsinet.com/dibaj/yusefi.html.

12. *Charisma News Service,* June 2005.

13. "Iran: Country Reports on Human Rights Practices—2001," released by the Bureau of Democracy, Human Rights, and Labor, March 4, 2002, and viewed at http://www.state.gov/g/drl/rls/hrrpt/2001/nea/8251.htm on February 22, 2006.

14. Yahya R. Kamalipour, "The Battle of the Airwaves: The Rise and Proliferation of Iranian Satellite TV Channels," *Transnational Broadcasting Studies,* as viewed at http://www.tbsjournal.com/Kamalipour.html on February 22, 2006.

15. Ibid.

10—Dreams and Visions in Iran

1. International Antioch Ministries (IAM) Press Release, accessed December 5, 2005 at http://www.iam-online.net/Press_release_PDFs/IAMTVrelease_FINAL.doc%20(Read-Only).pdf. Ellie Davidian, who heads the call center for Antioch Ministries, reported the information about dreams and visions.

2. John Gill's 10-volume *Exposition of the Bible* was first published in 1746–1766. It may be accessed today at http://www.freegrace.net/gill.

Index

Leadership Training School

The great outpouring of God's Spirit in Iran has resulted in the conversion of tens of thousands of Muslims. This ongoing influx of new converts has given rise to a great need for discipleship. The majority of these new believers are left on their own because there are no local churches to care for them. Since the beginning of our TV outreach in Iran in 2003, we have conducted short-term training schools for the believers in a country outside of Iran. We are now in the process of building a permanent Bible school and training Iranian pastors and leaders. These believers will become the leaders of the future of the Islamic world.

We need your prayers and support in this massive project. For more information, please contact our office at (918) 488-9645 or e-mail us at reza@rezasafa.com.

TBN Nejat TV

About ten years ago, the Lord spoke to me about the future of the Middle East and a great revival that will take place there. Part of that vision was a TV ministry that would bring forth the gospel to millions upon millions of unreached Muslims. At that time I had no knowledge whatsoever of satellite TV, yet TV ministry became a reality for us four years ago. After reading how we started Nejat TV, one must admit that this is a miracle and a great work of God. Satellite TV is being aired in the areas in the Middle East where no one and no other means have the possibility of reaching out with the gospel of Jesus Christ to the masses of unreached people. This is an open door by God. No governments or religious organizations can close this door. It is truly an open door for the gospel of God. I believe that in a few short years, we will see millions of Muslims convert to Christ through TBN Nejat TV and other Christian TV networks in the Middle East who preach a pure gospel message. To God be all glory forever.

I would like to encourage you to be a part of this great harvest machine that God has given to His church. For more information on TBN Nejat TV, please call us at (918) 488-9645 or visit our Web site: www.rezasafa.com.

Other Publications by Reza F. Safa

Books

The Rise and Fall of Islam
Inside Islam
Blood of the Sword, Blood of the Cross
Islam Awareness Seminar Handbook
The New Birth (Farsi)
Baptism in the Holy Spirit (Farsi)

Videos

"Day of Salvation" teaching programs
(Farsi), DVD/VHS
"Day of Salvation" teaching programs
(English), DVD/VHS
Healing Crusade programs, DVD/VHS

Audio Teaching Tape Series

"Condition for Promotion"
"The Church, God's Will in the Earth"
"Increase"
"Praying God's Will"
"The Mind of Christ"

and many more strong topics

For a complete listing of books, teaching tapes, and videos in both English
and Farsi, please contact the Harvesters World Outreach.